★ ★ ★ ★ ★ ★ ★ ★ ★ ★ ★ ★ ★ ★ ★ ★ ★ ★ ★ ★ ★ ★ ★ ★

## PRAISE FOR
# FIGHT HOUSE

★ ★ ★ ★ ★ ★ ★ ★ ★ ★ ★ ★ ★ ★ ★ ★ ★ ★ ★ ★ ★ ★ ★

"The White House is a dignified seat of government, but it is also bull-pen, cockfight, and viper nest. During the Johnson and Nixon presidencies, these rivalries, encouraged by both chief executives, yielded policies contrary to presidential and national intention. *Fight House* at once illuminates these conflicts and reminds us of their absurd, and sometimes tragic, results. *Fight House* is a fast read, full of both gossip and deep insight."

    —Amity Shlaes, author of *Great Society: A New History*

"Tevi Troy presents such a vivid and accurate portrait of the strife, sniping, backbiting, leaking, and intrigue in the Reagan White House that I found it perfectly excruciating to read. I mean that as a compliment. Deeply researched, briskly written, and full of judicious, useful lessons, *Fight House* is just a marvelous book."

    —Peter Robinson, the Murdoch Distinguished Policy Fellow
        at the Hoover Institution and a former speechwriter and
        special assistant to President Reagan

"*Fight House* is an outstanding contribution to presidential history that reminds us that bitter conflicts within administrations are the norm, not the exception. Because he is that rare combination of historian and former White House aide, Tevi Troy is able to make the behind-the-scenes battles between cabinet officials and presidential aides come alive with deep political insights mixed with subtle wit. This book is a must-read for political junkies, historians, and all future White House transition teams."

    —Vincent J. Cannato, associate professor of history at the University of Massachusetts Boston and author of *The Ungovernable City: John Lindsay and His Struggle to Save New York*

"Everything about working in the White House is magnified—and nowhere is that more true than in the intensity of staff infighting. Tevi Troy tells the tale of the personalities who played hardball and the warring factions that shaped the modern presidency. It's a fun and fascinating book—essential to anyone who aspires to serve in the highest office in the land."

—Anthony Scaramucci, founder of Skybridge Capital and former White House Director of Communications

"Tevi Troy has done a superb job of chronicling infighting in the modern White House. I saw it firsthand from the Nixon White House and can vouch for the phenomenon. People already in positions of immense power almost inevitably seek even more. Troy's analysis is must-reading for any fan of 'inside politics' or presidential history."

—Geoff Shepard, former senior member of President Nixon's Domestic Council staff and author of *The Real Watergate Scandal*

# Fight House

# FIGHT HOUSE

## Rivalries in the White House from Truman to Trump

## TEVI TROY

REGNERY
HISTORY

Regnery History™ is a trademark of Salem Communications Holding Corporation
Regnery® is a registered trademark of Salem Communications Holding Corporation

ISBN 978-1-62157-836-9
ebook ISBN 978-1-62157-837-6

LCCN: 2019955272

Published in the United States by
Regnery History
An imprint of Regnery Publishing
A Division of Salem Media Group
300 New Jersey Ave NW
Washington, DC 20001
www.RegneryHistory.com

Manufactured in the United States of America

10 9 8 7 6 5 4 3 2 1

Books are available in quantity for promotional or premium use. For information on discounts and terms, please visit our website: www.Regnery.com.

*The only thing new in this world is the history you haven't read yet.*
—Harry Truman


*What has been will be again,*
*what has been done will be done again.*
—Ecclesiastes 1:9


*Look around. There are no enemies here.*
*There's just good old-fashioned rivalry.*
—Bob Wells

*To my friend and teacher Rabbi Levi Shemtov,*
*who guided me through my own White House experience*

# CONTENTS

# PREFACE

**W**hen Dr. Tevi Troy approached me about writing *Fight House* for Regnery History, I had long thought a well-documented, entertaining history of modern White House rivalries was needed. I also knew that Tevi would do an excellent job.

As Tevi shows, White House infighting is nothing new. In fact, it is the rule; for there are many reasons for the legendary, often searing, rivalries. Some appointed to serve the president fight for their point of view; some fight to advance their careers, while others fight because it is in their nature. And Tevi didn't just dust off a few books to learn about White House infighting. He saw it firsthand while serving in the George W. Bush administration.

What's more remarkable is the depths to which the fighting can sink. Harry Truman's secretary of state, George Marshall, for example, would not speak to the younger White House aide Clark Clifford, or ever mention his name again, after one bruising encounter. Over thirty years later, Reagan administration officials sank to planting leaks using the speaking styles of colleagues so that they could escape blame.

While many White House aides chronicled in these pages were, and many still are, listed in any Who's Who of Washington, from Arthur

Schlesinger Jr. to Henry Kissinger to Donald Rumsfeld to Richard
Cheney to Valerie Jarrett, there are many more figures, important in their
day but now long forgotten, whom Tevi describes in gripping, and often
humorous, language.

When Tevi mentioned to me that he would be using among his
key sources columns written by my father, Robert Novak, and his
partner, Rowland Evans, I was delighted. Not only because of the
family connection, but because for fifty-plus years, Evans and Novak
produced multiple weekly columns that contained news for the record,
remarkable by the journalistic standards today. Most of the news they
were reporting came from the sausage factory that is Washington,
D.C. And many of the factory workers, as it happened, worked at the
White House. The Evans and Novak columns were often the first
thing read by Washington insiders to see who among them was up,
who was down, and what the inside scoop was for that week. They
would also eagerly read them to see if they were mentioned as a source
or, more importantly, as a target.

My father and Rowly would press sources for information, starting
early, having as many as two breakfasts a day or long lunches so they
could meet more sources and obtain greater information. Which, of
course, begs the question: Why do sources make themselves available
like this—a risky activity—when White House officials from the president on down can use their extraordinary powers to stop it? What I
learned from my father, and in Tevi's book, is that any leaker's motives,
so central to White House infighting, can range from the noble to the
petty, from furthering a policy agenda to making themselves look good
at the expense of others to getting back at their own administration for
perceived slights, or just to feel like a big player in the game.

Tevi has done a wonderful job of incorporating the Evans and
Novak columns in addition to dozens of other sources to give the reader
a front row seat at the White House ring. I hope you enjoy reading it
as much as I enjoyed publishing it.

Alex Novak
Publisher, Regnery History

# INTRODUCTION

Looking at media coverage of President Donald Trump's White House, a dominant theme is staff dysfunction. The Trumpian "soap opera," like popular soap operas, does have a notable cast and gripping drama. The opening act centered around chief strategist Steve Bannon. Bannon was an intellectual street fighter with an idiosyncratic worldview at odds with both major political parties. From his White House vantage point, Bannon declared war on two fronts—against political moderates and establishment Republicans. He would launch criticisms of moderate, non-ideological New Yorkers, like Trump's daughter, Ivanka, and her husband, Jared Kushner. He also took on former Goldman Sachs executive, Gary Cohn, who became head of Trump's National Economic Council. Bannon referred to them, derisively, as "the Democrats" or "the Globalists." Kushner had trouble understanding why Bannon, with whom he had allied during the 2016 presidential campaign, was suddenly his White House opponent.

Bannon told CNBC after he left the White House, "On the campaign, we got along great. It's just that Ivanka and Jared—look, I respect them for this. They are progressive Democrats and globalists." Given their political differences, Bannon felt an obligation to fight them internally. As he recalled, "I was there for one reason. I'm a populist and I'm a nationalist. And if people are going to try to fight those policies internally, I don't mind a knife fight. Right? I just don't mind it. I'm there to win."[1]

Bannon's opposition to the "Democrats and Globalists" in the White House might have made him a natural ally of GOP conservatives on the Trump team. Yet Bannon had a problem with mainstream conservative Republicans too, represented by White House Chief of Staff Reince Priebus and Press Secretary Sean Spicer. Priebus, from Wisconsin, was a former chairman of the Republican National Committee (RNC) and a close friend of then–GOP House Speaker Paul Ryan. Spicer was the communications director and chief strategist at the RNC under Priebus. But Bannon fought with them over immigration policy and the merits of free trade, among other issues associated with traditional GOP conservativism since the Reagan presidency.

The existence of three White House factions—globalist Democrats, conservative Republicans, and Bannonite populists—made for a series of shifting alliances on issues key to President Trump. Evenly matched ideological factions were not typical of past administrations, which exacerbated rivalries and added to the Trumpian soap opera.

In addition, a revolving door of White House employment mirrored Trump's famous television show *The Apprentice*, where he delivered the catchphrase "You're fired!" White House turnover dwarfed that of other administrations and did not end with Steve Bannon's abrupt departure in August of 2017. In the first two years of the Trump administration, the key positions of chief of staff, national security advisor, press secretary, economic advisor, White House counsel, and communications director all changed hands at least once, with the communications director slot turning over multiple times. In the first two years of the George W. Bush administration, only one of those positions changed hands, as Communications Director Karen Hughes left to return home to Texas. In the Trump White House, short tenures and frequent departures were the rule and a key part of the drama.

Alongside Bannon's fate, consider the brief but explosive tenure of White House Communications Director Anthony "The Mooch" Scaramucci. The unorthodox Scaramucci tried to impose order in the leak-heavy communications shop. At one staff meeting, Scaramucci threatened to fire everyone but himself and newly minted Press Secretary Sarah Huckabee Sanders. He also had problems with Steve Bannon, telling the *New Yorker*'s Ryan Lizza in crude terms that Bannon leaked to the press to pleasure himself. Later, long after his eleven-day stint in the White House, Scaramucci would detail some of Bannon's targets, including the president himself. As Scaramucci explained, Bannon "was dramatically and incredibly divisive in the White House.... He was leaking on everybody...You don't leak on the president if you're the president's senior adviser."[2]

Political rivalries are nothing new to our Republic. The hit musical *Hamilton* features the bitter rivalries of George Washington's cabinet set to rap lyrics, and the show ends with Aaron Burr killing his rival, Alexander Hamilton, in a pistol duel. Similarly, Abraham Lincoln's cabinet was filled with challengers to the president, whom Doris Kearns Goodwin famously called out in her 2005 book, *Team of Rivals*.

Pistol duels aside, some believe that internal tension can be good for an administration: Goodwin suggested that the "Team of Rivals" showed creative tension among smart people could bring about better results than a team of yes-men or yes-women. Franklin D. Roosevelt would famously set advisors against each other with contrasting policy positions, then asked them to resolve their differences. This led to a reputation of slipperiness, which Roosevelt found useful. Incumbent President Herbert Hoover, Roosevelt's 1932 election opponent, mocked FDR as a "chameleon on plaid."

For the first 150 years of U.S. history, presidents relied on their cabinet secretaries to formulate policy and rivalry mostly occurred among them. The White House staff was, like the government itself at the time, small and highly focused. The big personalities, chief policymakers, and visionary thinkers were heads of the most prestigious cabinet agencies—typically the Departments of State, Treasury, Justice, and War.

In the 1930s, this changed under Roosevelt. The key drivers were the expansion of government under the New Deal, America's ascendant influence and power after 1939, and the growing importance and power of the presidency itself. The development of a large White House staff naturally followed, aided by Roosevelt's style and his preference to be at the center of decisions. The first entity to recognize this new challenge was the Brownlow Committee on Administrative Management, set up by Roosevelt in the summer of 1936, largely because the New Deal brought an increase in political tension and deadlocked government. The committee considered how to reshape the executive branch: "There is need for improvement of our governmental machinery to meet new conditions and to make us ready for the problems just ahead." In 1937, the committee issued its famous four-word conclusion: "The president needs help." Initially, this help would come via "not more than six administrative assistants" and the movement of the Bureau of the Budget into the White House operations. These six "executive assistant" positions would "remain in the background, issue no orders, make no decisions [and] emit no public statements." Chosen by the president, all assistants had to be "possessed of high competence" and a "passion for anonymity." The committee's recommendations found their way into law when Congress enacted the Reorganization Act of 1939, which created the Executive Office of the President (EOP). The EOP comprised a new White House Office, as well as the existing Bureau of the Budget, which had been lodged in the Treasury Department. The famous four words of the Brownlow Committee had set in motion a decades-long expansion, leading to the current White House operation of more than 1,600 people and the creation of the modern White House staff; now a glamorous group inspiring novels, TV shows, movies, and generating many prominent careers, from ABC News' George Stephanopoulos to billionaire philanthropist David Rubenstein.

Growth of the modern White House staff took time to develop after Roosevelt, however. Both Harry Truman and Dwight Eisenhower followed the old ways and looked to their cabinet secretaries to formulate policies, using a tightly structured, loyal staff organization to tamp down rivalries. By the 1960s, however, both John F. Kennedy and Lyndon

Johnson, following Roosevelt's model, made policymaking a White House prerogative, hiring prominent and experienced presidential aides. This has continued in every presidency since then, in one way or another. And since the Kennedy administration, presidential aides could also become political and media heavyweights with lucrative careers later.

Bitter and legendary rivalries soon followed White House staff growth and any "passion for anonymity" was soon relegated to the past. These rivalries have shaped not only the reputations of those involved, but the image of presidents, their policies, and the modern presidency itself. To the extent that rivalries disrupt, even cripple presidential administrations—and they have—studying them can help future presidents and other leaders understand how to prevent what James Madison called in *The Federalist* No. 10 the "disease" of faction.

Since the Roosevelt administration, three leading causes of White House staff infighting have been ideology, process, and presidential tolerance of staff infighting and turmoil itself. History shows an ideologically unified administration will have fewer internal debates. Yet too much unity brings with it challenges of its own. As political scientist, senator, and former White House aide Daniel Patrick Moynihan observed, "In unanimity one often finds a lack of rigorous thinking." On the other hand, a White House divided along clear ideological lines is prone to the disease of faction.

Process is also important. It is easy to make fun of officious nerds talking about "process fouls" and the like, but process governs White House policy operations. The president may be the ultimate decider-in-chief, but process determines how information is presented before final decisions are made. Process determines questions such as who attends the key meetings, what information is required, and what is the timeline for decision-making. Poor processes set up administrations for unhealthy dissent, such as leaking, but also long-term problems in the form of historical score-settling by White House staff and cabinet secretaries both before and after a president has left office.

Finally, presidential tolerance for and use of dissent among White House staff is an important lever. A healthy White House is characterized by a degree of staff collegiality during policy debates. When a president sets staff against each other, establishing clear winners and losers, rancor and dysfunction often follows.

History gives presidents and their staffs clear guidelines on how to structure an administration, from both management and ideological perspectives. For presidents, as for so many others, the search for wisdom begins with an examination of the past, for presidential history is rich in case studies.

# CHAPTER 1

# TRUMAN AND IKE
## The White House Staff Emerges, and Conflicts Follow

**B**oth Harry Truman and Dwight Eisenhower ran tightly controlled operations that gave little room for White House staffers to shine as individuals. They kept the focus on cabinet members, and thereby minimized rivalries. Truman also followed Franklin Roosevelt's lead, by employing a spokes-on-the-wheel system, in which aides reported to a centralized hub in the form of the president himself.

Even though he was following Roosevelt's lead in his staffing, Truman was the first to enter office following the creation of the EOP. Roosevelt had a tumultuous internal process, embracing contradictions and treating staff disagreements with a light touch. The New Deal was complicated, with new agencies and new governmental authorities creating conflicting lines of authority.[1] The presidential scholar and former White House aide Stephen Hess put things starkly: "Roosevelt had designed his whole theory of management on conflict."[2]

Truman, however, abjured Roosevelt's conflict-centered approach, returning to the traditional concept of a cabinet-centric government. As an unnamed Truman intimate told *U.S. News* during the administration, Truman "likes things to run smoothly" and "doesn't like his advisers to disagree."[3] Historian Alonzo Hamby observed that while Truman's "staff was no freer than any other from ordinary tendencies toward turf battles, personality conflicts, and back-biting, such episodes were minimal." This was so, Hamby explained, because Truman "loathed" such conflicts to the point that "however forced the cordiality may have been between some persons, they all maintained in it their dealings with each other—or found themselves leaving."[4]

What Truman inherited from Roosevelt was not aligned with his personal preferences toward conflict or slipperiness. Yet when presented with a Brownlow-recommended White House staff as a concept and reality, Truman was determined to use it to his advantage. This meant that at least some conflict would be inevitable. In these early days, the structure of the White House staff was informal. To quote Clark Clifford, who served as Truman's special counsel, "There was no hierarchy within the White House. There was no organization chart...I never received any instructions from any other staff member; I got them from the President." Truman saw the White House staff as a team of equals. As Clifford wrote, "The organization of the White House was a group of individuals, and they were individuals who were equal in status." Truman could have chosen to create a more formal structure but pointedly did not. Clifford attributes this conscious decision to Truman's time in the Senate and the personal, oral way he liked to be briefed while there: "The President got more from personal contact than he did from other forms of contact."[5]

Truman's approach had its advantages, but it could be off-putting to those not equipped to deal with oral briefings or White House egalitarianism. There was the risk that traditionally higher-ranking individuals, such as cabinet secretaries, might resent the fact that, as Clifford observed, there seemed to be "no particular rank...between the persons in the White House."[6]

The title "Special Counsel" itself was born in a controversy that began in the Roosevelt administration. Roosevelt had wanted to bring Samuel Rosenman in to serve as his White House Counsel—the same

Harry S. Truman and Clark Clifford in Key West, Florida. Clifford would later recall that he "never received any instructions from any other staff member; I got them from the president." *Courtesy of the Harry S. Truman Library and Museum*

role Rosenman held when Roosevelt was governor. Attorney General Francis Biddle objected, thinking that the attorney general of the United States effectively held the role of counsel to the president. To placate Biddle, they came up with the title of special counsel for Rosenman, but fearing the title modification would not suffice, Roosevelt also aimed to make the announcement at a time that Biddle would be unable to object: "We'll call it Special Counsel to the President, and I'm announcing it next Wednesday when Francis Biddle is in Mexico City."[7] As things would turn out over time, cabinet members like Biddle were right to be worried.

Despite the title and the existence of a predecessor in Rosenman, Clifford's job was ill-defined. As Clifford himself wrote years after both he and others had served in the position, "there is no blueprint for the job."[8] This seems to have been the case for getting the job, too. Clifford's qualification for the job may have been based more on personal connections than on his record. This is, of course, not unusual for political aides. To this day, there is no clear-cut educational or professional path to the position of White House aide, and in that respect, Clifford was not uncommon. A graduate of Washington University in St. Louis—both for college and law school—Clifford was already in his late thirties when the Second World War began. He joined the navy, commissioning as a lieutenant junior grade and working on readiness assessment for West Coast naval bases. He became a naval aide to Secretary of Defense James Forrestal and then moved over to the White House after making a point of being useful to Rosenman while Truman was away at the 1945 Potsdam Conference. Rosenman noticed this effort and, after Truman's return, said to the president, "Let's keep that young fellow here."[9]

Clifford continued to make himself useful at the White House, eventually following Samuel Rosenman as Truman's special counsel. He also became a valued political advisor to the president, a role that would bring him into the crucial presidential decision over whether to recognize the State of Israel in 1948. Many books are still written about this incident, which has had enormous political and policy implications for decades. While an obvious decision to many now, given the closeness between the United States and Israel, at the time it was exceedingly controversial, so much so that nearly the entire national security establishment opposed the decision, particularly Secretary of State George Marshall.

Truman faced enormous pressure on both sides of the recognition question. Politically, the Jewish vote was important, particularly in New York, which was then a hotly contested state in presidential elections. There were also complicated geostrategic issues at play. Those opposed to the recognition pointed out that the surrounding Arab populations vastly outnumbered the small number of Jews in Israel and around the world. As Clifford put it, "I remember at that time the argument being made that there were approximately twenty or thirty million Arabs and a million and a half Israelis, and that the day would come that the Israelis would be pushed into the Mediterranean. Obviously also, the oil was a matter of important military consideration."[10] The Zionists were, however, more "Western," and had the potential to be allies in a strategically important region. Nascent Cold War politics played a role as well. Both the U.S. and the Soviet Union, which voted with the Jews in favor of partition in 1947 at the United Nations, hoped to make the new state into an ally. There also was the issue of destiny. Truman, well-versed in the Bible, had some sympathy for the position that the Jews had a right to return to their ancestral homeland.

Given the complexity of the decision, Truman had a meeting in the White House to discuss the situation. As Clifford recalled, the president came to him and said, "I want to have a conference on this problem of Israel. I would like you to prepare yourself and you be the lawyer for the position that we should recognize Israel." Truman knew that Clifford would be facing opposition by taking this stance, saying, "I am inclined to believe that General Marshall is probably opposed to it, but you get ready and we'll set up a meeting."[11] As Truman wrote in his memoir, he was always aware of the fact that "not all my advisers looked at the Palestine problem in the same manner I did."[12]

Truman was right about Marshall. At the meeting, which took place on May 12, 1948, Marshall went first and made the expected case against recognition. Marshall's argument focused on the geostrategic elements of the situation, particularly the likelihood that the Arabs would defeat the outnumbered Israelis. Clifford went next, ushering in a cinematic Oval Office confrontation. Clifford, who had prepared for the meeting like the trial lawyer he was, gave a formal presentation, "with an introduction and a body to the argument…and ended up with a ringing peroration." Despite the quality of the presentation, or perhaps because of it, "it infuriated General Marshall."[13] Clifford remembered that even during his presentation, "he noticed the thunder clouds gathering" and "Marshall's face getting redder and redder."[14]

When Marshall did respond to Clifford's presentation, it was dismissive and personal. Addressing the president, Marshall said, "I don't even know why Clifford is here. He is a domestic adviser, and this is a foreign policy matter. The only reason Clifford is here is that he is pressing a political consideration." Truman lashed back quickly: "Well, General, he's here because I asked him to be." Not done yet, Marshall said, "I fear that the only reason Clifford is here is so that he can press for a political solution of this issue. I do not think that politics should play any role in our decision."[15]

Already stretching the boundaries of appropriate behavior in a meeting with the president, Marshall went even further: "I said bluntly that if the president were to follow Mr. Clifford's advice and if in the elections I were to vote, I would vote against the president." As Clifford recalled, Marshall's disloyalty to the president "was so shocking that it just kind of lay there for fifteen or twenty seconds and nobody moved."[16]

Marshall's comment created an awkwardness that effectively ended the meeting. Afterwards, Truman said to Clifford: "Well, that was rough as a cob," adding, "That was about as tough as it gets. But you did your best."[17] For the next two days Clifford worked behind the scenes with Undersecretary of State—and future Secretary of Defense—Robert Lovett to hammer things out in such a way that Truman could recognize Israel without embarrassing Marshall and the State Department too badly. Truman would recognize the State of Israel two days later, shortly before the Soviet Union did the same.[18] Despite Clifford and Lovett's efforts, the State Department was not pleased. Truman recorded that he "was told that to some of the career men of the State Department this announcement came as a surprise." He was unbothered by this; for he wrote, "It should not have been if these men had faithfully supported my policy."[19] Even Lovett, who would fondly recall their working together, still inserted a memo to the file explaining that "I can only conclude that the President's political advisers, having failed last Wednesday afternoon to make the President a father of the new state, have determined at least to make him the midwife." Clifford wrote in his memoir that "I knew exactly whom Lovett meant when he referred to 'the President's political advisers.'"[20]

Lovett, at least, was civil. Marshall was irate. Going into the meeting, Marshall did not like Clifford, but things clearly worsened after the meeting. As Clifford later wrote about Marshall, "Not only did he never speak to me again after that meeting, but, according to his official biographer, he never again mentioned my name." To be fair, Clifford did not seem to like Marshall much either, writing in his memoir that "George Catlett Marshall was a man of the strictest rectitude, with little noticeable sense of humor."[21] But at least he was willing to use Marshall's name.

The May 12 meeting was one of the starker exchanges to take place in the Oval Office. Yet the disagreement between Clifford and Marshall was not strictly a rivalry, mainly because of the power disparity between the two men. Marshall was one of the leading generals of the Second World War, a national hero and someone whom, as Hamby noted, Truman "revered...as he did no other man in public life."[22] Truman thought Marshall would "probably go down in history as one of the great men of our era, not because he was the chief military brains in winning the war, but because he is also a great statesman and diplomat."[23] In fact, when Clifford suggested that the U.S. effort to rebuild Europe be called the Truman Plan, Truman balked and insisted it be called the Marshall Plan.[24]

Despite Clifford's anonymity at the time and Marshall's iconic status, Clifford won the fight over Israel. For this reason, the conflict merits inclusion because of the way it highlights the shifting power from cabinet officials to the White House. Of course, there was another important reason for Clifford's victory: Truman himself wanted to recognize Israel. He had read the Bible as a child, as well as a book called *Great Men and Famous Women*, which celebrated, among others, the Persian king Cyrus who returned the Israelites to their land after the Babylonian exile.[25]

Beyond the influence of Truman's boyhood reading, it is important to examine the structural explanation for his decision. Clifford may not have had the same status as Marshall, but he did have one huge advantage over him, that of propinquity. As Stephen Hess wrote eloquently in his *Organizing the Presidency,* Clifford's effectiveness "illustrated that proximity to the President was a blessing of no small value." The access close White House staffers like Clifford had could overcome the obvious power disparities between them and congressionally constituted cabinet officials like Marshall.

Another related development during Truman's presidency was the beginning of the erosion of what Hess called the "distinction between Cabinet officers (policy advocates and managers) and White House aides (facilitators, mediators, and performers of personal and political services)." Clifford played no small role in the beginning of its disappearance, as his "performance during five years under Truman was of a different magnitude: since he acted primarily as a presidential adviser on policies and programs rather than on ways and means, the theoretical line between Cabinet and White House staff began to blur." As Clifford's experiences illustrate, the law of propinquity is apt to govern.[26]

Clifford, always an astute observer of power relations, recognized what was going on even as he was in the middle of it. As he observed, "Marshall's attitude towards me foreshadowed the conflicts between the State Department and the National Security Council, which would later become a standard part of the Washington landscape."[27] Unsurprisingly, Marshall had similar concerns, worrying in 1947 that the nascent concept of the National Security Council would cause "fundamental changes in the entire question of foreign relations."[28] They were both right. Following the emergence of the concept of a permanent White House staff, able to supply its own guidance to the president in a way separate and sometimes different from the cabinet officers, it was inevitable that conflict would follow. It was clear that this same dynamic began to apply in domestic affairs as well. Hess notes that Truman's vetoes of legislation related to the Office of Price Administration and the Taft-Hartley Act were "both actions urged by Clifford and opposed by almost the entire cabinet."[29]

George Marshall clearly did not like the new national security superstructure or younger political aides like Clifford interfering with his empyrean geopolitical judgments. Nor was it coincidental that the chief exception to Truman's desire for comity and obedience among his staff was a military man and war hero, whom Truman (a major in the First World War) revered along with the American public. This ability of a high profile and politically popular official to get away with behavior that White House staffers could not was not limited to the Truman White House. It has become a recurring issue in many presidencies. The fear of this phenomenon is one reason the Brownlow Committee suggested that one of the characteristics of a presidential assistant should be "a passion for anonymity."

If Truman liked order, his successor Dwight Eisenhower loved it. The mercurial Truman saw order as professionally necessary. Eisenhower saw it as a way of life. He entered the Oval Office with none of the hindrances Truman inherited as a relatively unknown vice president to the popular Roosevelt. Like Roosevelt, Eisenhower was also politically popular and respected globally. He was not just a successful general, he was the architect of victory in Europe, which meant that leaders, whether political, business, or military, did not intimidate him.

Eisenhower was even critical of what he perceived as Truman's lack of order. He felt that Truman "didn't know any more about government than a dog knows about religion."[30] What Ike did like was organization, as he thought that "disorganization can scarcely fail to result in inefficiency and can easily lead to disorder."[31] With this approach in mind, he delegated authority. Eisenhower was one of the first presidents to have a chief of staff, Sherman Adams; he was also the first president to appoint a national security advisor, Robert Cutler, and held regular meetings of his national security team. For his part, Truman thought Eisenhower was overly rigid in his organization, joking that Ike was slow to react to the 1959 Cuban revolution as "he was probably waiting there for his chief of staff to give him a report, and he'd initial it and put it in his out basket. Because that's the way he operated."[32]

Eisenhower also believed in cabinet government and gave his department heads leeway to run things as they saw fit. He would even get annoyed if cabinet heads came to him too often with what he considered minor problems. His cabinet was largely unknown to him before the selection process began, but nearly all had similar backgrounds as successful executives before coming to government, including CEO of M. A. Hanna Company, George Humphrey; CEO of GM, Charles Erwin Wilson; and president of Procter and Gamble, Neil H. McElroy. Critics derided his cabinet as being composed of "nine millionaires and a plumber." As a result, Hess noted, "basic differences among the cabinet were minimal.... The like-mindedness of the department heads ensured it."[33]

As for the White House staff, they tended to be younger and far more likely to have a prior connection to Eisenhower than the cabinet secretaries. With both the White House staff and the cabinet, Eisenhower sought amicability, or what the historian Fred Greenstein called "friendship as the lubricant of leadership."[34] While minimizing conflict generally worked throughout the administration, Eisenhower did sow the seeds of conflict in future administrations. By increasing the size of the White House staff from thirty-two to fifty over the course of his presidency, he made disagreements between the White House staff and the cabinet more likely in the future. As Hess noted, "the larger the staff, the greater the temptations to try to run the departments from the White House."[35]

## Tension at State: Dulles versus Stassen

Within the Eisenhower administration, Ike's desire to avoid friction ensured relative concord among the staff. There was at least one exception, albeit one initiated by Eisenhower because he wanted to put pressure on one of his cabinet members, Secretary of State John Foster Dulles. On March 19, 1955, Eisenhower, concerned that Dulles was moving too slowly on disarmament negotiations with the Soviets, appointed Harold Stassen, a former Minnesota governor, and quixotic presidential candidate, to the newly created position of Special Assistant to the President for Disarmament. The statement detailing Stassen's appointment indicated that the position would be of cabinet rank, and that it would have "the responsibility for developing, on behalf of the President and the State

Department, the broad studies, investigations and conclusions which, when concurred in by the National Security Council and approved by the president, will become basic policy toward the question of disarmament."[36]

The *New York Times* editorial board dubbed Stassen's position the "Secretary of Peace," which annoyed the fussy and officious Dulles. Dulles grumbled about the sobriquet: "If he is the secretary of peace, what am I—secretary for war?" In addition, the cabinet rank rankled and interfered with the chain of command. While equivalent to Dulles in terms of having cabinet rank, Stassen was simultaneously under Dulles when it came to handling negotiations with foreign governments. As the historian David Tal wrote, "Stassen was thus at the same time equal to

Governor Harold E. Stassen, Ike's "Secretary for Peace," a designation that annoyed Secretary of State Dulles, who wondered if that made him the "Secretary for War." *Courtesy of the Library of Congress*

Dulles and under him, a situation that allowed Stassen to defy the clear hierarchy that had been established with his recent appointment."[37]

The situation was bound to create a rivalry. Stassen, to his credit, was deferential in the beginning. According to Eisenhower speechwriter Emmet Hughes, Stassen would be sure to issue reassuring statements like, "Whatever you think, Foster" and "Under your leadership, Foster."[38] Regardless of the politesse, the clashes were inevitable. Stassen was twenty years Dulles's junior, and had nowhere near the foreign policy credentials of the older man. Despite his relative lack of experience, Stassen had little doubt about his own abilities. As Hughes observed, "Many of [Stassen's] cabinet colleagues were impressed, and not appreciatively, by the exceedingly high importance that Stassen seemed to attach to his words and his own ambitions." Stassen also came to the office believing he had some kind of mandate from Eisenhower to accelerate disarmament talks with the Soviets, concluding that Ike was "frustrated by Dulles's inability to 'break through the stalemate of the Cold War and [he] moved far too slowly.'"[39]

Dulles brought his own flaws to the relationship. According to Stassen, "My best summary of Dulles is that he always *knew* he was absolutely right. Further, he *knew* that anyone who disagreed with him was, of logical necessity, always wrong. And finally, he could not understand how anyone could dare question the fact that he was *always* right [italics in original]."[40] It wasn't just Stassen who had a problem with the priggish Dulles, though. As Supreme Court Justice William O. Douglas once said, "I'm not sure I want to go to heaven. I'm afraid I might meet John Foster Dulles there."[41] Some U.S. allies had misgivings about Dulles as well. Harold Wilson, a British member of Parliament and future prime minister, once mocked Dulles's propensity to try to be everywhere all the time: "I heard they are inventing an airplane that can fly without Dulles! They hope soon to get it into production." Winston Churchill himself once famously mocked Dulles via declension: "Dull, Duller, Dulles...."[42]

Whatever the flaws of and personal difference between Stassen and Dulles, the two men had a fundamental philosophical difference on arms control policy. Stassen favored a more ambitious approach, supporting

Secretary of State John Foster Dulles, about whom Supreme Court Justice William O. Douglas once said, "I'm not sure I want to go to heaven. I'm afraid I might meet John Foster Dulles there." *Courtesy of the Library of Congress*

a nuclear freeze. Dulles was more cautious, wanting slower movement overall, with trust-building steps like mutual inspections. Eisenhower went with a third approach, in between the two, called Open Skies—a proposal that would allow the Americans and the Soviets surveillance flights over each other's territory, as a way to reassure each side that neither side was planning an attack. The Soviets rejected it, but it effectively became U.S. policy. Still, Stassen and Dulles disagreed over how to implement Open Skies, leading to continual and even personal strife between them. In one comical incident in 1955, Dulles had his security team take away Stassen's assigned car at a foreign policy gathering. In a not-so-subtle example of Washington territoriality, he then offered Stassen a ride in what was supposed to be his own car.[43]

Stassen's undoing was semi-comical as well. During the 1958 arms discussions in London, Stassen shared his own position on arms control with Soviet diplomat T. K. Zorin, implying it was the American position. Dulles, Eisenhower, and the British were angered. Dulles called Stassen back to Washington, demoted him, and gave him a career state department official as his minder. In another embarrassment, Stassen's staff was moved out of the White House to a different location. Stassen did not last long after that, handing in his resignation to Eisenhower, not Dulles, on February 18, 1957. Ike's statement on his departure noted his deep "regret that you are leaving the Federal government, effective today, and that our five-year association together in government service is to terminate."[44]

Here again, the power disparity was important. Dulles was the Secretary of State; if he acted to the president's liking, he was bound to win out. But Stassen brought advantages too, as a young and dynamic governor, and a former and future presidential candidate. (He would end up running a record ten times for president.) Eisenhower bore some blame as well, giving Stassen at least the impression that he wanted to push Dulles, convoluting his usually buttoned-down organization chart by giving a White House staffer cabinet rank. The Stassen-Dulles contest was not exactly a fight among equals, but it did show what such a fight between a cabinet official and a sufficiently senior White House staffer could look like.

In later years, struggles like the one between Dulles and Stassen would have generated more attention and media fireworks. The issues of turf, ego, and control, which would govern most internal staff conflicts in the future, were evident in the conflicts under Eisenhower. Both Truman and Eisenhower presided over governments in the early days of the White House staff. In this period, the Brownlow Committee's recommended "passion for anonymity" largely reigned among White House aides. The conflicts within the administrations came in areas where the presidents themselves were willing to tolerate dissension over substantive policy disagreements, such as Israel or arms control. And they were worsened by perceived affronts to the normal process. These three factors—presidential tolerance for conflict, internal ideological disagreement, and challenges to the established order of doing things—would serve as combustible ingredients for conflicts to come.

# CHAPTER 2

# JOHN F. KENNEDY
## Passion for Anonymity on the White House Staff?
## Not So Much.

The feuds in the Kennedy White House reflected changes in the presidency and society at large. The power of television was instrumental in electing Kennedy, as modern celebrity culture began to influence the world of politics. While the concept of aides with a "passion for anonymity" still existed, it was certainly not what the Brownlow Committee had expected. Furthermore, complicated questions of influence and status began to hinge on more than position and title, as closeness to the president, fame, and even familial ties began to play a larger role in the power equation.

### True Hatred: RFK and LBJ

The best-known feud in the Kennedy administration was not between White House staffers but between two people at "the principals' level." Over the course of the administration of the thirty-fourth president, Attorney General (and president's brother) Robert "Bobby" Kennedy and Vice President Lyndon B. Johnson squared off in a legendary feud, characterized by the kind of drama and fury that would make for an excellent Netflix series.

17

At the beginning of his book on the White House staff, Bradley Patterson observed that the vice president and the first lady were the "two key players whom the President cannot remove."[1] Mrs. Kennedy was a powerful first lady, a celebrity in her own right. Similarly, Kennedy could not get rid of Lyndon Johnson as he was elected with him. Yet Johnson was miserable as vice president after an illustrious career as Senate majority leader. Plus, he craved power—and the presidency—for himself and would not resign under any circumstances. Johnson's predicament was worsened by the fact that the Kennedy administration had a third category of person who could not be removed: the president's brother.

It is unusual to have a relative serve in a presidential administration. There are good reasons for this, and today they are written in law. But even before there were statutes against it, there were political reasons for avoiding this circumstance. A president needs to be able to fire people, and direct relatives are hard if not impossible to fire. This is not to suggest that Kennedy had any interest in firing Bobby. In fact, Bobby was one of his most effective cabinet secretaries. But Bobby's feud with Vice President Johnson created an awkwardness that persisted throughout the administration—and beyond. Since he could not fire either of them, Kennedy did not have the leverage required to deal with the problem. But if Kennedy had lived to complete two terms, his 1964 re-election might have forced a final showdown between his brother and the vice president.

From the moment they met, Johnson and Bobby detested each other. In 1953, Bobby was sitting at a table in the Senate cafeteria with his boss, Senator Joe McCarthy, and some of McCarthy's other aides. Johnson entered and McCarthy stood to greet him, as did the other aides—all except for Bobby. Johnson noticed Bobby's snub and stood over Bobby with his impressive height until Bobby reluctantly stood and shook Johnson's hand. Johnson "won" the encounter, but at the high price of a thin-skinned man's eternal enmity.[2] As Bobby's father once said, with an odd sort of pride, "Bobby's my boy. When Bobby hates you, you stay hated."[3]

There was little interaction between them while Bobby served as a lowly Senate GOP staffer. Johnson at the time was ruling the institution

Secretary of State Dean Rusk, Vice President Lyndon B. Johnson, Attorney General Robert F. Kennedy, and President John F. Kennedy in the Oval Office. Attorney General Kennedy was far more influential than Vice President Johnson while President Kennedy was alive, and he was not above tormenting Johnson, who hated his time as vice president. *Courtesy of the John F. Kennedy Presidential Library and Museum*

as one of the most powerful Senate majority leaders in history. But in 1959, Jack Kennedy sent Bobby down to Johnson's ranch to learn of Johnson's presidential intentions and possible support for his 1960 presidential bid. Bobby was already angry about the things Johnson had been saying about Kennedy in the press, including allusions to Kennedy's poor health and to Joseph Kennedy's softness towards Hitler before World War II. But things worsened on Bobby's trip to Texas. In one famous encounter, Johnson took Bobby hunting on his ranch. When the recoil from Bobby's rifle sent him sprawling to the ground, Johnson helped him up but not before condescendingly quipping, "Son, you've got to learn how to handle a gun like a man."[4] Bobby may have been good at maintaining hatreds, but Johnson was showing that he had a talent for staying hated.

The feud escalated at the Democratic Convention in 1960. In a period that the historian and Kennedy White House aide Arthur Schlesinger described as governed by "confusion," Johnson and Kennedy engaged in an ambivalent dance around Johnson's place in the vice-presidential slot on the 1960 Democratic ticket. Bobby visited Johnson three times to negotiate some agreement between the Johnson and Kennedy camps. The enmity between the two was plain before they even sat down. When Bobby called to announce his intention to come by for the first visit, Johnson said, "Whatever it is, I don't want to see him." Bobby was reluctant to offer Johnson the vice presidency, and Johnson was reluctant to take it. Bobby, beyond his personal dislike for Johnson, was concerned that having Southerner Johnson on the 1960 ticket would alienate Kennedy's liberal supporters.[5]

Johnson, meanwhile, was concerned about the loss of power that the move from senator to vice president would entail, saying, "I wouldn't trade a vote for a gavel." On the third visit, after Johnson had already accepted the nod, Bobby later recalled trying to convince Johnson to withdraw from the ticket. A wary Johnson then spoke to Jack Kennedy himself, who kneecapped his own brother by saying that "Bobby's been out of touch and doesn't know what's been happening." Later, the Kennedy team tried to make it sound as if Johnson was eager if not desperate for the job, with Schlesinger recording Kennedy as saying, "I didn't offer the Vice Presidency to him. I just held it out like this and he grabbed at it."[6]

Tensions often diminish when people from different campaigns converge in an administration, but this did not happen when both men joined the Kennedy administration. Johnson was now vice president. To outsiders, it is a position of great prestige, but to a power player like Johnson, the former Senate majority leader, it was a comedown. By most accounts, including his own, he was miserable. As Johnson recounted, the vice presidency "was filled with trips around the world, chauffeurs, men saluting, people clapping, chairmanships of councils, but, in the end, it is nothing. I detested every minute of it."[7] As vice president, Johnson had a special phone installed in his office for calls from the White House, but the phone rarely rang.[8] Indignities like this made him so miserable that, per Press Secretary George Reedy, "He couldn't bear to appear on television," forcing Reedy to become ever more creative in explaining Johnson's sudden media shyness.[9]

Bobby's slights intensified Johnson's misery. These happened most often in the area in which their jurisdictions overlapped, that of civil rights. RFK, both as attorney general and as President Kennedy's top advisor, was deeply involved in the issue, even at a cost to the administration. The fact that Kennedy was the president's brother complicated the administration's political standing in the South.[10] For understandable reasons, Kennedy wanted his vice president involved in the civil rights issue, with its special sensitivities in the South. As the president told White House aide Lee White about civil rights issues, "Look, you work with Lyndon Johnson and you make sure that he knows about all these things. I want him here. I think he can do a lot."[11]

Johnson may have been involved, but Bobby did not make that involvement pleasant. In one meeting with civil rights leaders at the White House, Johnson was speaking and RFK was impatient for him to finish. He called over Louis Martin, an African American and top official at the Democratic National Committee, and asked him to get Johnson to expedite matters: "I've got a date and I need to get on this boat in a few minutes. Can you tell the Vice President to cut it short?" Martin's reaction to this request was understandable. He ignored it. But this non-response did not satisfy RFK, who called over Martin for a second time, and showed less patience this time: "Didn't I tell you to tell the Vice President to shut up?" Martin then dutifully but reluctantly went over to Johnson, who was still talking, and whispered to him, "Bobby has got to go, and he wants to close it up." Johnson glared at Martin but kept on talking. It is unclear whether Kennedy made it to his "date."[12]

On another occasion, RFK took over a meeting Johnson was chairing for the president's Commission on Equal Employment Opportunities. Johnson was already sensitive about his chairmanship of the CEEO since Kennedy had inadvertently changed its composition without telling him.

This oversight stung Johnson so profoundly that Lee White recalled that "I've never seen a more surprised, disappointed and annoyed guy than Lyndon Johnson when the president of the United States issued an executive order changing the jurisdiction of his committee." Johnson's attempt to keep his composure impressed White, who called it "about as good as a guy can get when he gets a mackerel in the face!" At the meeting, RFK came in and impatiently grilled the participants over what he saw as insufficient progress, which made Johnson look inept. Johnson later complained bitterly about Kennedy's behavior, saying "he humiliated me."[13]

Kennedy and his friends also hurled a torrent of personal digs at Johnson. Bobby's residence in McLean, Virginia, is known as Hickory Hill, and Bobby's friends and allies, known as the "Hickory Hill Gang," gave Johnson no quarter. At one party, a voodoo doll meant to represent Johnson caused great hilarity. Oh-so-witty guests asked smart-alecky questions such as "Whatever happened to Lyndon?" In addition, nicknames for Johnson abounded at both Hickory Hill and at fancy Georgetown parties, such as "Rufus Cornpone," "Judge Crater"—referring to a judge who had disappeared—and, for the vice-presidential couple, "Uncle Cornpone and his Little Pork Chop." They howled upon hearing that Johnson mispronounced "hors d'oeuvres" as "whore doves," and on the rare occasions when the Johnsons did come to Hickory Hill, Uncle Cornpone and Mrs. Pork Chop would get placed at the "loser's table" by Ethel, Bobby's wife, who despised Johnson. Her nickname for the vice president was Huckleberry Capone.[14] Sometimes spouses moderate the worst and most competitive instincts of their partners. This was not the case with Ethel Kennedy, who hated Johnson even more than Bobby did, which is saying a great deal.

These petty anti-Johnson activities ate at Johnson. He had his own nicknames for the Kennedys, including "the boy" and "Johnny" for JFK, and "Sonny boy" for his brother. Johnson also had a derisive nickname for the entire Kennedy crowd, calling them "the Harvards." Years later, when Johnson aide Joe Califano reported to Johnson that the 1968 race riots were threatening Georgetown, Johnson replied, "Goddamn! I've waited thirty-five years for this day." Clearly, the slights of Bobby, his wife, and his entourage during this period both irked and stuck with Johnson.[15]

The historian Jeff Shesol characterizes the Kennedy presidency as a period of an "uneasy peace" in the Bobby-LBJ relationship. It was—at least compared to the ugliness that was to follow in the Johnson administration and in the 1968 campaign. Listing all the slights and counterslights between Kennedy and Johnson has filled more than one book. The important thing here is not to recount every poisonous interaction but to understand the shifting power dynamic. Johnson, as a powerful senator, was on top at first, and not shy about letting Bobby Kennedy know it, even if their interactions were infrequent. The power differential shifted as RFK's brother sewed up the presidential nomination in 1960, but both players were on equal and shifting ground during the confusing period of the Democratic convention in 1960. Johnson wanted the vice-presidential nod despite his conception that trading a "vote for a gavel" would be disempowering. Bobby's reluctance to have Johnson on the ticket showed in his discussions with the senator and his team, and JFK ended up undercutting his own brother to secure Johnson's agreement to join the ticket. Once they were both in the Kennedy administration, they saw each other more often, and RFK made the most of his closeness to the president in his efforts to humiliate Johnson. The dynamic shifted again after Kennedy's assassination, and Bobby ended up serving unhappily under the thumb of the man he had tormented. Finally, Bobby would later take advantage of Johnson's political unpopularity and run to succeed him in 1968. The lesson from all this to future aides and officials is to tread carefully. Washington has a ladder that goes up and down, and those you kick beneath you on the ladder might—will—kick back harder when they are on an upper rung.

The Johnson-Kennedy feud was unusual in the history of White House rivalries in that it involved a vice president and a presidential sibling. Furthermore, the typical levers of presidential power did not apply here, as the nature of the feud went beyond process or ideology, and a noted lack of presidential tolerance for anti-Johnson behavior had little impact on RFK's behavior. After all, Jack Kennedy needed Lyndon Johnson to carry vote-rich Texas in the Electoral College. But the feud also had elements that fit certain recurring patterns. While the vice president is technically senior to the attorney general, RFK's closeness to the president gave him an edge over Johnson, at least for the period in which JFK remained president. Ego was at stake in their clash, as in most rivalries, and the efforts to humiliate one another took place in both professional and social situations. And, as with most rivalries at the White House level, standard tactics for resolving internal disagreements would have been inadequate. President Kennedy even tried to make sure that his staff treated Johnson with respect, but no president could realistically police every action between two senior officials, even if one was his brother.

## Within the White House Staff: Schlesinger and Sorensen

Just as the LBJ-RFK feud would continue and even escalate after Kennedy's tragic assassination, so would another Kennedy-era feud, this one taking place at the White House staff level. When John F. Kennedy came to the White House, he brought a bigger team with him than earlier presidents. Roosevelt had already been elected twice by the time the Executive Office of the Presidency was created; Truman entered office on Roosevelt's death, and therefore inherited Roosevelt's structure and much of his staff; Eisenhower, while entering with a clean slate after the 1952 election, was a relative newcomer to politics and did not bring a large coterie of longtime aides with him.

Kennedy was different. Elected after eight years of Republican rule, it was expected that he would bring his own people with him. In fact, Kennedy had two main groups he was bringing with him, the "Irish Mafia" and the "Intellectuals." The Irish Mafia were political pros like Ken O'Donnell and Lawrence O'Brien, who had worked on Kennedy's campaigns, and had risen with him in the world of Massachusetts politics. The "Intellectuals" were people like law professor

Archibald Cox, economist John Kenneth Galbraith, and especially Pulitzer Prize–winning Harvard historian Arthur Schlesinger Jr., who brought intellectual credibility, a sense of history, and current ideas from the academic world to Kennedy's campaign.

There had been an expectation among outsiders in the press and elsewhere of a feud between the Irish Mafia and the Intellectuals. But these expectations rested on a fundamental misunderstanding of the loyalty of both groups to Kennedy. Ted Sorensen made this point quite explicitly in his memoirs, dismissing "outside observers" who "attempted to divide the staff into two camps." According to Sorensen, "No such division, in fact, existed." As Sorensen observed, the misunderstanding was based on the fact that "those with primarily political roles were men of high intelligence. Those who came from primarily academic background often had political experience. Many could not be simply classified as either intellectuals or politicians (and I insisted I had a foot in each camp)."[16]

There is something immensely self-serving about Sorensen's analysis, here and elsewhere in his memoir. In fact, Sorensen himself makes clear at the very beginning of his book that it was not going to be a tell-all nor was it going to make the late president or his administration look bad. As Sorensen notes: "[Kennedy] expressed disdain for the reliability of most government memoirs and diaries. He thought that Emmet Hughes, a part-time speech writer for Eisenhower, had betrayed the trust of Republican officials by quoting private conversations against them. 'I hope,' said Kennedy, 'that no one around here is writing that kind of book.'" Sorensen then made his intentions clear, writing, "This is not that kind of book."[17]

Yet despite Sorensen's goal to downplay feuds or indeed any problems between administration insiders, he was right that the two groups largely did not take potshots at each other. The intellectuals in the administration were too committed to Kennedy and his goals to create any separation between a political and an intellectual operation. "The fight never came off," Stephen Hess wrote, in large part because "the intellectuals in residence did not place politics lower in the scheme of things."[18]

President John F. Kennedy meets with Special Assistant to the President Arthur M. Schlesinger Jr. (left). The famous historian found himself relegated to the East Wing in the Kennedy White House. *Courtesy of the John F. Kennedy Presidential Library and Museum*

In addition, more than any administration before it, the Kennedy team viewed themselves as separate and apart from the growing federal civil service. The federal workforce, which stood at 699,000 in 1940, had reached 1.8 million by 1960—not that far from the current two million, and proportionally more when you take into account the smaller population of the 1960s.[19] With the larger federal workforce came suspicion. As Hess notes, "The staff's suspicions of the civil service, however, steadily increased in the Kennedy White House."[20] Arthur Schlesinger noted his distrust of the civil service on several occasions. He felt that the agencies "remained in bulk a force against innovation with an inexhaustible capacity to dilute and delay, and obstruct presidential purpose. Only so many fights were possible."[21] More specifically, he felt that they had "convincing evidence that the president required people in the State Department whose basic loyalty would be to him, not to the foreign service or the Council on Foreign Relations."[22] With this comment, he expressed his skepticism not only of the career bureaucracy but of the D.C. intellectual establishment as well.

At the same time, there were certainly some disagreements between the camps. In Schlesinger's Pulitzer Prize–winning memoir, he notes that during the presidential campaign, "a chronic tension existed between the Sorensen-Goodwin-Feldman operation and the Cox office," i.e., the Academic Advising Committee (AAC), which was set up to solicit thoughts from top academics. Schlesinger further described this as a natural tension, "since the men on the road, sensitive to the ebb and flow, the very vibrations, of the campaign, found little sustenance in the weighty and academic material they received from Washington."[23] As Sorensen himself wrote of the AAC, "not all their material was usable and even less was actually used."[24] Furthermore, when discussing the makeup of the White House staff, Schlesinger reported that Kennedy and his team felt that "some neutral figures ought to be introduced in order to relieve what he feared might be a tension between the Sorensen and O'Donnell groups."[25]

Adding to this tension was the fact that the Kennedy presidential campaign itself was a rough, sharp-elbowed environment. When Harris

Wofford was trying to convince the campaign to have Kennedy call Coretta Scott King, the wife of the imprisoned Martin Luther King Jr., he found that he could not get his calls to campaign headquarters returned. When he did finally get the opportunity to argue his case in front of Kennedy, O'Donnell warned him starkly about what he faced internally from the campaign staff: "If it works, you'll get no credit for it; if it does not, you'll get all the blame." Then after the call, Bobby Kennedy tore into Wofford's internal ally, Sargent Shriver, who happened to be Kennedy's own brother-in-law, saying that "Jack Kennedy was going to get defeated because of the stupid call." As it turns out, the "stupid call" ended up being a political masterstroke, as the goodwill it engendered for Kennedy within the African-American community was indispensable in the close election against Richard Nixon in 1960.[26]

Part of the challenge in both the campaign and the White House was that Sorensen was a prickly sort whose ego required frequent massaging. When the tensions flared between Sorensen and Cox, even Kennedy himself was aware of the problem. According to Schlesinger, JFK "regretted the problems between Sorensen and Cox"—but he was not eager to do much of anything about it. Sorensen was just too valuable a player to risk alienating him. In explaining his reluctance to get involved, Kennedy told Schlesinger that "Ted is indispensable to me." Schlesinger agreed. In one of the many passages in which Schlesinger praised Sorensen just a little too effusively, the professor wrote that "from his long experience with Kennedy and his superb service for him, Sorensen had come to feel that no one else knew the candidate's mind so well or reproduced his idiom so accurately." Yet Schlesinger also knew that Sorensen was thin-skinned and needed careful handling. After the fulsome praise of Sorensen, Schlesinger added, "Justifiably proud of his special relationship, he tended to resent interlopers."[27]

Kennedy knew about Sorensen's sensitivities as well. At one point, Kennedy told Schlesinger to punch up a speech that he found lacking, but to make sure his efforts were kept quiet. His instructions to Schlesinger were revealing: "[R]ework this a little, but don't tell Ted I asked you."[28] On another occasion, when Sorensen was trying to block Schlesinger's edits from inclusion in a final draft, Kennedy himself knowingly joked that "Ted certainly doesn't go for additions to his speeches!" When some of Schlesinger's words did make that speech, and those words made the *New York Times'* "Quotation of the Day," Kennedy recognized that Sorensen would be put off, telling Schlesinger that "Ted will die when he sees that."[29]

Kennedy's "adhocracy" approach left room for internal disagreement. Even if the warring camps expected by the press did not arise, there were certainly disagreements among individuals within the two broad camps, if not outright enmities. In the case of Sorensen and his friendly rival Schlesinger, there was more of an ebb-and-flow in their rivalry. It's clear that Schlesinger in the White House was more focused on Sorensen than the other way around. In their respective memoirs, Schlesinger pays far more attention to Sorensen than Sorensen does to Schlesinger. Furthermore, when Schlesinger does mention Sorensen, he tends to be more descriptive and more apt to praise Sorensen and his closeness to Kennedy, as well as to issue the occasional subtle digs. Sorensen's fewer mentions of Schlesinger are more neutrally written.[30]

This disparity in attention stems from a core reality. Sorensen was a much more important player in the Kennedy White House than was Schlesinger. Sorensen was closer to Kennedy, knew the president's mind and rhetoric, and was more of a political operator. Overall, he was indeed indispensable, as Kennedy himself said. Therefore, Sorensen's role was more senior and more important within the Kennedy operation. As budget director David Bell put it, Sorensen was "the strongest man in the White House on all matters except foreign policy."[31]

Yet Schlesinger was indisputably the more famous one. He was the celebrated Pulitzer Prize–winning intellectual whose fame derived from his own impressive accomplishments rather than from his closeness to a politician. Looking back at their fame disparities decades later, Sorensen dismissed the idea that he could have seen Schlesinger as his competition: "Competitor? It could be as easily asked whether I regarded

Ted Sorensen, Kennedy's top aide in the White House. He had more areas of responsibility in the White House than any aide in the modern era. *Courtesy of the John F.
Kennedy Presidential Library and Museum*

tennis champion Arthur Ashe as a competitor! Arthur Schlesinger was
an intellectual giant, liberal champion, prodigious writer and leading
scholar while I was still figuratively in knee pants."[32]

On one level, Sorensen was right. But it is also important to remember that these gushing words were written decades after the fact.
Sorensen's more contemporary comments on Schlesinger were much
more careful and nuanced, not to mention occasionally negative. Inside

the White House, there was little competition between the two men, since it was Sorensen who was so much more integral to the Kennedy operation. This gap was most clear in the differences between their job descriptions in the Kennedy White House. Sorensen had the title of Special Counsel, the same job that Rosenman and Clifford held under Truman.[33] As Richard Neustadt, who advised the Kennedy transition, wrote, Sorensen's assignments "encompassed drafting all the public documents through which the president defined and pressed his program: speeches, messages to Congress, drafts of legislation, statements on enrolled bills, executive orders. This put the counsel at the center of domestic affairs."[34] The 1960 campaign chronicler Theodore White put it more simply, but no less expansively, writing that Sorensen served as "JFK's intellectual chief of staff."[35] After the Bay of Pigs, Sorensen's responsibilities expanded even further, including foreign affairs as well.[36] Sorensen's role was so expansive that Commerce Secretary Luther Hodges tried to lodge a complaint about him at a 1961 cabinet meeting, putting it on the agenda under the title, "A candid discussion with the president on relationships with the White House staff." Kennedy ended the meeting without allowing the topic to come up.[37] Sorensen's tremendous roster of responsibilities would be unmanageable today, and more than any White House staffer could realistically hope for since.

Schlesinger's responsibilities, in contrast, were modest and vague. Ken O'Donnell and Dave Powers described Schlesinger's role as that of a "special assistant without a special portfolio, to be a liaison man in charge of keeping Adlai Stevenson happy, to receive complaints from the liberals, and to act as this sort of household devil's advocate who would complain about anything in the administration that bothered him." Sorensen also focused on the liaison aspect of the Schlesinger role, seeing him as the administration's contact person with "liberals and intellectuals both in this country and abroad, as an advisor in Latin American, United Nations and cultural affairs, as a source of innovation, ideas and occasional speeches on all topics and incidentally of the lightning rod to attract Republican attacks from the rest of us." Sorensen's use of the word "occasional" to describe Schlesinger's role in speechwriting is revealing, especially given how protective Sorensen was of his role as Kennedy's wordsmith. Richard Goodwin, another Kennedy speechwriter, used the same word to describe Schlesinger's role, writing that "occasionally when a Sorensen speech draft was unsatisfactory, Kennedy would give it to Arthur Schlesinger." Attorney General Robert Kennedy recalled that JFK "liked Arthur Schlesinger, but he thought he was a little bit of a nut sometimes. He thought he was sort of a gadfly and that he was having a hell of a good time in Washington. He didn't do a hell of a lot, but he was good to have around." RFK further recalled, also dismissively, that Schlesinger "wasn't brought in on any major policy matters, but he'd work on drafts of speeches." RFK did not bring out the word "occasional" here, but he might as well have.[38]

Looking at their respective job responsibilities makes it clear: Sorensen was a major player in the White House, while Schlesinger was more of secondary one. As Schlesinger's biographer Richard Aldous put it, "By 1963 Sorensen was clearly in command and Schlesinger on the bench."[39]

Yet even with this clear disparity in roles and responsibilities, a rivalry had developed. Aldous, who said the two had a "prickly relationship," suggests that the rivalry dated back to Schlesinger's comments on Sorensen's draft of *Profiles in Courage*, the Kennedy Pulitzer Prize–winning book, largely written by Sorensen. Neither talked too explicitly about the incident, as the Kennedy apparatus supported the fiction that Kennedy, not Sorensen, had written the book. Thus Sorensen acted as if he did not write it, and Schlesinger acted as if he had a minor role in the whole affair, saying that his "only assistance [to Kennedy] was to suggest some books that he might look at."[40]

The truth is more complicated. Sorensen authored the book's first draft. When Schlesinger offered a detailed 2,000-word critique of the draft, he was providing both Kennedy and Sorensen with a critique of *Sorensen's draft*. This meant that Kennedy was unlikely to be offended by Schlesinger's criticisms but not Sorensen. Schlesinger may have naively thought he was giving feedback to Kennedy, but he was really criticizing the prickly Sorensen.[41]

When this was going on, the two men were also in different Democrat Party camps. Schlesinger was not officially on Team Kennedy, and plainly not to the degree Sorensen was. Schlesinger was an Adlai Stevenson man and had worked as a speechwriter for Stevenson's failed presidential campaigns in 1952 and 1956. Schlesinger's first interactions with the Kennedy campaign were as a sort of spy who could update the Kennedy team on Stevenson's activities. Sorensen wrote that Schlesinger "quietly kept us informed on thinking within the Stevenson camp."[42] Schlesinger also wrote about meeting Sorensen via his association with Stevenson. This was during the 1956 Democratic convention, when the Kennedy team was unwilling to use the Stevenson operation's draft for Kennedy's speech to the convention. This impasse required a conclave in which Schlesinger led the negotiations on behalf of the Stevenson forces. As Schlesinger recalled, "It was then that I first saw the Kennedy-Sorensen team in operation. There was no question which was the dominant partner, but there was no question either that in Sorensen Kennedy had found a remarkably intelligent, sensitive and faithful associate."[43]

This passage reveals several important points. First, Schlesinger clearly acknowledges how talented Sorensen was and how close he was to Kennedy. Second, even as Schlesinger praised Sorensen, he felt the need to make clear just who was the "dominant partner." Third, this early interaction foreshadowed much of their future relationship under Kennedy, as Sorensen jealously guarded his ability to write the words that came out of Kennedy's mouth and was extremely reluctant to cede his monopoly to anyone.

The differential in power was palpable on both sides of the Schlesinger-Sorensen divide. Sorensen and his allies mocked Schlesinger's marginality to the operation and even his physical location within the White House. Goodwin uncharitably recalled that Schlesinger resided "on the other side of the mansion, in the East Wing." Press Secretary Pierre Salinger joked about Schlesinger's placement that the "calmer atmosphere he must have found more congenial to his cerebra-tions." Aldous quotes an unnamed Kennedy staffer as saying, "You have to understand that *Arthur* was over in the *East Wing,* drinking with *Jackie.*" Aldous argues that JFK intentionally placed Schlesinger near Jackie "as a way to circumvent the kind of toxic jealousies so perfectly illustrated by that petty remark." If that were the case, then Schlesinger seemed uncertain of Kennedy's intent. When feeling positive about things, he called his location in the White House a "more luxuri-ous, but more remote domain." When feeling less good about it, as Schlesinger recalled to his daughter Christina, he complained that "his office was in the East Wing and, as you know, the West Wing is where everything was happening."[44]

Beyond the disparity in roles was their disparity in effectiveness. In one sticky personnel situation, the Kennedy administration struggled with what to do with Chester "Chet" Bowles. Bowles was a Connecticut politician and foreign policy advisor to the Kennedy presidential cam-paign. He was undersecretary of state—the number two official at the time—serving under Secretary of State Dean Rusk. Unfortunately, Bowles was ineffective in the job, someone who liked meandering memos and discussions more than decisive action. As Sorensen wrote, Bowles "preferred exploring long-range ideas to expediting short-gap expedi-ents."[45] Bowles also told his friends and allies—known as the Chet Set—that he was not involved in planning the Bay of Pigs fiasco and was opposed to it when he did hear of it. As the columnist and Georgetown party regular Joseph Alsop put it, "Bowles was in great agony and telling everyone and sundry that only he had been right about Cuba and other endearing things of that kind."[46] More broadly, the president didn't like lengthy reports. As National Security Council staffer Robert Komer recalled, "Chet couldn't resist writing these eleven-page cables to the president. Neither Kennedy nor Johnson could stand that sort of thing."[47] A great Jules Feiffer cartoon, which Schlesinger dutifully shared with Kennedy, had Bowles coming to a staff meeting late, and explaining to Kennedy, "Sorry I'm late, Chief. I was finishing up a book review." To this, the cartoon had Kennedy reply: "Try to be prompt, Chester. The rest of us manage to get our book reviews done on our own time."[48]

The question was: how to handle the problem of Bowles's ineffectuality? Bowles did have his Chet Set allies in the administration and in the press, and he was none too anxious to leave. Alsop cattily wondered whether Bowles's interest in staying in Washington "wasn't because Bowles spent such a lot on his house in Georgetown and didn't wish to vacate it." As if in a biblical story, Kennedy sent two messengers to address the problem. The first was Schlesinger. As Alsop put it, more than a little contemptuously, "They sent young Arthur over to make peace with Bowles." Schlesinger did talk to him, but not much beyond the status quo came out of it: Bowles would keep his position but without the management responsibilities—leaving Bowles with "the perfectly empty title of Under Secretary with none of the authority." Kennedy did not think much of this. As Alsop recalled, "Of course, the proposal that was made to the president filled him with perfect contempt. 'Imagine suggesting that,' he said to me."[49]

The new arrangement was clearly unworkable and did not last long. Bowles would have to leave State, but the problem of his unhappiness remained. This time, Kennedy sent Sorensen to speak to him, "to hold his hand a little, as one 'liberal' to another, after Rusk breaks the news to him."[50] As Bowles wrote in his memoir, Sorensen "had apparently been asked to stand by in the White House with his political fire extinguisher."[51] It was a strange scene. Sorensen recalled that he "found Bowles sitting disconsolate and alone in his office." As the two men talked, "It grew darker and darker, but neither of us moved to turn on the lights." Finally, Sorensen wrote, "a solution began to emerge." Bowles would leave the State Department altogether for a new post, that of "Special Representative and Adviser for Asian, African, and Latin-American Affairs." The position brought with it a White House office and staff, a pay hike, a car and driver, in addition to White House mess privileges—but no real responsibilities. As Sorensen wrote, "It was not a real post, as became clear to all later." However, "it was a post which saved faces and prevented fights in November, 1961."[52] As Alsop recalled, this "second Bowles crisis" was "handled by Mr. Sorensen rather more ruthlessly" than Schlesinger had handled the first one.[53] Kennedy himself was pleased with the resolution and appreciated Sorensen's work on it, telling him, "Good job, Ted—that was your best work since the Michigan delegation."[54] Even when both Sorensen and Schlesinger worked on the same issue, Sorensen was clearly the more effective one.

While Kennedy was president, the roles were clear. But after Kennedy's tragic death, things changed a bit. Sorensen had lost his patron, the source of his power, while Schlesinger had his well-known and well-established body of work to fall back on. Both stayed briefly in the Johnson administration—each leaving in early 1964—and then set out to write their own memoirs of the Kennedy administration. In January of 1964, Schlesinger wrote in a letter to his parents that "I am inclining more and more to the idea of writing a book about the Kennedy administration, though I understand that Ted Sorensen has this in mind too." Schlesinger acknowledged Sorensen's advantages—a head start in writing and a closer relationship with Kennedy—but Schlesinger had assets of his own. In a line that revealed much about their respective places in the Kennedy orbit, Schlesinger wrote that Sorensen "was much more involved in a wider range of policy than I; but I still think I might have something to contribute."[55] The race was on.

This contest between the two men to get a book out first both fascinated the media and chilled their relationship. Even though tensions existed almost since their first meeting, Sorensen observed that media interest in their rivalry dated to "1965, when our two books on JFK were rivals for publication and public attention."[56] In this period, Sorensen acknowledged, "Our friendship was temporarily strained."[57]

There was some effort by Sorensen to effectuate a deal between them so that they could, as he wrote to Schlesinger, "conclude a pact on the timing of our books, thereby relieving some pressure from us both and better serving JFK's memory with better books." He was not really suggesting much of a truce, though, as his proposal was that Schlesinger stand aside and let Sorensen go first. Unsurprisingly, Schlesinger balked, and tried to write faster to beat Sorensen to the finish line.[58]

In the end, Sorensen finished first, and his book—*Kennedy*—hit number one on the bestseller list. Schlesinger's book—*A Thousand Days*—came second, and it also hit number one, displacing Sorensen. Sorensen reacted to being leapfrogged by sending Schlesinger a chipper note: "Welcome to the number 1 slot. As number 2, we try harder."[59]

Once the books were out, there were disagreements over what each book revealed. Jackie Kennedy told Schlesinger that some of his revelations were "too personal."[60] Rusk, annoyed that Schlesinger had written that the "Buddha-like" Rusk would say little in White House meetings, would retort that he was silent in Schlesinger's presence because he knew of Schlesinger's propensity for gossiping on the Georgetown cocktail circuit.[61] Columnist Drew Pearson recalled discussing "the Schlesinger-Sorensen books on Kennedy and the current feud between them." According to Pearson, Sorensen "said that Schlesinger should not have told all, especially Kennedy's plans to fire Rusk." Schlesinger "shot back by publishing a letter that Sorensen had written him, praising his book and saying he wouldn't change a word."[62]

In some ways, the loss of Kennedy reestablished the natural order between the two men. Schlesinger has gone down as one of Kennedy's most famous aides, even if he was not one of the more senior ones during the administration. Schlesinger's book—not Sorensen's—won the Pulitzer Prize, and it was Schlesinger's second prize. Sorensen may have been closer to John F. Kennedy, but Schlesinger was closer to the surviving Kennedys, namely Jackie Kennedy and Bobby, about whom he later wrote an even more glowing book than the one he wrote about JFK.

There can be little doubt that in that shining moment of Camelot, there was a rivalry between Schlesinger and Sorensen. It was an unusual rivalry, in which there was little day-to-day sniping, and in which it was obvious who was on top during Kennedy's presidency. But in the seeds of the Schlesinger-Sorensen rivalry, there were visible aspects of White House rivalries to come: competing memoirs; sniping over position titles; reveling in small victories like getting one's words in a speech; getting praise from the president for doing a job better than one's rival; or being in a position considerably more significant than someone long more famous and successful. For those thousand days of the Kennedy administration, it was Sorensen who held the upper hand in that rivalry, proving once again the rule of propinquity when it comes to interpersonal relations in the White House. Just as Bobby Kennedy's fraternal closeness served him well in a position technically below that of Lyndon Johnson, so too did Sorensen's mind-meld with Kennedy serve him well for the years in which he was special counsel to the president. But the aura only lasted so long as the source of their status remained in power.

Inadvertently or not, Kennedy allowed certain tensions to surface in his administration. He brought Lyndon Johnson in as vice president, even though he had to know his brother and Johnson did not get along. That decision would have significant consequences both in and beyond the Kennedy administration. As for Schlesinger and Sorensen, even though it was a lower profile rivalry, the fact that there was tension between the two men could not have escaped Kennedy's attention.

The Kennedy administration was a bridge administration between the buttoned-down teams of the 1950s and the open warfare of some more recent administrations. Tensions were there in the Kennedy administration, but they had to do with jealousies and ego, rather than serious ideological disagreements. In addition, Kennedy did have the advantage of dealing with a different kind of media atmosphere than would future presidents. While the fights happened, and the jealousies and hatreds were real, they rarely made the headlines or caught the wider attention of the American public and were confined more to Georgetown party gossip. If the media were willing to overlook Kennedy's sexual escapades, they would naturally take a similar approach to intra-administration feuding, meaning that some of the fighting will be lost to history. At the same time, the higher profile people brought in by Kennedy would bring more baggage with them than earlier aides governed by the Brownlow-sought "passion for anonymity." Kennedy's administration differed from modern administrations to be sure, but it also foreshadowed many of the tendencies that would appear in later years.

# CHAPTER 3

# LBJ

## Johnson's Kennedy Obsession Continues

The central fact of the Johnson administration was that Lyndon Baines Johnson ascended to the presidency because of the Kennedy tragedy. While Johnson had long desired to become president, he certainly did not expect to ascend to the position in the way he did. As a result, the Kennedy assassination—not to mention Johnson's miserable experience serving under Kennedy—markedly shaped how Johnson ran his administration and the policies he pursued. It also shaped the rivalries that took place within his administration, with Johnson standing tall at the center of most of them.

The succession from Kennedy to Johnson was only part of the story. Lyndon Johnson was a larger-than-life personality, a fact that would make his ego, insecurities, and crude manners an outsize determinant of the relationships and rivalries that formed over the course of his administration. Johnson's eccentricities and bullying of staff put him at the heart of his administration's rivalries, and he was often an active participant in the most challenging relationships that developed. This made his administration unusual as rivalries were president-focused rather than staff-focused. Rivalries were not based on who had access to the president so much as who the president targeted.

Johnson's White House was, by Johnson's own design, a difficult and hard-charging environment. Johnson himself famously worked herculean hours, best exemplified by his two-shift workday. Under this system, Johnson would begin working at six in the morning, using the phone to check in with key staff and legislators. As Johnson aide Jack Valenti described it, "He would be on the phone during these early morning hours, always to [Secretary of State] Rusk and [Secretary of Defense] McNamara. Within an hour or so, he would sweep the West Wing clean, calling each of his top aides with an opening line 'What do you know?' which meant he wanted to dredge them for information."[1]

Johnson would work continuously until about two in the afternoon, at which time he would take a walk and a nap. Then, refreshed from his exercise and rest, he would go back to work until midnight, and often even later. As Johnson's long-time personal aide Mildred Stegall recalled, "People often asked me if LBJ wasn't hard to work for. I would always answer, 'Not if you were willing to work.' It seemed as though he never ran out of steam—work, work, work."[2]

It was not easy for staff to accommodate themselves to Johnson's style. Johnson needed five secretaries to keep up with him and his demands. His immediate predecessors Eisenhower and Kennedy each had only two people in those roles.[3] Staffers acutely felt the fast pace. Johnson Press Secretary George Reedy recorded that "those who were in the Johnson administration during the early days will always think of the White House as an indoor stadium hosting a perpetual track meet." This sense of constant racing put a form of peer pressure on the staff, in which everyone always had to be working. As Reedy put it, "Only the president himself dared to walk through the corridors empty-handed. For anyone else, it was either a confession of impotence or a gesture of defiance."[4]

There was something of a method to Johnson's challenging approach. His hard-charging style predated his time as president, although the presidency exposed his methods to a much larger staff. But those who had served with him before recognized the style. As one long-standing Johnson aide said, LBJ "ran the White House as he had his Senate office, under his hat."[5]

Johnson's habitual use of the telephone had a purpose beyond getting information. Kent State Professor James Best, who did an analysis of Johnson's phone usage, suggested that Johnson's frequent calls and his expectation in those pre-cellphone days that aides would be by their desks served "as an instrument of staff control; staff members could never be too far from their phones." In addition, Best saw the constant phoning and haranguing as a form of vetting, of trial by fire. Subjecting aides to Johnsonian harassment taught Johnson whom he could rely on and, more importantly, who could be trusted.[6]

Johnson had the self-awareness to recognize that he rode his staff hard. Referring to his trusted aide and White House Press Secretary Bill Moyers, Johnson said, with a touch of sympathy and perhaps even appreciation, "That boy has a bleeding ulcer. He works for me like a dog, and is just as faithful."[7] Johnson wanted the same dedication from others, saying "An eight-hour man ain't worth a damn to me." He also had little patience for family considerations getting in the way of work: "I don't want some wife at home complainin' that the cornbread's gettin' cold while her husband's doin' somethin' for me."[8] Johnson also had what his Senate colleague and future vice president Hubert Humphrey called a need "to have people around him." As Humphrey put it, "If you weren't there, he'd just reach a little further to get you. And if he couldn't get you physically, he'd pick up the phone and get you."[9] Lady Bird Johnson put things a little more starkly, observing that "the thing Lyndon hated most was to be by himself."[10]

Johnson's brother Sam Houston Johnson suggested that Johnson's demanding style derived from their Texas roots. According to Sam Houston, Johnson's belief was that "an employee owes complete loyalty to his employer." As a result, Johnson believed that "any shade of criticism or lack of enthusiasm from any staff member could be suspect. A staffer's duty was to carry out instructions, not to challenge them." When a staffer appeared to deviate from this level of slavish dedication, Johnson could be brutal. Former Johnson aide Bill Brammer authored his successful book *The Gay Place* while serving as a Johnson staffer. Brammer told him, after Johnson confronted him, that the book was not written on staff time but "at nights and on weekends." This answer did not placate Johnson, who told him: "You ought to have been answering my mail."[11]

In addition to imposing heavy work demands, Johnson also belittled his staff on a regular basis. As Doris Kearns Goodwin, who worked in the Johnson White House, reported, "Johnson commanded, forbade, insisted, swaggered, and swore." He picked on and highlighted people's weaknesses and kept his special hatred for the intellectuals and the so-called Georgetown elites, both on his staff and elsewhere. As Texas playwright Larry King wrote, Johnson "had the old chauvinistic instincts indigenous to the *macho* country boy, and one of his worst insults— invariably directed at the Bundys, the Goldmans, and the Schlesingers, the polished intellectuals—was to sneer that such-and-so fellow 'probably has to squat to pee.'" Harry McPherson, a close aide who was buffeted by Johnson's mercurial nature, recalled, "When I was in favor, I was on top of the world; when I was out of favor, I was in the dumps." As a result, McPherson would later have to leave Johnson's orbit to "save [his] sanity." Johnson's vice presidential aide Charles Boatner summarized working for Johnson thus: "When you were working for Johnson, you were caught up in the Johnson scheme of things."[12] All of this berating and mood swinging came from Johnson's own sense of inadequacy. He had to undermine others for his own peace of mind. As Kearns Goodwin wrote, "It seemed as if Johnson *needed* to make his staff look ridiculous; that he was strengthened by his exposure of inadequacies in others."[13]

Another way in which Johnson rode hard on his staff was in his relentless pursuit of leaks. He demanded that his administration be leak-proof, an impossible standard. As Johnson's domestic policy advisor Joe Califano recalled, "Even minor leaks irritated Johnson."[14] Johnson invited only a few choice aides to key meetings to minimize the possibility of leaks and engaged in what columnists Rowland Evans and Robert Novak called "gumshoe tactics" to try to identify and root out leakers.[15] These tactics included having White House operators monitor callers and recipients on White House phone lines and having White House drivers record the destinations of White House staffers headed to meetings in official vehicles. Johnson even suggested building a wall between the West Wing and the Old Executive Office Building to separate reporters from staff physically. Marvin Watson, the Johnson aide in charge of the anti-leak efforts, took preliminary steps to start building the wall before better judgement took hold and the project came to a halt.[16] Overall, recalled Attorney General Nick Katzenbach, "[Johnson] occasionally acted in an almost childish manner when news he had been planning to announce leaked out."[17]

Sometimes Johnson's anti-leak crusade would lead to humorous results. Katzenbach recalled steering a *Washington Post* reporter off a false, damaging—and unfortunately now forgotten—story by explaining to the reporter what was really happening. The reporter put Katzenbach's less harmful yet accurate version of the story on the front page, without attribution to Katzenbach. Johnson, recognizing that the item had clearly come from the Justice Department, called Katzenbach and demanded, "I want you to find who leaked that story and fire him." Katzenbach responded, "I'm afraid I can't do that, Mr. President." Johnson was taken aback, and angered, by this rare instance of staff resistance to his demand, "What the hell do you mean you can't do that?" Katzenbach explained, "Mr. President, you're the only person who can do that. I leaked the story." This response prompted what Katzenbach described as "Silence, then a chuckle," followed by, "By God, that's the first leak in government I've ever uncovered."[18]

The Katzenbach story had a happy conclusion, but it was atypical. Johnson's demanding, belittling, and mistrusting behavior had the intended consequence of asserting Johnson's dominance. And there is no doubt that President Lyndon Johnson was a dominant figure, in the

White House or on Capitol Hill; as the *Christian Science Monitor*'s Richard Strout wrote, "Rarely has one man so dominated Washington as President Johnson now does."[19] Johnson's method was successful in that it allowed him to pass the monumental Great Society legislation, as well as to pursue a large land war in Vietnam that would, over time, garner intense public opposition.

Johnson's difficult interpersonal methods had an unintended consequence as well. They made the Johnson White House a paranoid, defensive place, where staffers would be wary of bucking the president with contrary advice. No doubt there are others who, hearing the horror stories, never even submitted job applications. For those who stayed, they felt they had to toe the line to avoid angering their hypersensitive and overreactive boss. The approach may have worked when things were going well, but it made it hard to give the president difficult but necessary advice when things went poorly.

## Johnson and the Kennedy Staff

As challenging as Johnson was with staff in general, he was particularly paranoid about the Kennedy staff. These included staffers he suspected—or knew—had loyalty or even ties to the Kennedy family. Katzenbach had been Bobby Kennedy's deputy at the Justice Department before moving up when Kennedy left to run for Senate. But Katzenbach successfully proved his loyalty and his effectiveness to Johnson, so much so that Johnson used to ask his other staffers, "Why can't you be like Nick Katzenbach?"[20] Other staffers with even a whiff of loyalty to the Kennedy dynasty would hear about it. Regarding Press Secretary Bill Moyers, Johnson told his speechwriter Richard Goodwin, "That boy's like a son to me, even if he did go work for those Kennedys." Despite this affectionate claim on one occasion, however, on another he shouted at Moyers and National Security Advisor McGeorge Bundy, "That's the trouble with all you fellows. You're in bed with the Kennedys."[21] The comparisons of aides' performances under Kennedy and under him started early. In December, just one month after Kennedy's assassination, Johnson chided a group of press aides, including Kennedy's Press Secretary Pierre Salinger, snapping, "You're not getting my picture on the front page the way you did Kennedy's."[22]

Johnson once engaged in a legendary humiliation of Salinger at a luncheon. When Salinger did not eat the beans on his plate, Johnson noticed, saying, "Pierre, you haven't eaten your beans." Salinger's response was eminently reasonable: "Mr. President, I happen not to care for this variety of beans." But Johnson pressed the point, demanding, "Pierre, eat your beans!" Johnson got Salinger to eat the beans, but he also got him to quit, which might very well have been Johnson's intent.[23]

Immediately following the assassination, though, Johnson felt that he needed to keep the Kennedy staff on board. This feeling may have been in part because of Kennedy's popularity, but also because the Kennedy staff had the experience and knew how the White House ran. Johnson made that pitch to multiple Kennedy aides, including Bobby, whom he told on the day of the assassination: "I need you more than the president needed you." Beyond the individual pitches, Johnson in a meeting asked for the whole Kennedy staff to remain shortly after the assassination: "I want you all to stay on. I need you," he told them.[24] No doubt with some disingenuousness or posturing, Johnson suggested that he felt unable live up to Kennedy's legacy, to win over the Kennedy loyalists. He even told Ted Sorensen, "I want you to draw the threads together on the domestic program, but don't expect me to absorb things as fast as you're used to."[25] In fact, Johnson may have pressed the point too hard, potentially alienating his own staff. By making the case that he needed the Kennedy people—"that his own staff wasn't quite up to Kennedy's," as Rowland Evans and Robert Novak wrote—he irked his own people.[26]

With Schlesinger, Johnson took an even more extreme version of this approach, warning him that if Schlesinger acted on his November 26 resignation letter, "I will have you arrested." Schlesinger withdrew the letter, but was not given much to do by the new president, who apparently valued him more as a symbol than as an effective aide.[27] As Lee White described Schlesinger's view of working for Johnson: "It was not his dish of tea. Arthur did not have a sort of operating responsibility. He was at the ballpark, but he wasn't in the ball game."[28]

Johnson's pleas to keep the Kennedy staff around gave him some needed stability, but it also led to some staffing anomalies. He kept the Kennedy cabinet, with no changes for his first thirteen months. Ten of the twenty-five cabinet secretaries who served under Johnson had originally been Kennedy secretaries.[29] No Kennedy person left before Sorensen did in late February, with Schlesinger following shortly after. Overall, as Evans and Novak wrote, "The key faces of the new frontier remained in Washington into 1965 and even beyond."[30]

At the same time, Johnson also doubled up responsibilities to make sure he had people he trusted to do what was needed. Johnson aide Eric Goldman described the result as a Noah's Ark staff: "There's two of everybody."[31] There was a cost to keeping the Kennedy people, in terms of actual dual loyalty but also in terms of a perceived dual loyalty. In Goldman's view, the Kennedy staff viewed Johnson as "a usurper, and an ignoble one at that." According to Goldman, there was also a sense among the Johnson staff that the remaining Kennedy aides "snickered and sniped, half performed their tasks, and engaged in acts of petty sabotage."[32]

Johnson shared his staff's views on the Kennedy team. Even though he felt he needed the Kennedy people for symbolic and political purposes, he distrusted them, and made sure people knew it. His closest, most loyal aides, probably offended by Johnson's obsequiousness towards the Kennedy people in the earliest days of the Johnson presidency, acted to make clear that Johnson was in charge. When Goldman, a Princeton professor thought by some to be a sort of White House intellectual, came on board, Johnson loyalist Walter Jenkins told him definitively that he should not view himself as a replacement for his Harvard counterpart Schlesinger. As Jenkins put it: "You are not the Johnson Arthur Schlesinger. Nobody is going to be the Johnson

Schlesinger. Nobody is going to be the Johnson anything of Kennedy. *This is a different administration* [sic]."[33] Marvin Watson, in addition to staving off leaks, recalled in his memoir that he was also in charge of funneling the Kennedy men out of the administration—after an acceptable time period, of course.[34]

No Kennedy holdover caused Johnson more agitation than Kennedy's brother Bobby. The two men had had a fraught relationship for years (see previous chapter). Johnson did beg Kennedy to stay on—but the two quickly found themselves in disagreement over Johnson's succession to the presidency. Bobby felt that Johnson consolidated his new position too quickly and too eagerly, and without sufficient compassion for those displaced by Kennedy's death, staff and family alike. Johnson felt that Bobby did not give him the respect deserved by his new position, and moreover suspected that Bobby did not accept the legitimacy of the succession itself. Johnson even believed that Bobby "seriously considered whether he would let me be president, whether he should really take the position [that] the vice president didn't automatically move in. I thought that was on his mind every time I saw him in the first few days."[35] Even once the succession was cemented and in place, Johnson thought that Bobby "acted like he was the custodian of the Kennedy dream, some kind of rightful heir to the throne."[36]

Those first few days were truly awful on the RFK-LBJ front, worse than the 1960 convention and far worse than the awkward cold peace that existed between them while Kennedy was president. During Johnson's vice presidency, Johnson was indeed miserable, but Bobby was not obsessed with him. Bobby was busy being attorney general and the president's top advisor. Sure, Bobby treated Johnson disrespectfully and would on more than one occasion embarrass him, but their interactions were inherently limited. Furthermore, Johnson did have the elevated title of vice president, and President Kennedy would insist—albeit with limited success—that the staff treat Johnson with respect.

Once Kennedy was killed, though, RFK became a direct report to Johnson. As a result, things quickly worsened between the two men. The extent of the mutual distrust prevented any kind of a healthy interaction from happening. While the enmity began earlier, it was that initial period after Kennedy's death that turned their rivalry into something much worse. As Bobby characterized it, "There were three or four matters that arose during the period of November 22 to November 27 or so which made me bitter—unhappy at least—with Lyndon Johnson. Events involving the treatment of Jackie on the plane trip back and all that kind of business—when he lied again and where he treated Jackie, the whole business, very badly."[37]

Of course, Johnson had his issues with Bobby as well. Bobby famously—and rudely—rushed by Johnson when Air Force One returned to Washington with the new president. He came late to Johnson's initial cabinet meeting shortly after the assassination. Johnson was sure the tardiness was intentional, claiming that Bobby told an aide, "We won't go in until he has already sat down."[38] The two men had a meeting on November 27 to clear the air regarding the accusations and counter-accusations—but the attempt failed. Afterwards, they did not see each other again for almost two months.[39] This absence of encounters would not be unusual in ordinary circumstances, except for the fact that Kennedy was and remained Johnson's attorney general in that period.

Kennedy would stay on as attorney general until he quit to run for the Senate from New York in 1964. The next major flashpoint in their tempestuous relationship was over the vice-presidential slot on the presidential ticket in 1964. On the surface, this should not have been an issue, as neither man in their right mind should have wanted to share the ticket with the other. From Johnson's perspective, Kennedy was a political threat, and uncooperative and disrespectful to boot. From Kennedy's perspective, he saw how miserable a vice president could be in an administration where the president's staff did not respect him. For these reasons, the idea was doomed from the start, but that did not prevent the existence of the opening from creating additional intrigue and mistrust between the two men.

The groundswell to add Kennedy to the ticket was so frequent and so intense that it became known within the White House as "the Bobby problem." Johnson felt that he could not get away from the talk. As he recalled, "Every day, as soon as I opened the papers or turned on the television, there was something about Bobby Kennedy; there was some person or group talking about what a great vice president he'd make." In addition to the media speculation, there was also the constant stream of people making "helpful" suggestions to add Bobby to the ticket. Johnson recalled that "a tidal wave of letters and memos about how great a vice president Bobby would be swept over me."[40] Such suggestions and media speculation, of course, made it less likely that Johnson would want to pick Bobby. Beyond the personal dislike and Johnson's generally contrary nature when it came to all things Kennedy, there was also the matter of Johnson's political and historical standing. At one point, Johnson told Kennedy holdover Ken O'Donnell that "I don't want history to say I was elected to this office because I had Bobby on the ticket with me." Even here, though, he did give a nod to political necessity, adding, "But I'll take him if I need him."[41] At other times, he was more adamant, though, insisting that "if they try to push Bobby Kennedy down my throat for vice president, I'll tell them to nominate him for the Presidency and leave me out of it."[42] In the end, Bobby did not join the ticket, but instead became senator from New York, a fact that entailed its own torments for President Johnson.

As with many rivalries at this level, the RFK-LBJ feud would have larger implications in Washington. Johnson had told Minnesota Senator Hubert Humphrey that he was almost certain to be the nominee, but Johnson left him dangling while the Bobby drama lingered on. At times Johnson was encouraging, but he would also retreat, suggesting other senators as candidates. As Doris Kearns Goodwin wrote, "This emotional seesaw took its toll on Humphrey." Humphrey would pathetically compare himself to the high school girl desperate for the attention of the captain of the football team. In the woeful tale, the football hero would constantly ask the poor girl what he thought of other girls, but never ask her on the date she so desperately wanted. The episode, Kearns Goodwin wrote, "reinforced the psychological dependency long rooted in Humphrey's relationship with Johnson."[43]

Johnson's on-and-off flirtation with Humphrey should have prepared the Minnesota senator for the tribulations of serving under Johnson. Johnson cruelly imposed some of the misery he experienced as vice president on his own vice president. George Reedy put it starkly: Johnson's "treatment of Humphrey was very bad." Johnson kept Humphrey out of the loop, so much so that Humphrey somewhat pathetically had to rely on Reedy for news on developments at the White House: "The vice president received what little information about the White House that came his way by calling me daily." Johnson would also not only make Humphrey wait for meetings with him, but staff members like Califano would also leave Humphrey waiting for meetings as well. This sort of thing is unlikely to happen without the president's tacit approval. Reedy even speculated that "it may have been that he felt keenly the indignities that he believed had been visited on him as vice president and he wanted to take them out on someone else."[44]

Outsiders noticed Humphrey's plight. The irony of Johnson doing to Humphrey what had been done to Johnson was not lost on observers of the political scene. The comedic lyricist Tom Lehrer even memorialized the situation in a 1965 song. As Lehrer sang:

> What ever became of Hubert?
> Once a fiery liberal spirit,
> but now when he speaks he must clear it…
> Did Lyndon, recalling when he was VP,
> Say "I'll do unto you like they did unto me?"[45]

Joe Califano had initially thought that "because of the way [Johnson had] been humiliated, I thought Johnson would treat Hubert Humphrey differently." It was not to be. Johnson removed responsibilities such as civil rights from Humphrey's portfolio in a peremptory manner, and even

Lyndon Johnson did not follow the golden rule when it came to Vice President Hubert Humphrey, pictured above. He treated Humphrey as he was treated by the Kennedy staff, not how he wished he had been treated. *Courtesy of the Library of Congress*

tried to make it look as if the diminution of responsibilities had been Humphrey's idea. Humphrey, however, put on a game face for the press. When a reporter asked him if, "With these posts being eliminated you no longer have an official title," Humphrey archly responded: "That is correct, except vice president."[46] Still, the experience hurt him deeply.

## LBJ and Vietnam: Rivals Within and Without

The Humphrey torment was only one way in which the Bobby-Johnson rivalry had an impact beyond that on its participants. The most significant consequence to come out of the feud was its impact on the Vietnam War. The curious thing about Johnson's actions on Vietnam is that they were shaped in many ways by Kennedy people, both from within and without. Inside the government, it was the people Johnson inherited from Kennedy, including Dean Rusk, McGeorge Bundy, Walt Rostow, and Robert McNamara, who shaped the Johnson administration's approach to Vietnam and America's deepening involvement in that conflict. Johnson felt that the Kennedy aides gave him cover. Whatever they recommended had the apparent blessing of the late president, and so Johnson generally followed their advice.[47]

Outside the administration, the specter of Bobby loomed. Concerns about Bobby made Johnson feel that he had to be more hawkish than he wanted to be, even as it was Bobby's dovishness later in the administration that put additional pressure on Johnson in the other direction. But in the early days, Johnson worried that Bobby would be pressing Johnson from the right and using his brother's legacy to press the case. Johnson feared that "there would be Robert Kennedy out in front leading the fight against me, telling everyone that I had betrayed John Kennedy's commitment to South Vietnam. That I had let a democracy fall into the hands of the Communists. That I was a coward. An unmanly man. A man without a spine. Oh, I could see it coming, all right."[48]

While the Kennedy aides mostly adopted a hawkish approach, ironically some Johnson people were more skeptical, including Bill Moyers and Harry McPherson.[49] But there were two main reasons why their skepticism had little impact on the White House's approach. First, Moyers and McPherson were political aides, not foreign policy experts. As Kearns Goodwin later put it, "The only individuals whose opinions on foreign policy could carry weight were those whose positions tied them in on a daily basis to the decisions made about Vietnam."[50] The experts were overwhelmingly Kennedy people, and they favored the gradual escalations. Second, and more important, was Johnson himself. His core premise, expressed to his foreign policy advisors in a meeting two days after the assassination was, "I will not lose in Vietnam."[51] Given this direction from the top, it is unsurprising that the advisors pursued policies that they believed would prevent the U.S. from "losing" Vietnam.

The only exception among the initial group of top foreign policy advisors was George Ball. Ball, who was undersecretary of state—the number two official in the Department—under Kennedy and then under Johnson, had been skeptical of increased American involvement in Vietnam under Kennedy. When he warned that the U.S. would end up with 300,000 troops in Vietnam, Kennedy dismissed him, saying, "George, you're just crazier than Hell.... That just isn't going to happen."[52] As it turned out, Ball underestimated things, as the number of American troops in Vietnam would exceed half a million by 1968.

Kennedy's dismissal of Ball's views was mild compared to what dissenters would experience in the Johnson White House. Ball had it better than most, as he had the appearance of official sanction for his role as the in-house objector to the Vietnam War. Johnson acknowledges this in his stiff and over-edited memoir, *The Vantage Point*. Johnson writes, with some degree of understatement, that "Ball had been less than enthusiastic about some prospects of our involvement in Southeast Asia." Johnson further explained that Ball had a designated role in this regard, and that "often in our meetings he spoke in opposition to one proposal or another. Especially from 1965 onward he played the role of devil's advocate frequently."[53]

Marvin Watson suggests that Ball's mandate to be in-house skeptic was more explicit, noting that Johnson called in Ball and specifically asked him to take a contrary position. According to Watson, "From that moment on, in every private moment among the president's principal advisors, George Ball became the articulate spokesman against American policy in Vietnam." Watson acknowledges that this did not make Ball popular with the rest of the Johnson staff: "The arguments he expressed—always calmly but forcibly stated—were, to say the least, annoying to the president's other advisors." But at the same time, Watson paints a picture of a president more amenable to dissent than other accounts suggest, writing that the other Johnson aides "were amazed that a president they always viewed as impatient and intolerant of dissent never took any action to suppress Ball."[54]

Ball's presidential blessing, though, was not enough to protect him from colleagues. Ball's first memo outlining his concerns about Vietnam, which he shared with staff but not the president, angered Defense Secretary McNamara. McNamara could be a tough cookie, with a hard stare and a general impatience for having his time wasted in any way. He insisted, for example, that his briefings be written rather than oral. When an aide asked why, the staffer got a glare, and a cold response: "Because I can read faster than they can talk."[55] McNamara also disliked when other staffers meddled in what he saw as his business. As NSC staffer Bob Komer put it, McNamara "damn well doesn't want you monkeying around in his cabbage patch." McNamara also had no compunctions about telling people off when he disagreed with them. As Komer recalled, McNamara "read me the riot act more than anybody else in Washington, with the exception of McGeorge Bundy."[56]

McNamara, one of the key architects of the Vietnam strategy, intensely disliked the first memo Ball wrote raising questions. As Ball put it, McNamara "treated it like a poisonous snake.... He really just regarded it as next to treason." Ball had other staff problems as well. According to Komer, "There was an obvious coolness between George Ball and Bundy on occasion."[57] These kinds of internal pressures from the Johnson staff led even Ball to mute the full brunt of his concerns. As Dean Rusk remembered, "George Ball didn't come into my office every other day saying, 'Look, we've got to do something radically different in Viet Nam.'"[58]

Other doubters had it worse than Ball, who at least had the presidential dispensation for his heresies. When USIA Head Leonard Marks suggested later that Johnson pursue Vermont Senator George Aiken's idea of declaring victory and going home, Johnson did not want to hear it. As Marks put it, "He looked at me—he had a way of staring at you—and finally I blinked, I said, 'What do you think?' He said, 'Get out of here.' I picked up my papers and left."[59] Skeptics within the State

Secretary of Defense Robert McNamara was famously impatient, eschewing oral briefings because he could read faster than his staff could talk. *Courtesy of the Library of Congress*

Department had a "Non-Group" that met unofficially to avoid Johnson's attention.

Overall, Johnson wanted a narrow circle advising him on Vietnam, ostensibly to prevent leaks, but also to limit dissent. For this reason, he created the "Tuesday Group" of six foreign policy advisors to discuss Vietnam policy. Many domestic players, including cabinet secretaries, had their concerns, but they had no forum in which to express their opinions. As Doris Kearns Goodwin suggested, for those outside the group, "The rules of the game restricted all other players from real participation in decisions on Vietnam, thus inhibiting an expression of views on the basis of domestic considerations."[60] This approach may have limited leaks and explicit dissent, but it also famously led to "groupthink" as well as bad blood after the administration. Many later memoirs and accounts are critical of Johnson on the Vietnam issue because the authors felt that they could not express their concerns out loud at the time. This is a recurring problem in White House management. If staff members do not feel there is a forum for dissenting views, they will find other pathways, including leaking, whispering about the president behind his back, and writing unfavorable memoirs. Meanwhile, those who took the contrary view learned that their days were numbered. As Kearns Goodwin wrote, "Johnson protected himself from contrary arguments and discussions by dismissing the doubters from his staff. First McGeorge Bundy left. Then George Ball. Then Bill Moyers."[61]

For those who were on board with Johnson's Vietnam approach, it was even harder to express dissenting views. McNamara was an early proponent of escalation but soured on the war over time. By 1967, he had become a war skeptic, imperiling his relationship with Johnson, who saw this development as evidence of disloyalty. Johnson expressed his unhappiness with McNamara both verbally and non-verbally. In response to one McNamara memo suggesting a bombing halt, Johnson said "You've never seen such a lot of sh*t." On another occasion, after McNamara admitted to the Senate that he could not bomb North Vietnam into submission, the president subjected McNamara to a three-hour screaming session.[62] Johnson also let others know of his displeasure, complaining to them that he had been "suckered" by McNamara into a Christmas bombing halt. At a meeting with Democratic leaders, where it was clear that Johnson and McNamara were in different places, Johnson tartly acknowledged, "We do have differences of opinion."[63] Johnson also periodically reduced his accessibility to McNamara as the defense secretary's skepticism increased, culminating in McNamara's eventual termination in 1967. To cover his move, Johnson announced that McNamara would take over as president of the World Bank. This was a difficult decision. Johnson had felt that Treasury Secretary Henry Fowler was "the man who deserved that bank job all along." Fowler was so unhappy about being passed over that he allegedly cried on learning he did not get the job. Even with all this, Johnson still gave the position to McNamara. He felt that McNamara's caviling over Vietnam left him in a position where "I had no choice" but to let him go.[64]

Secretary of State Dean Rusk, President Lyndon Baines Johnson, and Secretary of Defense Robert McNamara. The three men agreed on Vietnam until McNamara changed his mind, prompting Johnson to replace McNamara with Clark Clifford. *Courtesy of the Library of Congress*

As always, Johnson attributed the McNamara problem to his real enemy: Kennedy. As Johnson remembered, "McNamara's problem was that he began to feel a division in his loyalties. He had always loved the Kennedys; he was more their cup of tea, but he also admired and respected the presidency." Johnson was right. Socially, McNamara was more in line with the Kennedys and their friends. He would even play the hide-and-seek variant "Sardines" with Bobby and Ethel Kennedy and Supreme Court Justice Byron Whizzer White at Hickory Hill. Initially, Johnson thought, McNamara remained loyal to Johnson, but the affection he felt for Johnson was still "not so deep as the one he held for the Kennedys but deep enough...to keep him completely loyal for three long years."[65] As things in Vietnam worsened, though, "the Kennedys began pushing him harder and harder. Every day Bobby would call up McNamara, telling him that the war was terrible and immoral and that he had to leave."[66]

Of course, Vietnam qualms from Kennedy and his allies were unlikely to sway Johnson in the desired direction. Bobby recognized this fact and was quieter than he wanted to be in the Senate, in part because he felt that his criticisms on Vietnam would be unhelpful in getting Johnson to change his approach. As Bobby told the journalist Jack Newfield, "I'm afraid that by speaking out I make Lyndon do the opposite, out of spite. He hates me so much that [if] I asked for snow, he would make rain, just because it was me."[67]

With McNamara gone, Johnson turned to Clark Clifford to run the Pentagon. Clifford, who had turned down the attorney general position a few years earlier, was no longer the junior staffer whom George Marshall tried to intimidate during the Truman administration. He was now a so-called Washington Wise Man, and Johnson initially had great faith in him. As Undersecretary of the Air Force Townsend Hoopes recalled, Johnson "had looked forward to Clifford's coming aboard as a means of reestablishing solid group harmony." Unfortunately, things did not work out that way. Clifford took a fresh look at what was happening and became an internal critic of the Vietnam policy. Johnson and the key staff were angry and confused; as Clifford observed, it seemed that "this Judas appeared." The disagreement over Vietnam affected their personal relationship. Hoopes felt that "the warm, long-standing friendship between the two men grew suddenly formal and cool." To Johnson, Hoopes wrote, "nothing counted more than personal loyalty."[68] Clifford felt the rift acutely, recalling Johnson's "sense of personal hurt that I was doing this to him."[69]

Clifford's position was different from Ball's in that Johnson did not authorize Clifford to play the thankless devil's advocate role. He had expected Clifford to be a loyal soldier. Yet when Clifford did not play that role, he found himself standing against both Johnson and the Johnson staff. From Johnson, Clifford met a "sense of personal hurt."[70] From the staff, he felt singled out as well. As Hoopes wrote, "On the almost daily meetings on Vietnam at the White House, Clifford continued to find himself outnumbered '7 or 8 to 1....'"[71]

The ostracism and the cooling of his relationship with Johnson did not deter Clifford. He continued to press for a move toward a negotiated settlement with the North Vietnamese, using the Clifford manner—"deliberate, sonorous, eloquent, and quite uninterruptible," as Hoopes wrote—that he had also used in his internal fight with Marshall over Israel during the Truman years.[72] But the difference from the Truman experience was that Truman wanted Clifford to take a position contrary to that of his senior foreign policy advisors. Johnson, in contrast, wanted Clifford to be on the same page as the other advisors. Even though Clifford was eventually successful in helping to bring about talks in Paris between the two sides, it brought him little credit from Johnson. As George Reedy recalled, "Lyndon Johnson later denied heatedly that Clifford played any real role in the unexpected decision to bring the Viet Cong and the North Vietnamese to the table in Paris." It appeared that Johnson's denials were based on personal pique; as Reedy noted, "Frankly, I could not take his protestations seriously."[73] Clifford understood that his skepticism within the administration came with a cost. As a result of Clifford's opposition to Johnson's war, Clifford wrote in his memoirs, "Our long friendship would never be the same again."[74]

In the end, the defining dysfunctional relationship of the Johnson administration was not between any warring White House staffers or between the staff and the agencies, but between the president and Bobby Kennedy. Even though Kennedy only served under Johnson for a brief period, he colored Johnson's thinking on key issues like Vietnam and his relations with his subordinates. With things going poorly in Vietnam, for example, Dean Rusk's job security was enhanced by virtue of Kennedy's disenchantment with him, even as Bundy recalled that "Rusk's style soon irritated [Johnson], and those who were around him detected a very subtle patronizing of the Secretary."[75] Being disliked by Bobby appeared to be weightier than any annoyance Rusk may have caused Johnson. As Califano wrote, "No testament to Rusk's loyalty could be more persuasive to Johnson than Kennedy's desire to see the Secretary fired."[76]

Of course, Kennedy added to Johnson's torment by threatening to challenge the president in the 1968 Democratic primaries. Kennedy did not to enter the race until after Johnson withdrew from the contest in March of 1968, but he certainly received internal encouragement to run before that point. His wife Ethel—who somehow hated Johnson even more than her husband did—encouraged and assisted the Kennedy children in putting up "Run Bobby Run" signs at the family house at Hickory Hill. Arthur Schlesinger and Ted Sorensen were rivals once again on this issue, with Sorensen warning Bobby against running and Schlesinger issuing an equally dire letter warning against not running.[77]

Johnson was a bully. He berated his staff in his need to dominate his surroundings. His style led to a bullying staff as well, in which those who deviated from Johnson's view on Vietnam were derided, ganged up on, or even dismissed. The lesson is clear: presidential tolerance for abusive or backstabbing behavior creates an environment in which such behavior flourishes. Furthermore, the ideological divide between being a Kennedy or a Johnson Democrat, later a hawk or a dove, on Vietnam, further contributed to internal disagreement.

Another lesson from the Johnson administration is that bullying is not always a one-way street. The Johnson period revealed that bullies could be intimidated as well, as Johnson was by Bobby Kennedy. Bobby caused Johnson to doubt the loyalty of his aides, doubt his policy instincts, and doubt himself. Johnson's obsession with Bobby and the whole Kennedy clan contributed to his sense that he was trapped on the Vietnam issue. In this very real sense, America's most unpopular war was shaped by one of American politics' bitterest rivalries.

CHAPTER 4

# NIXON
## Kissinger-Rogers and the Dangerous Quest for White House Control

Richard Nixon is largely remembered today for the Watergate scandal: the event that forced him to resign office rather than face the prospect of being the first U.S. president impeached by the House, found guilty by the Senate, and removed from office. But Nixon was also one of the most experienced people ever to become president, and he had definitive thoughts on how the executive branch should work. He expressed a belief in cabinet government and policy generated by departments and agencies.

Nixon supported cabinet government, but he was also preternaturally suspicious of others. He distrusted the federal bureaucracy and wanted to keep decisions under his and his closest aides' control. These countervailing and contradictory tendencies would have profound implications for the interpersonal relations among his staff. In other White Houses, disagreements lead to unhappiness with policy outcomes, unpleasant nicknames, premature resignations, or badmouthing in the press and in memoirs. In the Nixon administration, people ended up in prison. The Nixon staff had some of the bitterest rivalries in the White House staff era, and the dysfunctionalities behind those rivalries usually reflected the personality of the suspicious Nixon.

## Kissinger versus Rogers: Proximity versus Position

The defining feud of the Nixon administration was the one between National Security Advisor Henry Kissinger and Secretary of State William Rogers. On the surface, Rogers had all the advantages. He was a decade older than Kissinger and had a long-standing friendship with Nixon dating back to his time as Eisenhower's attorney general. When Nixon would visit Washington after serving as vice president, Rogers would lend him a desk in his law office.[1] As secretary of state, Rogers was also a cabinet secretary, a title which had until then carried greater weight in policy discussions than the national security advisor.

Kissinger was an upstart on multiple levels, having served as a consultant to the Kennedy administration and as an aide to Nixon's GOP rival Nelson Rockefeller. The staff was acutely aware of his ambition and past loyalties. White House speechwriter Pat Buchanan described him as follows: "Henry Kissinger, a Harvard professor with a reputation for being a brilliant and ambitious courtier, Nelson Rockefeller's man, was our national security advisor."[2]

Kissinger was also an immigrant, German-born with a heavy accent. Even though he was Jewish, and therefore victimized by the Nazis, his accent nevertheless revealed ties to a nation that while now an ally, had bitterly fought the U.S. twice in the preceding half century. To many, Kissinger's accent was a defining aspect of his persona, and he was capable of mocking it along with others. At one point, Kissinger joked that he was close to *National Review* editor William F. Buckley despite their political differences because they were both well-read, ambitious, multilingual, and "spoke with accents unfamiliar to their audiences."[3] This jibe obviously poked more fun at Buckley's *sui generis* accent, a mixture of New England, Southern, and British inflections, and was funny because of the universal recognition of Kissinger's Teutonic tones.

Kissinger's Jewishness was another recurring White House and media theme, especially compared to Rogers's more traditional Republican, upstate New York, WASP background. Nixon even kept Kissinger out of Middle East policymaking for much of his first term out of a mistaken concern for Kissinger's Jewish bias. He was also known to call Kissinger "my Jew boy" behind his back.[4]

Yet Nixon was unbiased in recognizing the talented Kissinger. The German Jewish refugee came out on top in the dispute with Rogers, and resoundingly so. At the time, Missouri Senator Stuart Symington cruelly referred to Rogers as "the laughing stock of the cocktail party circuit" in that Kissinger "had become Secretary of State in everything but title." This development, according to Symington, had a worrisome implication, namely "a resultant obvious decline in the prestige and position" of the office of the secretary of state.[5] Similarly, the *New York Times'* Bernard Gwertzman wrote that "Mr. Rogers was nominally the president's top advisor on foreign policy but in reality was overshadowed by Mr. Kissinger."[6] In just one of many more recent assessments, historian Niall Ferguson concluded in his analysis of Kissinger's social network that "Secretary of State William Rogers is a very unimportant node…despite the fact that in the org chart of the Nixon administration he was superior to Kissinger."[7]

## Nixon's Approach to Governing

It is important to recognize that the Kissinger-Rogers feud did not just exist because of Kissinger's overweening ambition. Beyond Kissinger's sharp-elbowed and widely recognized paranoid approach was the fact that at heart Nixon wanted the feud to happen. Nixon may not have wanted the sniping, the backbiting, or the bad blood, but he did want policy run out of the White House rather than Foggy Bottom. Having the White House run policy would necessarily elevate the national security advisor, whomever he or she might be, at the expense of the secretary of state and other cabinet level national security team members, such as Secretary of Defense Mel Laird. As the *New York Times'* Milton Viorst wrote, Nixon "never intended to use Rogers as the chief formulator of foreign policy." Nixon had held high office before, had long thought about the presidency, and knew how he wanted to run foreign policy as president. Rogers himself made clear that he was aware of Nixon's intentions going in, telling Viorst that "the president himself started out with great interest and great ability in foreign affairs. I knew that when I took the job. I understood that he would be making foreign policy—that's his constitutional responsibility."[8]

Nixon knew what he wanted and it had little to do with personnel. It stemmed from his experience under Eisenhower and his views of how Kennedy and Johnson ran things. The result was, "From the outset of my administration...I planned to direct foreign policy from the White House." Beyond Nixon's recollections, he also made this clear to the national security staff at the time. General Andrew Goodpaster, who was a national security aide to Nixon, recalled that both he and Kissinger wanted interagency national security groups chaired by a White House staff person. The State Department resisted, despite Rogers's disingenuous claim that he was fine with the White House running foreign policy. The disagreement reached the president and, as Goodpaster put it, "Nixon stood fast and said, no, the chairing would be done—in other words the agenda would be set—by somebody from the White House. So, the die was cast."[9]

More broadly, the White House chief of staff's office was aware of the president's desires and was willing to enforce them. Larry Higby, a top aide to Nixon's powerful chief of staff H. R. Haldeman, recalled the dictum that "policy was going to be decided in the White House." Given that clear marching order, the chief of staff's office understood that it "was the job of the cabinet to execute. And there were mechanisms put in place to make sure that follow-up and execution did take place."[10]

The implications of the Nixon approach became clear even before Nixon's inauguration. In December of 1968, Kissinger and his aide Morton Halperin prepared a nine-page memo for Nixon called "Proposal for a New National Security Council System." Nixon received and approved this memo before he even met with Rogers and Secretary of Defense-to-be Mel Laird in Key Biscayne to discuss the structure of the national security team. Before they had even met or started work, Kissinger—with Nixon's blessing—had already undercut Rogers's authority.[11]

Nixon's structural views shaped much of the conflict to come over the next few years, but those views were not the end of the story. Kissinger suggested that it was not a structural issue so much as a confidence issue. His personal closeness to Nixon, and the trust Nixon had in him, were the determinative factors in Kissinger's power and his ability to bypass or even ignore Rogers. As Kissinger wrote, "The influence of a presidential assistant derives almost exclusively from the confidence of the president, not from administrative arrangements. My role would almost surely have been roughly the same if the Johnson system had been continued."[12] There is certainly some truth to this: Kissinger was uniquely qualified to be a geo-strategic thinker in a way that Rogers was not equipped to be. Yet Kissinger's analysis does not recognize that Nixon demanded rules of operation that enabled him to win bureaucratic struggles more easily. By focusing power in the White House, Nixon gave a huge advantage to the national security advisor over the secretary of state, regardless of who filled those roles. If the NFL allowed, say, the New England Patriots to deflate footballs, that allowance would remain an advantage regardless of whether they were playing a Super Bowl contender or a college-level team in an exhibition game.

The irony of the Nixon method is that he did not originally intend to disempower his cabinet members. He had even made noises about cabinet government and delegating authority to cabinet officials. In 1968, before becoming president, Nixon said he wished to "disperse power," and that he planned to "operate differently from President Johnson. Instead of taking all power to myself, I'd select cabinet members who could do their jobs, and each of them would have the stature and the power to function effectively." Nixon's stated desire for this kind of government stemmed not just from structural reasons, but from principles of good management as well: "When a president takes all the real power to himself, those around him become puppets. They shrivel up and become less and less creative . . . your most creative people can't develop in a monolithic, centralized power set-up."[13] Similarly, despite Higby's orders to the contrary, Haldeman had also declared that "our job is not to do the work of government, but to get the work out to where it belongs—out to the Departments."[14]

It is clear from what later occurred that Nixon and Haldeman were not being candid about cabinet government. They quickly developed instead a more corporate style system. As Assistant to the President for Domestic Affairs John Ehrlichman described it, "It should be like a corporation, where the executive vice presidents (the cabinet officers) are tied closely to the chief executive, or to put it in extreme terms, when he says jump, they only ask how high."[15] Nixon got what he wanted from a process if not an interpersonal standpoint. As Roger Porter, a political scientist who worked in multiple Republican White Houses, observed, "The Nixon-Kissinger National Security Council staff and the Nixon-Ehrlichman Domestic Council staff are frequently considered the most notable examples of a highly systematic centralized management approach to policy formulation."[16]

This "highly systematic centralized" White House approach understandably left some unhappy cabinet members. Ehrlichman, who was in part behind the system that disempowered the cabinet, had the *chutzpah* to ask "What Went Wrong with the Nixon Cabinet?" in his memoir. In answering his own question ("Surely something did"), Ehrlichman revealed a great deal about a system guaranteed to make cabinet members, all accomplished individuals, extremely dissatisfied. Ehrlichman had the self-awareness to recognize that "most of the Cabinet members were discontented most of the time, and many of them failed to manage their departments well." In addition, he wrote, "There was constant friction between the White House and the Cabinet."[17]

The specifics Ehrlichman laid out make it clear why the cabinet members were unhappy. According to Ehrlichman, "Nixon could never understand why a secretary needed to be courted and cultivated. There was no reason for a secretary to be anything but loyal and eternally grateful. Nor was there a reason for a Secretary to need to see the president all the time." Like the Persian King Ahasuerus in the ancient Book of Esther, Nixon felt that secretaries should see the president when, and only when, the president called for them and should never invite themselves. When secretaries inevitably and unsurprisingly complained about these unrealistic expectations, Nixon called them "crybabies." After Vice President Spiro Agnew made the mistake of arguing on behalf of cabinet consultation, Nixon was irate, saying, "The damn crybabies just want therapy, of course. They'll say, 'Oh, help us' and 'protect us.' Imagine that damn Agnew!"[18]

## Kissinger the Operator

Cabinet secretaries had it bad in the Nixon administration, but none had it worse than William Rogers. This was in part because of the system, in part because Kissinger was smarter and more determined than Rogers, but also because Kissinger acted territorially. Kissinger's challenging and egotistical behavior would have been intolerable if exhibited by other staff members. By making himself the indispensable lynchpin of the administration's foreign policy, Kissinger was able to get away with a great deal of unacceptable behavior.

Kissinger's worst excesses may have come in dealing with his subordinates. Al Haig recalled that Kissinger was very tough on his staff— he drove away over a third of them in the administration's first nine months. He was particularly rough on Lawrence "Larry" Eagleburger. Eagleburger was a smart but also sensitive aide who would briefly become Secretary of State under George H. W. Bush. According to Haig, when Kissinger once demanded a specific document from an overworked Eagleburger, "Larry stood up, turned deathly pale, swayed, and then crashed to the floor unconscious." Such a collapse would have concerned and even given pause to an ordinary person, but not Kissinger. As Haig recalled, "Kissinger stepped over his prostrate body and shouted, 'where is the paper?'" As it turned out, Eagleburger was fine—he had been suffering from a bout of nervous exhaustion—but the story is indicative of Kissinger's hard-driving manner while in the White House.[19]

In fact, the view that Kissinger was mentally unbalanced was a theme among those watching him closely. At one point, Nixon complained to Haldeman that "Henry's personality problem is just too goddamn difficult for us to deal [with].... Goddamn it, Bob, he's psychopathic about trying to screw Rogers." Things were so bad that Nixon, "quite shocked" about how Kissinger "ranted and raved" during a 1971 phone call with Al Haig, wondered about Kissinger's mental state. In 1972, Nixon read the book *The Will to Live* by Dr. Arnold Hutschnecker and suggested to Haldeman that it provided him with insight into "K's suicidal complex." Nixon, Haldeman wrote, "wants to be sure I make extensive memoranda about K's mental processes and so on, for his file." Nixon was not alone in wondering about Kissinger's mental state. Haldeman recalled that when Rogers would have dinner with Nixon, Kissinger "would seem paranoid, ranting that he couldn't understand why the president would want to talk to Rogers."[20] Press aide John Scali, in a classic statement, once complained that "Henry has practically taken leave of his senses."[21]

Kissinger also showed his eagerness for power in his manipulation of White House real estate. White House Counsel John Dean once saw evidence of this on a visit to Bryce Harlow's office on the first floor of the West Wing. Workers were building a new wall in Harlow's office, removing his private bathroom so that Kissinger's nearby office could be expanded. Harlow had a somewhat good attitude about his loss of space, as well as his privy, telling Dean with a smile that, "In a way, I'm glad to know the place I used to shit will be Henry's office. That tells me who's who around here."[22]

Office space was often taken as a signal of who stood where in the Nixon White House. As Dean put it, "Anyone who moved to a smaller office was on the way down. If a carpenter, cabinetmaker or wallpaper hanger was busy in someone's office, this was a sure sign he was on the rise."[23] White House aide and future Reagan campaign manager John

Sears learned this when exiled to the attic of the Executive Office Building, across the street from the West Wing. As Pat Buchanan wrote, the move to "that Tower of London" took place "to send him a message it was time to depart." Sears was philosophical about it as well, telling Buchanan, "I have a short, but impressive list of political enemies."[24]

Eagleburger and offices aside, Kissinger reserved his harshest antics for his fight with Rogers. He was determined to keep Rogers—and everyone else—out of the loop on the Nixon administration's groundbreaking opening of relations with China. To keep the secrecy of China discussions, Kissinger faked an illness on a trip to Pakistan. Then, with Nixon's permission, Kissinger clandestinely travelled to China to lay the groundwork for the official visit between U.S. and Chinese leaders. When Rogers found out that Kissinger did not have "Delhi Belly" and was indeed going to China, he turned white with shock.[25]

Kissinger's penchant for secrecy regarding the China trip had him force aides to create three separate sets of briefing books: for those actually going to China; for those not going to China but who were aware of the trip; and for those not going and not knowing. As Kissinger's overburdened aide Winston Lord recalled, "I swear to God, we'd get them all updated and I'd put my head on a pillow, and Kissinger would then wake up and look at it and want it redone again, and I've got to do all three all over again." In an amusing coda to the story, the overtaxed Lord ended up getting off the plane in China first, ahead of Kissinger, something for which Kissinger reportedly "never forgave" him.[26]

On the trip itself, Rogers suffered another major indignity as only Kissinger accompanied Nixon to the meeting with Chairman Mao. There was some thought that there would be a follow-up meeting in which Rogers would get another chance, but it was not to be. Rogers was understandably upset about this, and even Kissinger recognized what a terrible slight it was. Kissinger did, however, justify it in his memoirs by writing that "The neglect was technically unassailable but fundamentally unworthy." Still, it is hard to imagine that Kissinger felt too badly about things. Earlier, he had expressed concern to Nixon scheduler Dwight

Chapin about the China trip and "how he was going to be able to keep Secretary of State Rogers from attending various meetings."[27]

The recurring failures could lead one to underestimate Rogers. Reading the accounts of Kissinger's outmaneuvering, tricking, and playing "hide the ball" from Rogers makes Rogers sound like some kind of patsy, a combination of Wile E. Coyote and the Washington Generals basketball team that always lost to the Harlem Globetrotters. But Rogers was a serious person, a former attorney general, and was after all secretary of state. Rogers was also not above confronting Kissinger directly. In one instance, Rogers complained to Kissinger about the strife between them having the effect of sending mixed messages to the Israelis during Middle East peace negotiations, and giving the Israelis the impression that they could "forum shop," feel out both of their thoughts and go with whomever was inclined to treat them more favorably.

In August of 1970, Rogers conveyed his concerns on this front to Kissinger, telling him:

> Rogers: "This meeting last night screwed it up so badly."
> Kissinger: "Don't be ridiculous."
> Rogers: "I'm not being ridiculous."
> Kissinger: "You are being absurd. If you have a complaint talk to the president. I am sick and tired of this."
> Rogers: "You and I don't see alike on these things."

Rogers then added that the perception of "two channels to the president" let the Israelis "use them differently."[28] The argument is a fascinating one, as most of what happens in these high-level rivalries usually takes place behind others' backs in newspapers and complaints to fellow staffers. This exchange, in contrast, was an actual *mano a mano* argument. Rogers's "two channels" point shows that there were real implications for these disagreements in addition to the personal ones. The puerile nature of their shouting shows that even two very intelligent, highly educated Ivy League products (Kissinger went to Harvard and Rogers to Cornell Law) could engage in schoolboy taunting and shouting when dealing with the pressures of their jobs and their dislike for each other. Furthermore, it is important to recall that Kissinger was particularly sensitive on this subject because the Middle East was one area where Nixon initially gave Rogers the lead, as the president was concerned that Kissinger's "Jewishness" would prejudice him in favor of Israel. (As it turned out, this would not be a serious worry.)

Sometimes Rogers would get the upper hand, although this was usually when Nixon wanted to put Kissinger in his place. Nixon would invite Rogers and his wife to dine in the residence with the president and First Lady Pat Nixon. Such invitations would drive Kissinger nuts. First, Kissinger disliked the signal that Rogers was an actual friend of the president, while Kissinger would always, on some level, be "staff." In addition, Kissinger would worry about what Rogers might be telling Nixon while he had him alone. As Haldeman recalled, "Henry would brood and fume when Rogers was having dinner at the mansion." In addition to his complaints, Kissinger also had a good idea of what Rogers would be saying to the president: "He'd pace around telling me exactly what Rogers must be telling the president and how outrageous it was." When he made similar complaints to Nixon, the president would have little patience for them, telling Kissinger, "What the hell do you care how it gets to me? I'm going to make the decision myself, and I'm not going to be influenced one goddamn bit by Rogers."[29]

## Leaking and Counter-Leaking

In addition to complaining, Kissinger undercut Rogers in the press as well. The State Department was (and remains) notorious for leaking information that comes from the White House, especially if State considers White House policies to be infringing on State prerogatives. As former NSC staffer Peter Rodman wrote, "Leaks from State are thus a familiar and sometimes effective weapon in the bureaucratic wars."[30]

The Nixon administration was no different, and arguably worse given the testiness between Kissinger and Rogers. In fact, to Kissinger and Nixon, it was a given—and not an inaccurate one—that the State Department was a source of leaks. Nixon felt this way from the beginning of the administration. Shortly after the beginning of the administration, NSC aide Alexander Haig briefed Nixon about leaks that had come from the State and Defense Departments during the Johnson administration. Nixon wanted to know if his administration was doing a better job protecting information: "We have been more careful, haven't we? We have kept a lot from State, I know, and enough from Defense." Haig reassured him, noting, "Your White House papers are in very good shape," he added. Nixon liked hearing this, but he also knew the reason: "That's why we don't tell them anything." After some time in office, Nixon continued to hold this view. As he told Haldeman about State, "Since Cambodia, they've been taking on the P[resident], leaking, etc. These things don't just happen, and from now on, it's us or them. State can't be told anything, and that's the way it is."[31]

Kissinger was aware of Nixon's proclivities in this regard and would encourage them. In one phone call, Kissinger brought up former Secretary of State John Foster Dulles's concerns about the bureaucracy, telling him that "Dulles always used to say that he had to operate alone because he couldn't trust his own bureaucracy. Nixon liked this, and said, 'I just wish that we operated without bureaucracy.'" When this elicited a knowing laugh from Kissinger, who himself had expressed concerns about bureaucracy in his years as an academic, Nixon said, "We do.... Yeah, we do, we do, we do."[32]

Rogers recognized the leaking problem. In 1972, he told the *New York Times'* Milton Viorst that "one problem that stands between presidents and the Department of State has to do with leaking information.... The trouble I've found is that the more we appear to lack the president's confidence in deliberations, the more likely information is to leak." Rogers further explained efforts he was taking to limit leaks, telling Viorst, "I think I have improved that situation and increased confidence within the ranks. Yet to safeguard our secrets, I've often had to keep a great deal to myself."[33]

At the same time, Rogers was eager to show that there had been instances where State had gotten a bad rap. He told Viorst that an investigation of a leak of certain White House papers on India and Pakistan found that State was not at fault, and that the search for the leaker was ongoing at the likeliest sources, Defense and the NSC. As Viorst wrote, "Rogers could not conceal his delight" at these developments.[34] Rogers's glee at being able to demonstrate that this leak did not come from his Department demonstrates the degree to which the State Department's leaky reputation was harming Rogers in his bureaucratic wars with Kissinger and the NSC.

Despite Rogers's win in the India and Pakistan leak situation, the State Department remained in the cross hairs of suspicion. Kissinger was only too happy to leak to help himself, to harm the Department, or both. He leaked favorable stories about himself all the time and was close with many journalists and columnists, including the brothers Joseph and Stewart Alsop, as well as Tom Braden.[35] Kissinger also did not mind that the press highlighted that he was quite the playboy in his White House days, linked with numerous attractive and famous women, including feminist Gloria Steinem and "Bond Girl" actress Jill St. John. In fact, Kissinger's "swinger" reputation was such that Steinem got a laugh at the White House Correspondents Association dinner by saying, "I am not nor have I ever been a girlfriend of Henry Kissinger's." Kissinger, rarely at a loss for words, had his own *bon mot* for the situation, "I am not discouraged. After all, did she not say, 'If elected, I will not serve.'"[36] About St. John, however, there was no doubt that they had dated, and Kissinger even accused Rogers internally of leaking stories to the press about their relationship. The truth, however, was that Kissinger himself often leaked the stories and then issued the complaints. This devious act had two positive impacts: it hurt Rogers by adding to his reputation as a leaker and it helped Kissinger since, as he bragged, the playboy reputation served "to reassure people...that I am not a museum piece."[37]

It is not clear if Nixon was aware of Kissinger's trickery in the Jill St. John incident, but he wouldn't have minded. In fact, Nixon was not above his own strategic leaking to teach State a lesson. As Buchanan recounts, Nixon asked Buchanan to go to columnist Roscoe Drummond with Nixon's concerns about the State Department. Drummond dutifully took the material and wrote a column highlighting Nixon's anger with State, and implicitly with Rogers, for opposing Nixon's Romania and Vietnam visits, as well as the "Nixon Doctrine" itself.[38]

All of this leaking and counter-leaking raises a vital point: Leaking is part of governing. As Lyndon Johnson learned, it will never end, even with semi-police state tactics employed against one's own staff. The trick is to learn how to live with leaking and use it to your advantage. Nixon and Kissinger understood this, as shown by the Drummond and St. John stories, but they also allowed obsession with leaking to be the administration's undoing. The Plumbers' unit, specifically created to control leaking, morphed into a political hit squad, which led to breaking into the Watergate Hotel, home of the Democratic National Committee at the time.

President Richard Nixon with (left to right) Soviet leader Leonid Brezhnev, Soviet Minister of Foreign Affairs Andrei Gromyko, and Secretary of State William P. Rogers. Rogers would often be outmaneuvered by National Security Advisor Henry Kissinger in the development of U.S. foreign policy. *Courtesy of the Library of Congress*

## Nixon as Feud Stagemaster

Nixon may not have minded strategic, authorized leaking, but he showed little patience for the accompanying feuds, such as between Kissinger and Rogers. He complained that "I'm not going to have a couple of crybabies acting like this." He even called the conflict between the two men a "sh*t a**" business, telling Haldeman and Ehrlichman, "Did you know that Henry worries every time I talk on the phone with anybody? His feeling is that he must be present every time I see anybody important." When aide Bill Safire told Nixon his assessment that "each thought the other was an egomaniac," Nixon agreed, saying, "In a sense they're both right." He added, "It's a pity, really, I have an affection for them both."[39]

The Nixon staff also complained about Kissinger's behavior in the feud and would even mock his immature antics. During one tantrum, Kissinger made a list of impossible demands, and threatened to resign if they were unmet. Safire did not take the threat seriously, joking, "If you quit, Henry, you'll never get a phone call from a beautiful woman again. The secret of your attraction is your proximity to power." Kissinger stopped his complaining to respond, "You may be right about that Safire. It would be a tremendous sacrifice." As Safire noted, "Even amid a tantrum," Kissinger "was usually willing to consider a humorous or intriguing proposition."[40] During another tantrum, Haig, recognizing Kissinger's importance as well as his immaturity, asked, "How do you deal with a four-year-old genius?"[41] Clearly, the staff had little patience for Kissinger's shenanigans.

Kissinger's outlandish behavior raises the question of why he was able to get away with it. Why didn't Nixon fire him, or accept one of his many resignations, or side with his old friend Rogers? As Haig alluded to in his "genius" comment, Nixon and his team recognized Kissinger's exceptional talent and its centrality in Nixon's foreign policy strategy. In fact, before the administration even began, Buchanan predicted to fellow aide Raymond Price "that Henry would eat [Rogers's] lunch." Buchanan's reason for the prediction was twofold. First, "given Henry's lust for power and fame, his knowledge, bureaucratic skill, proximity to the president, and daily access, Rogers never stood a chance." More important, Kissinger was what Nixon wanted, someone he would learn from. In fact, Buchanan recalled, Nixon had said that "he wanted a foreign policy adviser who could teach him something, not someone he would have to teach. Rogers's problem was that his old friend, now the president, knew far more about foreign policy than he ever did."[42]

Beyond Kissinger's sheer brainpower, he was also a tireless worker and a relentless networker. As his biographer Niall Ferguson has argued, Kissinger's networking, both in and outside of government, was one of the secrets of his success. Kissinger's extra-governmental reach extended to academia, journalists, foreign officials, and even Hollywood. In this process, and in his quest to get things done, Ferguson found that Kissinger "was quite dismissive of the org chart of the federal government," going over or around other officials when he needed.[43]

Kissinger's talent was certainly part of the reason for his success in the Nixon administration and with Nixon himself, but not all of it. Part of the issue was that Rogers wasn't up for and wasn't fully engaged in the fight. As Nixon treasury secretary John Connally recalled, "Bill was a laid-back guy enjoying life and not looking for ways to be aggressive."[44] Historian Robert Dallek had a similar conclusion, observing that Rogers "was a very passive figure in the administration."[45]

Rogers did have his limits. When Nixon had Haig ask Rogers to submit his resignation in the summer of 1973, Rogers told Haig, "Tell the President to go f*ck himself," insisting that the request come from the President himself.[46] Nixon eventually managed to see Rogers in person over the matter, and Rogers handled the situation with grace. As Kissinger described it, "To everyone's surprise and Nixon's immediate intense relief, Rogers made it easy for his old friend. Without letting Nixon speak he submitted a letter of resignation free of recrimination or argument." In doing so, Rogers even won over his *bête noire* Kissinger, who had to admit that "it was a classy performance."[47] Rogers continued to maintain his silence long after leaving government, refusing to write a memoir as, he rightly observed, it is "hard to write interestingly without being critical of people."[48] He also may not have wanted to publish a chronicle filled with defeat and humiliation. While Rogers may have been classy in staying silent, Kissinger got what he wanted: control over Nixon's foreign policy and a much more powerful role as national security advisor, the legacy of which continues to this day.

## Kissinger's Other Targets

Rogers's relative passivity was no match for Kissinger's relentless aggression. The experience of some other aides suggests that a more creative and assertive stance could have more success in resisting Kissinger. Defense Secretary Mel Laird, for example, enjoyed standing up to Kissinger and often got his way over the powerful and wily national security advisor. As James Schlesinger, who also served as a Nixon defense secretary, assessed matters, "Mel was a match for Henry." In Schlesinger's analysis, Laird "was just as devious, but he also had a Midwestern pol's instinct for power maneuvers."[49] Even Nixon recognized that Laird was "a sneak," something he would understand and appreciate. Like Kissinger, he made himself so indispensable to the administration that he was above firing too, despite occasional instances of insubordination. As Ehrlichman observed, "Laird was so effective with his old Congressional cronies that everyone realized he was irreplaceable."[50]

Laird's abilities did not stop Kissinger from trying to circumvent and belittle him. National Security Council aide Larry Lynn recounted that "cutting out Mel Laird is what we did for a living." And he engaged in his preferred tactic of mocking Laird as well. According to Lynn, Kissinger would joke "about Laird's horrible syntax" and let aides eavesdrop on calls between the two while "Henry would predict accurately what Laird was going to say and then make gestures and smirk at us."[51]

Despite these efforts, Kissinger could not flummox Laird. Laird had his own spies to inform him what Kissinger was doing. Rodman notes that Laird's military assets in this quest were formidable: "The NSA intercepted back channel messages; the U.S. Army Signal Corps tracked White House telephone conversations; the Special Air Missions branch of the U.S. Air Force ran the fleet of aircraft that Kissinger used." As a result, unlike Rogers, Laird was aware of Kissinger's China trip before it took place.[52]

In Kissinger's memoirs, he acknowledged what a formidable opponent Laird was. As Kissinger wrote of Laird, "In working with him, intellectual arguments were only marginally useful and direct orders were suicidal." As a result, Kissinger changed tactics, learning "that it was safest to begin a battle with Laird by closing off insofar as possible all his bureaucratic or Congressional escape routes, provided I could figure them out, which was not always easy. Only then would I broach substance." Despite Kissinger's sharp elbows and keen understanding of the bureaucratic process, Laird was a worthy match. As Kissinger put it, "Even with such tactics I lost as often as I won."[53]

Another Nixon aide who figured out how to trump Kissinger on occasion was Pat Buchanan. He had learned that one of Kissinger's favorite stratagems was to hold on to documents, drafts, and papers in general until it was too late to change things. As Buchanan put it, "What Henry would do, when he got the briefing book from the NSC staff, would be to sit on it—until my deadline approached, then send it over, leaving me no time to rewrite." Buchanan found two ways around Kissinger's obstructionist tactic. First, like Laird, he found his own sources of information. Buchanan convinced a cooperative NSC staffer to share the draft briefing books earlier on an informal basis. The second approach was more challenging. When Nixon asked Kissinger to produce a paper on the U.S. incursion into Cambodia, his NSC staff drafted a paper and then, as usual, held on to it until the evening before the deadline. Buchanan stayed up all night rewriting all six thousand words (in the era before word processors) and then had his assistant bring it to Kissinger's office in the morning. On seeing the new paper, Kissinger did not react well, throwing the papers all around as a two-star general scrambled to pick them up. Nixon, however, liked what Buchanan had done, and told Haldeman that he wanted future papers done in the same format. Even though Buchanan got the better of Kissinger this time, he kept a grudging respect of Kissinger's abilities, concluding that "as a turf conscious bureaucrat, Henry had no equal."[54]

Kissinger was indeed a unique aide, brilliant but thin-skinned, and an incredibly skilled bureaucratic player. He knew how to get what he wanted and could get the best of anyone in government, even those who outranked him. This was especially the case if the president endorsed the state of play, or if he outmatched an opponent who, like Rogers, was not fully engaged in the game. As the Buchanan and Laird stories show, others could on occasion stymie Kissinger, but it required exceptional efforts from those with their own protections or presidential dispensations giving them cover.

## Moynihan versus Burns: A More Civilized Feud

The Kissinger-Rogers feud was far from the only major feud in the Nixon White House. Among others, two domestic aides, Pat Moynihan and Arthur Burns, were also rivals for both position and policy primacy. In some ways, the Moynihan-Burns feud had some surface similarities to Kissinger-Rogers. Like Rogers, Burns—a well-respected economist—had longstanding ties to Nixon dating to the Eisenhower administration, and he had a more august and prestigious title: counsellor to the president, with cabinet rank. Like Kissinger, Moynihan was a younger Harvard academic not previously known to Nixon, who began the administration in a lesser-ranked position, as executive secretary of the newly created (and no longer extant) Council for Urban Affairs, after having been an assistant secretary at the Labor Department in the Kennedy and Johnson administrations. Like Kissinger, there was bipartisan agility in his career with no strong links to the GOP other than a conservative reputation for a liberal, which appealed to Nixon.

Despite Burns's surface advantages, Moynihan dazzled the intellectual Nixon with his wit and his relentless stream of ideas and insights.

Moynihan would write Nixon long and fascinating memos on issues like the antiwar activists on campus and Leonard Bernstein's legendary fundraiser for the Black Panthers, immortalized in Tom Wolfe's *Radical Chic*. Nixon found Moynihan's memos intriguing, writing in response to the Bernstein missive that the Black Panther party showed "the complete decadence of the American 'upper' class intellectual elite." In response to another Moynihan note on developments among the intellectuals, Haldeman made a diary notation that Nixon was "impressed by a long Moynihan memo, gist of which is the lack of real intellectuals in the Administration." As Stephen Hess, a White House aide at the time, wrote, "Burns is boring," while "Pat's quick wit is immediately appreciated by the gray suits who are now his White House colleagues."[55]

Ambition also played a role in how the feud turned out. The go-getting Moynihan was constantly seeking an edge. As Hess put it, Moynihan, who had served effectively in both the Kennedy and Johnson administrations, "was expert at dealing with the president."[56] In contrast, Burns, who had turned down the position of Domestic Policy Advisor, was like Rogers in that he just did not seem interested in a fight.

While the Moynihan-Burns feud may have shared similarities with the Kissinger-Rogers rivalry, there were major differences. Both Moynihan and Burns were within the White House orbit, and Nixon declared them to be in putatively equal positions. Second, the arguments between them were mostly ideological, and less personal or positional, as with Kissinger and Rogers. The liberal Moynihan won out more often than the conservative Burns, especially on the key—and controversial—issue of winning Nixon's (reluctant) support for a Guaranteed Annual Income, a Moynihan priority. As a result, Moynihan outlasted Burns, who was sent to the Federal Reserve at the end of 1969, while Nixon elevated Moynihan to counsellor to the president, with cabinet rank.

Despite Moynihan's victories, there did not seem to be significant personal animus between the two men. Hess viewed their disagreements as "a gentleman's quarrel...rare, even unique in Washington's corridors of power." Both men wrote positively about the other in the aftermath, a contrast to Kissinger's score-settling memoir and Rogers's refusal to write because he did not want to criticize anyone.[57] In the end, the dispute, and Moynihan's victories, would have real impact on the policies of the administration. When Hess looked back at things decades later, he concluded that Moynihan had really mattered: "Pat changed the trajectory of domestic policies in a way Nixon never promised or expected."[58]

Moynihan succeeded in outmaneuvering the gentlemanly Burns, but Moynihan would eventually fall victim to staff intrigue. In early 1970, he wrote what would become his famous and controversial "benign neglect" memo, arguing that the best policy for advancing African American interests was backing off and deescalating racial rhetoric in order to allow for African American progress. Since the memo, by definition, did not call for any significant administration policy changes, it fell more in the category of an intellectual analysis rather than a plan for action. Six weeks after Moynihan wrote that memo, someone leaked it to the *New York Times*, which featured it under the headline, "'Benign Neglect' on Race is Proposed by Moynihan." Nixon was irate and asked Haldeman for "a complete freeze on *Times*, etc."[59]

Nixon's anger did not help Moynihan, whom the press and liberal groups blasted over the "benign neglect" phrase. Suspects in the leaking included White House aide Clark Molenhoff and Health and Human Services official—and future Democratic congressman and White House chief of staff—Leon Panetta. Moynihan was worried that the leak would ruin him in the Democratic Party, and he was right to be worried. Even though Moynihan was elected four times as a Democratic senator from New York State—serving from 1977 through 2001—the benign neglect charge would stick with him. As late as thirty years after the memo appeared, Al Sharpton, who ran against Moynihan for the Democratic Senate nomination, referred to his former opponent as Daniel Patrick "Benign Neglect" Moynihan.[60] As this episode shows, vanquishing one opponent in an intra–White House squabble does not inoculate one against subsequent backstabbing campaigns.

## Conclusion

Nixon differed from his immediate predecessors in that he encouraged conflict among his advisors. He may have complained about fighting among the "crybabies," but Nixon wanted full control over the decision-making process, which guaranteed conflict, and he knew it. The warring aides approach had political disadvantages too; it contributed to leaking, intra-staff enmity, and forum-shopping by foreign leaders. But history shows Nixon's results in the policy arena were far-reaching, advancing an ambitious, consequential domestic policy, and a foreign policy that both enabled a rapprochement with China and forced the Soviets out of the Middle East.

Despite these successes, the Nixon administration ended in failure, in large part because Nixon's obsession with control and his quest to end leaks led to the creation of the quasi-legal White House "Plumbers" unit and ultimately to the Watergate break-in. Ironically, Nixon's overarching need for control ultimately led him to lose control of what he desired most—the presidency itself.

# CHAPTER 5

# GERALD FORD
## Defined by Rivalry: Robert Hartmann versus Donald Rumsfeld and Dick Cheney

G erald Ford became president in August of 1974 with little executive preparation for an extremely challenging task. Although he had been a congressman from Michigan for decades, he had never run for president, and he is the only person to become president without running on a national ticket first. After ascending to the vice presidency via appointment, he only served in that position for nine months in a collapsing Nixon administration before taking on the top job. When he did so, he had to learn how to do the job, manage two competing staffs, and reassure a worried nation, all at the same time. As a result, while the Ford administration was one of the shortest in American history, it was also one of the most tumultuous in terms of staff infighting.

### Too Nice for the Job?

When one thinks of Gerald Ford the man, incessant conflict does not come to mind. In fact, a startling number of descriptions of Ford focus on what a nice guy he was. Brent Scowcroft, who would replace Kissinger as national security advisor, observed that "there is no guile, no convolution, no complexity with Gerald Ford. He was comfortable in who he was."[1] Ford's manner served him well in his tenure as a congressman from Michigan and as House minority leader, the post from which he gained the vice presidency. As Stephen Hess wrote, "As the House minority leader, Ford's skills as a consensus builder and compromiser were practically a job description."[2]

As president, though, Ford's niceness was part of the problem. Immediately after acknowledging that Ford had the right skills and temperament for his House job, Hess also noted that "running the White House required a more commanding approach."[3] Donald Rumsfeld, who served in the House with Ford before becoming his White House "staff coordinator"—the title the Ford administration gave to the chief of staff role—had a similar view. He explained that "President Ford came into office with wonderful training and success that didn't suit him for an executive function. He started out functioning basically like a legislator."[4] Robert Hartmann, a Ford loyalist and speechwriter who would be at the heart of much of the conflict in the Ford administration, told Ford directly and in his typically earthy way that Ford was too soft: "You don't suspect ill motives of anyone until you're kicked in the balls three times. As a human being, that's a virtue. As a president, it's a weakness."[5]

People like Rumsfeld and Hartmann saw Ford as too nice, but at least they had Ford's best interests at heart. Ford's political opponents, both inside and outside his party, believed that he was someone they could exploit. Lyndon Johnson was supposed to have said that Ford was so dumb that "he can't chew gum and walk at the same time." A review of the archives revealed that the quote was likely apocryphal, but that did not stop the *New York Times* from running it in a Ford profile in October of 1973, less than a year before he became president.[6]

Whether Johnson said it or not, it became part of the wider view of Ford. More worrisome was the view of the Nixon folks, many of whom would go on to serve in the Ford administration after Nixon resigned. Alexander Butterfield, a former Air Force officer who had served as

Haldeman's deputy, was brutal about Ford in later years, saying "Nixon had Ford totally under his thumb. He was the tool of the Nixon Administration—like a puppy dog. They used him when they had to—wind him up and he'd go 'Arf, Arf.'"[7]

Ford's niceness, coupled with the related issue of his perceived ineffectuality, was especially problematic given the task he had to face: the melding together of two disparate and distrustful staffs. The trouble started early. A Ford transition team recommended a significant reorganization of the White House staff. As always, the team called for more cabinet government and recommended keeping the Nixon policy structures, if not the specific personnel. This report, which made good sense, came on August 20, 1974, after Ford had been president for eleven days. This meant that Ford was already in the hot seat dealing with challenging issues such as the Cold War, Nixon's departure, and the roiling Arab-Israeli conflict. There's a reason that administrations typically go through transitions before they begin. In this case, though, as Hartmann put it, "We had no time for transition. One day Ford was vice president and the next day he was president. If anybody didn't like it, tough."[8]

## Choosing Teams: Nixon versus Ford

The truncated transition meant that the Ford team had to handle issues of staffing and responsibility on the fly. When it comes to the White House, this is akin to fixing a car while driving it on the Autobahn. The resulting confusion led to what Hartmann called "a natural conflict between Ford's vice-presidential staff and Nixon's leftover staff." The Nixon people had the governing experience, but the Ford people were there to serve the new president. As Hartmann described things, the Nixon staff "thought, and probably with good reason, that they knew more about running the White House than we did." This was all fine, Hartmann thought, "except that they weren't running it anymore. They had difficulty getting that through their heads."[9]

Even though the Nixon people were coming from a different place, they diagnosed the problem the same way. Nixon speechwriter Pat

Buchanan, who was close to Nixon holdover chief of staff Al Haig, recalled that Haig "was having a difficult time meshing the Nixon and Ford staffs."[10] David Gergen, who had been on the Nixon staff but held over and worked for Ford as well, acknowledged the obvious: "It was not an easy transition." Gergen saw problems on both sides of the divide and was willing to criticize the Nixon group from which he came: "There continued to be an arrogance and smugness on the part of the some of the Nixon people."

Beyond the arrogance, though, the Nixon people had a fundamental problem in the form of the Watergate scandal itself. As Gergen put it, "The scandal had engulfed us." Gergen had feared that being affiliated with the disgraced Nixon staff "was like playing for the Chicago Black Sox. I thought none of us would ever come back and we would be written off." As for the Ford staff, nearly all of them didn't like the Nixon people. What this meant in practice was that "they wanted to do everything different. If Nixon had walked on the left side of the road, they wanted to walk on the right side of the road. They didn't want a Haldeman around, they didn't want a strong chief of staff...."[11]

One of the first casualties of this anti-Nixon approach was Haig. He and Hartmann were at each other's throats from the outset. Haig was a four-star general who had already been serving as White House chief of staff. Hartmann, a hard-drinking former journalist who served as Ford's speechwriter, political counselor, and vice-presidential chief of staff, had the advantage of longstanding ties to Ford. In fact, of all the Ford staff, only White House Counsel Phil Buchen, who knew Ford from his University of Michigan days, had known Ford longer than Hartmann. The Hartmann-Ford relationship did not sit well with Haig. Even before the transition, Haig, angered at Hartmann's leaks to the press about him, grabbed a Hartmann aide by his collar and snarled, "If you have any influence over that fat Kraut, you tell him to knock it off or he's going to be the first stretcher case coming out of the West Wing."[12]

The two men intensely disliked one another. As Richard Norton Smith said in an oral history interview with David Gergen, "One senses that Hartmann and Haig were put on the planet to piss each other off. We talked to Haig before he died, and the thing that got him red-faced with anger, thirty-five years later, was Hartmann." In response, Gergen diplomatically acknowledged that "it was possible to hate Bob Hartmann."[13]

Personalities and blame aside, the situation with Haig and Hartmann sniping at each other was untenable. The two men were regularly leaking negative information about one another to the press. As Ford press secretary Ron Nessen, whom Hartmann had brought into the administration, recalled in his memoir, "Hartmann was 'knifing' White House Chief of Staff Alexander Haig in anonymous conversations with reporters."[14] Haig knew about it and even told Ford directly, "You've got to get this guy under control. Otherwise, I can't serve you."[15]

Leaks in the Ford White House were vicious and incessant. On September 9, 1974, only one month into Ford's tenure, widely read columnists Rowland Evans and Robert Novak wrote a column where Hartmann was the source about the "urgent feeling by President Ford's closest advisers that Gen. Alexander Haig must be removed as his chief of staff soon—perhaps immediately." The piece suggested disloyalty on Haig's part, and highlighted that he had not warned Ford soon enough about six hidden Oval Office microphones that, even while disconnected, still had the capacity to record White House conversations. Ford had pledged to end secret taping, and the continued existence of the microphones threatened to make Ford appear disingenuous if not outright dishonest. Evans and Novak also mentioned that a Haig staffer had told the General Services Administration to move furniture to the EOB for ex-Nixon staffers Steve Bull and Ron Ziegler, implying that they would be returning to duty. Rowland and Evans concluded, "If Haig indeed has put Nixon and his former aides above an undivided allegiance to President Ford, it is indefensible." The piece was also salted with quotes from unnamed Nixon aides saying anti-Haig things like "the White House staff run by Haig is still functioning in the interests of Richard Nixon and the walking wounded of a lost war" and "until that happens [i.e. Haig's departure] the president will be the Prisoner of Zenda in his own house."[16]

There was little doubt at the time that Hartmann was the source. In fact, decades later, Novak confirmed in his memoir that the quotes came from Hartmann.[17] Yet Hartmann appeared not to care. In an interview years after the administration, Hartmann freely acknowledged not only that he was a source for Evans and Novak, but that he often leaked information to them with Ford's consent. As Hartmann recalled, he would tell Ford before leaving the White House that "I'm going to have lunch with Evans and Novak or both, what do you want me to tell them?" Afterwards, "when I came back from the lunch, I'd tell him what we talked about and what I told them." Rumsfeld agreed that Ford was aware, noting that Ford "saw that the barbs being leaked to the media were flowing largely from Hartmann."[18] After the Evans and Novak story, Haig was gone twelve days later, on September 21, and was quickly appointed as Supreme Allied Commander Europe in December. As Hartmann later noted, Ford "got rid of Haig. He sent him off to NATO, which was actually a good career move for Haig."[19]

Media reports at the time identified leaking as part of the problem. As New York's Richard Reeves wrote after Haig's departure, "Dismissal by leaky innuendo has been the standard operating procedure in the Ford White House since August 9, 1974." Reeves specifically pointed to the sniping between Haig and Hartmann, noting that "almost any morning as the summer of '74 came to an end, Ford could read Haig-inspired columns about Hartmann's administrative incompetence and slipping status in the Oval Office and Hartmann-inspired columns about Haig's subversion of presidential directives." Amid all the leaking and counter-leaking, rumors also had it that Haig got orders by phone from Nixon in San Clemente—which was not actually true, but this would not be the first or last time that false stories in the press undermined a senior government official.[20]

The Ford people had plenty to complain about as well. While Haig was in charge, Ford people reported not getting offices or even West

Wing badges. This meant that aides to Ford could not work in or even enter the West Wing and had to do their work and meeting from the Executive Office Building across the street.[21] In addition, during this same period, Haig demanded that all staff memoranda be routed through him. The Ford staff, led by Hartmann, was used to communicating directly with their principal, standard in the House of Representatives, and refused to go along with Haig's demand.[22] Hartmann, who called Haig and his people "the Praetorians," would place his memos directly in the presidential inbox and get Ford to sign them, completely bypassing Haig and his procedures. Circumvention of the White House process is dangerous for the president but also guaranteed to create strife. Haig blustered, "We've got some people coming in with an in-box under their arm, papers falling out, and getting in there and we have no record of what was discussed or decided or anything else. We can't run the White House this way!"[23]

The status quo under Haig was untenable and could not have continued, a fact that led to his departure. At the same time, however, Haig's knowledge of White House operations was not easy to replace, which even his nemesis Hartmann reluctantly acknowledged. As Hartmann told Nessen, Haig was "the only one who knows how to fly the plane. We're not going to shoot him in the cockpit before we learn how to fly the plane, or design a new plane."[24]

## A New Chief of, Er, Staff Coordinator

With Haig gone, the White House needed a replacement who could try to make the Ford White House run. To Hartmann's chagrin, he was not going to be that replacement. Ford liked Hartmann and knew him well, and he did have some good political instincts, albeit not of the interpersonal kind. As Pat Buchanan recalled, "Hartmann was an acerbic individual, but one whom Nixon respected for his savvy."[25] Moreover, he was not well-organized. Hartmann's lack of organizational skill was plain even when he served as Ford's vice-presidential chief of staff, which came with much lighter duties than those of a White House chief of staff. Hartmann's lack of logistical ability forced Ford to bring on William Seidman to serve as assistant for administration, to handle the administrative tasks that were beyond both Hartmann's capabilities as well as his interests.[26]

Clearly, Hartmann could not be chief of staff, as much as he may have wanted the job. Instead, Ford hired Donald Rumsfeld to serve as "staff coordinator"—the aversion to Haldeman's style as chief of staff extended even to the title. White House aide Roger Porter recalled that Hartmann was "crushed" when he was passed over twice for chief of staff, first when Haig got the job and then when Rumsfeld replaced Haig.[27] Nessen had a similar recollection, noting that Hartmann "lost out in the White House power struggle" and "took it badly."[28]

Bringing on Rumsfeld certainly had merit. He was a talented bureaucratic operator. As Nessen observed, Rumsfeld "brought order out of anarchy in the White House."[29] At the same time, the Rumsfeld move did not solve the larger problem of general warfare within the Ford staff. When incoming Press Secretary Ron Nessen asked Haig about the problem of the "Ford loyalists fighting with the leftover Nixon people," Haig explained that he had diagnosed the problem incorrectly. According to Haig, "The real problem was Ford loyalists fighting with other Ford loyalists." With Rumsfeld on board, that only meant a new faction with which to contend. According to Nessen, infighting among staff members became even more complex and divisive, with Rumsfeld's coterie, the Hartmann faction, and the Kissinger team engaging in a "daily struggle for influence." As for Nessen, he found that the feuds were so intense that neutrality was not a choice: "I tried to stay out of the never-ending staff feuds. But that was not possible."[30]

Rumsfeld had considerable experience with political maneuvering. In 1965, as a congressman from Illinois, he had helped Ford overthrow House Minority Leader Charles Halleck. This move not only boosted Ford in the House, but also built a close bond of trust between Ford and Rumsfeld. It also showed Ford that Rumsfeld had the tactical and political ability to maneuver as White House chief of staff.[31]

Qualified though he was, Rumsfeld was reluctant to take on the chief of staff role. In late September, Ford reached out to Rumsfeld, who went to Illinois following the death of his father. Rumsfeld returned to Washington to meet privately with Ford, where he expressed his reservations directly to the president, telling him "I'm not the guy to do it, and I don't have any desire to do it." At the same time, he was quite adamant that Ford needed help, bluntly warning that not having a strong lead staff person would be "your quickest way to lose your credibility because even though you are honest the fact that you don't know what you are doing misleads people and once you lose your credibility, you can't govern."[32]

Rumsfeld's studied reluctance may have been a way to make sure Ford gave him all the power he needed in the job. Rumsfeld understood Ford's desire to get away from the Nixon system, with all its dysfunction, but he also made it clear that he would only take the job if it was Haldeman-like in scope. As he told Ford, "I know you don't want a Haldeman-type chief of staff, but someone has to fill that role, and unless I can have that authority, I won't be able to serve you effectively." Rumsfeld also stressed the importance of an orderly staff process, something the Ford White House was sorely lacking. He explained his view of the position to Ford in stark terms: "There has to be order, and...I would consider it my job to see that there was order."[33] Ford agreed and gave Rumsfeld the job, less than two months into his presidency.

## Hartmann: The "Fat Kraut"

As the new "staff coordinator," one of Rumsfeld's first moves was to try and handcuff Hartmann. It would not be easy. Shortly after Ford ascended to the presidency, Hartmann squatted in an office next to—and sharing a door with—the Oval Office. Ford even granted Hartmann access to the private presidential toilet, an unusual dispensation to say the least.[34] This perch so close to the Oval Office facilitated Hartmann's efforts both in circumventing the process and strategic leaking. As Dick Cheney, who served as Rumsfeld's deputy, recalled, Hartmann would get Ford to sign off on things that the rest of the staff, including the staff secretary, who is supposed to control the paper flow to the president, had never seen. Beyond that, Hartmann would also pilfer the presidential inbox to find memos he did not like, which he would promptly leak to the press. White House staffers could even detect Hartmann's incursions via "the appearance of some strategically leaked information in a newspaper item by Rowland Evans and Robert Novak." Per Cheney, Hartmann's practice was as follows: "Finding an internal memo whose drift he had not cared for, Bob simply conveyed its contents straight from the president's desk to the appreciative hands of Washington's most-read columnists."[35]

At Cheney's suggestion, Rumsfeld went to Ford and recommended moving Hartmann away from his plum location. Despite Hartmann's closeness to Ford, and Ford's knowledge that Hartmann would leak to Evans and Novak, the president must have recognized that Hartmann's Oval Office shenanigans were causing problems. As Cheney recalled, when presented with the recommendation of using the Hartmann-occupied space as a private presidential study—which was how Cheney wisely framed it—"Ford quickly warmed to the idea."[36] Hartmann was moved.

Cheney and Rumsfeld may have succeeded in moving Hartmann from next to the Oval Office, but Hartmann remained both in the West Wing and a source of rancor and rivalry. It is astounding how poor Hartmann's reviews are from his colleagues in the Ford White House. His nickname in the White House, besides Haig's "fat Kraut," was "SOB," which Hartmann himself jokingly insisted stood for "Sweet Ol' Bob." David Gergen was relatively kind in saying that "Hartmann had outsized influence, and he was also erratic, so you never knew quite where you stood with him."[37] Tom Korologos acknowledged that Hartmann was polarizing, describing him as "large and in charge," which was probably a dig at his girth as well.[38] Ron Nessen, a Hartmann neighbor in the Washington suburbs recruited to the White House by Hartmann and who used to ride in to the White House in Hartmann's chauffeured limo, recalled that Hartmann was "very polarizing" and "a difficult man."[39]

Rumsfeld somewhat diplomatically described him in a memo as "an unusual human being. He simply seems not to work well with other people."[40] Even his protector Ford acknowledged that he was "suspicious of everyone" and told Rumsfeld he was concerned about the "Bob Hartmann issue." It is therefore not surprising that the *Washington Post*'s Sally Quinn said that Hartmann had "more enemies than any other man in Washington."[41] One wonders what kind of therapy Hartmann would have been mandated to attend in today's hugely different world.

Denied the chief of staff post and removed from presidential inbox proximity, Hartmann asserted himself as speechwriter. This was an area in which he had both experience and flair. He had long worked for the *Los Angeles Times*, serving for a time as Washington Bureau Chief, which was where he first met Ford. He transitioned over to government work and became a communications staffer for the House Republican leadership, which was how he came to know Ford so well. Ford valued his writing skills and political acumen, bringing him over to the White House when Ford became vice president. Roger Porter described him as "a wonderful speechwriter" and as "extraordinarily loyal to the vice president."[42]

Despite Hartmann's sharp elbows, he proved his value to Ford in the earliest days of the presidency. Hartmann wrote Ford's inaugural speech to the American people, including its most memorable line: "My fellow Americans, our long national nightmare is over." Not only did he write the line, he also fought for its inclusion over a reluctant Ford, who considered it too "harsh." Upon reviewing the speech, Ford said, "Bob, I think we ought to strike that." Hartmann threatened to resign if it was removed. As he told Ford, "Junk all the rest of the speech if you want to, but not that. That is going to be the headline in every paper, the lead in every story."[43] He was right: the "national nightmare" line is still Ford's best-known quote.

Shortly afterwards, Hartmann strongly advised Ford against the September 8 Nixon pardon. Issuing the pardon may have been the right move for the country, but it was disastrous for Ford politically, and may have cost him the 1976 presidential election. Haig had circumvented Hartmann and discussed the matter directly with the president. When Hartmann found out that a pardon was in motion, he looked to delay it, asking, "What's the rush? Why must it be tomorrow? Why not Christmas Eve, or a year from now...?" In both matters, Hartmann had Ford's best interests in mind.[44]

These important contributions did not mean that Hartmann always added value to the speechwriting process. In fact, Robert Goldwin, an intellectual Rumsfeld brought onto the staff who often helped in speechwriting, did not think that Hartmann had much talent in the speechwriting department. According to Goldwin, "Hartmann saw no need for continuity in a speech. He felt that each sentence had to carry its own weight, and that no overall theme need be developed." But the real issue with Hartmann and speechwriting was not writing skill so much as his own need for control. He felt that he should have the primary pen on all speeches, and, like Kissinger, he would hold on to drafts until it was too late to change them. Hartmann also used his closeness to Ford to ensure speechwriting would be his domain. He was constantly paranoid, and suspicious of all others who tried to involve themselves in the process. As Cheney later put it, "One of the problems we always had, frankly, was trying to integrate the speechwriting process with the policy process. And with the political process."[45]

Rumsfeld identified the problem early in his tenure. After seeing the process for a few months, he described it as "the dumbest operation known to man." According to Rumsfeld, "Each time we go through this hassle at the end, with a big group. Hartmann making snotty remarks to everyone else. The president pacifying and coddling Hartmann, and getting madder by the minute, and getting at it with other people."[46]

The crazy process led to mixed results, for Hartmann and everyone else. On the 1975 State of the Union, the entire top staff fought over what it should look like. Cheney and Gergen pushed for a thematic address, in contrast to a long-winded catalog of statements. Unfortunately, according to Gergen, Hartmann's first draft was "a total laundry list, which is exactly what the bulk of the people around the president didn't want." Rumsfeld had Gergen and new economic advisor Alan Greenspan prepare a different, more thematic draft, but Hartmann was committed to his original. With little time left, they had what Gergen described as "a showdown meeting in the Oval Office…[with] like sixteen of us in the room in a big circle." The advisors read the competing drafts, gave the pros and cons of each one. Gergen apparently did not think much of Hartmann's contributions to the discussion, recalling in his oral interview that "Hartmann was 'Urff, urff.'" At the end of the discussions, Ford asked for a vote, saying, "I'm going to go around the circle and ask each one of you which one you prefer." As Gergen described the result, "The vote was fourteen to two in favor of the Greenspan/Gergen draft." Unfortunately for Greenspan and Gergen, "the two votes against were Hartmann and Jerry Ford. And guess which speech he gave."[47]

Hartmann may have won that round, but his victory here did not serve the interests of the president. Ford knew it. He was angry about the whole process, breaking a pencil and barking, "The speech isn't ready and it should have been ready." Even worse, the speech was not what he wanted from a content perspective. Ford complained that "it was short on specifics and long on rhetoric; worse, it didn't have a clear and central theme." On top of everything, the dysfunctional process gave him little time to prepare or to rest for an enormously important speech. He had only three hours of sleep the night before he spoke to an anxious nation hearing its new president's first State of the Union.[48]

Another Hartmann-related blowup involved the WIN—Whip Inflation Now—slogan. Hartmann created this slogan that very quickly became the butt of jokes. He managed to slip it into a speech using his standard procedure of inserting it in a late draft and not letting anyone else see it before Ford delivered the address.[49] People with any basic understanding of economics were appalled. Treasury Secretary William Simon called WIN "ludicrous" and was determined to kill it. When Greenspan finally got to review a draft, he found a half dozen factual errors in it. The "surreal" experience almost caused him to quit, recalling that "I was the

only economist present, and I said to myself... 'What am I doing here?'"
Even Ford, Hartmann's patron, dismissed WIN as "too gimmicky."[50]

Hartmann felt that opponents did not understand the concept as
they were too young to recall Franklin Roosevelt's voluntary Blue Eagle
program from the 1930s. Hartmann also resented Simon and his allies'
efforts to undermine the idea, using what Hartmann called "every dirty
trick in their considerable bag to make it fail." But when the program
did, as expected, reflect poorly on the president, Hartmann did not
accept the blame, feeling that "the scorn and ridicule [Simon] assiduously
relayed to the media... severely embarrassed and undercut the president
of the United States."[51] Regardless of who was right, WIN was indeed a
disaster. Decades later, the Associated Press's Martin Crutsinger would
describe the WIN campaign as "one of the biggest government public
relations blunders ever."[52]

Hartmann's outrageous behavior often rebounded against him. The
best example of his paranoid and controlling approach to speechwriting
backfiring took place in the period before the Bicentennial celebrations
of 1976. In advance of the celebration, Goldwin began to collect the
thoughts of some of the nation's top conservative intellectuals, such as
Irving Kristol and Daniel Boorstin, for a Ford address on the nation's
birthday. Hartmann was concerned that knowing the names of the draft-
ers would bias the reviewers of the ideas, and potentially prejudice Ford
against Hartmann's own contribution. Hartmann's solution was to produce a code system that substituted the names of the outside thinkers for
numbers, allowing for anonymous reviewing. His trick failed in an unan-
ticipated and weirdly incompetent way—he lost the codes. As Hartmann
himself recalled, "In fooling Ford, I also fooled myself and history. I have
lost my code key and cannot match all the names with the numerals."[53]

### Rumsfeld and Cheney: Asserting Control from Above

The extent of Hartmann's idiosyncrasies raises the question of why
Ford tolerated him. He had some talent as a writer to be sure—witness

his long experience as a reporter and the famous national nightmare line. At the same time, Goldwin's comment about his speechwriting weaknesses and even Ford's complaints about the inadequacy of product proved that he was not a speechwriting genius in the way that Kissinger was allowed to be a coddled genius in the Nixon White House. Hartmann was not indispensable, as White House aides from Sherman Adams to Bob Haldeman to Don Regan to Steve Bannon have learned. The answer to Hartmann's staying power lies in Ford's loyalty to him. As Roger Porter remembered, "I never heard him once disparage Bob Hartmann and that was in the face of many other people making comments that were less than flattering. Ford was very loyal to Bob Hartmann."[54]

The other reason for Hartmann's staying power is the general chaos of the Ford administration. Rumsfeld and Cheney, despite considerable effort, were never able to stop all of the infighting, which helped Hartmann. As Cheney acknowledged in a C-SPAN interview in 1984, "I'd like to say that there was never any bickering or competition at all in the Ford administration but it wouldn't be true."[55] Consequently, Hartmann, who would remain in the White House until the end of the Ford administration, remained a challenge, especially in speechwriting. But Rumsfeld and Cheney were able to tame the rest of the White House, including Hartmann, enough to allow Ford to place him at a distance and keep the staff functioning. One measure of their success was that Hartmann ended his year-long practice of skipping morning staff meetings and once again became a regular attendee.[56]

These controls manifested in several ways. First, Rumsfeld limited the number of staffers who had direct one-on-one access to the president. What was once a free-for-all ended with only Kissinger and Greenspan being allowed to meet with Ford alone. This step curtailed Hartmann's ability to get Ford to sign off on initiatives that had not received staff clearance. Related to this was a demand that meetings would begin and end on time. Even Kissinger was not exempt from this one. After one too many late arrivals, Rumsfeld warned him that tardiness would be assumed as cancellation.[57]

Some efforts targeted Hartmann. To deal with the recurring speech-writing difficulties, Cheney created a shadow speechwriting operation, separate and apart from Hartmann. Instead of doing it in an *ad hoc* fashion, as they had done with Greenspan and Gergen for the State of the Union, in late 1975, Cheney brought Gergen back from the Treasury specifically to handle speechwriting. He did this contrary to his guarantee to Hartmann that he would put an end to "wildcat" speechwriting separate from the official operation.[58]

Maneuvers like these sidelined Hartmann and minimized his toxicity. Porter recalled that Hartmann, for all his skills, "was one that I think Ford kept at a bit of a distance."[59] More importantly, from Rumsfeld and Cheney's perspective, was that they had set things up so that Hartmann could gripe, but not really do very much about his griping. Under Rumsfeld-Cheney, getting targeted by Hartmann was no longer necessarily paralyzing as it was for Haig. As Cheney recalled it, Hartmann "had the knives out for Kissinger always. It was just continuous. He was always chopping away at Henry. But you know, it didn't have that big an impact on Kissinger."[60]

Part of the reason that Rumsfeld and Cheney were successful in bringing about more order is that they were good at their jobs. CBS's Bob Schieffer called Cheney "the best staff man I ever dealt with."[61] Ford clearly liked him as well. Shortly after Rumsfeld introduced the two men, he asked Ford what he thought. Ford was enthusiastic, gushing, "Dick is great! He comes in, he's got ten items to cover, he covers them and he leaves." Rumsfeld, to his credit and in contrast to many a staffer before and afterwards, was not jealous but thrilled. As he wrote in his memoir, "I was pleased that the two seemed to get on so well, because I was hoping Cheney not only would be able to take more of the burden off of me, but also might eventually replace me."[62] As it turned out, he would.

Rumsfeld and Cheney's methods, while effective, were far from perfect. Together, the two men developed a spokes-on-the-wheel system for the Ford White House. This system was less hierarchical than a traditional chief of staff–led system. It made for a messy operation, with different aides of equivalent power and authority maneuvering for access

President Ford chats with Chief of Staff Donald Rumsfeld and Rumsfeld's deputy Richard Cheney. The two men tried to control the fighting in the Ford administration and would long remain influential in Republican political circles. *Courtesy of the Gerald R. Ford Library*

and input. Unsurprisingly, Hartmann disliked it: "It didn't work very well because some people were headstrong and took the ball and ran with it as hard as they could; others were happy to just rock along and try to keep the waters calm."[63] Hartmann was not wrong in his assessment. More recent analysts like Chief of Staff chronicler Chris Whipple, and historians Karen M. Hult and Charles E. Walcott, who studied speechwriting operations, gave it poor reviews as well.

Hartmann should have liked the spokes-on-the-wheel system more than he did. Only two of the eight "spokes" were Nixon people, meaning that the Nixon team was purged within three months or so of Ford taking over. Hartmann, however, was not one of the eight, which must have rankled him. On the other hand, he may have at least appreciated that Ford people had at last supplanted the Nixon team. He was so obsessed by this distinction that his memoir included an appendix that had lists of Ford's presidential and vice presidential staffs. Hartmann underlined Nixon folks and placed stars next to those chosen few who had been with Ford before his presidency began.[64]

## The Halloween Massacre

Skilled as they were, Rumsfeld and Cheney also overreached at times. The best example of this was the infamous Halloween Massacre of November 1975. The tensions within the Ford administration precipitated action. Outside advisor Bryce Harlow, who had served on two earlier White House staffs, told Ford that stories of "internal anarchy" in the Ford White House were harming the administration and that he had to get things under control. As Harlow told Ford, "Now Mr. President, if you have to fire 'em all, you have to put a stop to it."[65]

At the same time, Ford was having troubles with Vice President and former New York Governor Nelson Rockefeller. Rockefeller was unpopular with conservatives and, unwisely, told that he would control domestic policy. Rockefeller was widely to the left of where Ford and his team were. The result was that Rockefeller would promote liberal initiatives and the Ford team would work to scuttle them.

On October 28, Ford told Rockefeller that he wanted him to remove himself from the ticket in 1976. Rockefeller was reluctant to go. Then Ford refused to give fiscal aid to a bankrupt and spendthrift New York City. Ford's decision, while understandable from a policy perspective, was extremely unpopular in New York and prompted the legendary *New York Daily News* headline "Ford to New York: Drop Dead." Rockefeller, angered by the way Ford treated his home state, finally wrote a letter withdrawing from the ticket.[66]

On November 2, the massacre commenced, led by the announcement that Rockefeller would not be joining Ford on the ticket in 1976. The rest of the staffing decisions were less prominent, but still extremely consequential for the Ford administration. Rumsfeld replaced James

Schlesinger as secretary of defense and Cheney took over for Rumsfeld as chief of staff. Kissinger lost his national security advisor role but remained secretary of state. Director of Central Intelligence William Colby, known for testifying on Capitol Hill about controversial CIA practices, was also ousted. Colby's testimony was so damaging that Kissinger had joked, "Every time Bill Colby gets near Capitol Hill, the damn fool feels an irresistible urge to confess to some horrible crime."[67] In his place came former Texas congressman and RNC Chairman George H. W. Bush, who had shortly beforehand served as the U.S. liaison in China.

The moves were too much at once and looked desperate. In getting rid of Rockefeller, it seemed as if Ford was kowtowing to conservatives. Some of the faces promoted to top positions were too fresh for Americans. Cheney recounts in his memoir that on November 3, Ford was given a stack of notecards with expected questions on the staff changes. One of the cards read, "Who the hell is Richard Cheney?" Even as a joke—which Cheney insists it was—the question rang too true.[68]

Ford was unhappy with the massacre as well. He looked back at it regretfully, saying, "I was angry at myself for showing cowardice in not saying to the ultraconservatives, 'It's going to be Ford and Rockefeller, whatever the consequences.'" Overall, he thought the massacre to be "the biggest political mistake of my life." Worse, he thought it to be "one of the few cowardly things I did in my life."

The massacre hurt Ford politically and probably contributed, like the Nixon pardon, to his defeat in the 1976 election. At the same time, circumstances were such that he could not have failed to act. Staff rivalries and internal strife kept the Ford White House off balance throughout its short, rocky tenure. The elevated levels of tension needed strong interventions from the top, both at the presidential and the chief of staff level. As the massacre showed, not all these interventions worked, but the tumult of the White House meant that they needed to try new and different approaches, and take their chances.

## Conclusion

Part of the problem with the Ford administration was Ford himself. He started out with the wrong skill sets, to be sure, but as Rumsfeld noted, he was on the path to progress towards the end: "Every day he was president he got better at being an executive. Within a year he became an exceedingly good executive. He began to delegate effectively, to become more strategic, instead of being consumed with what was in his inbox."[69] Still, the deficit was too great, and the time too short, to turn things around.

Furthermore, once again the trio of ideology, process, and tolerance played a key role in the dysfunction. Rockefeller's liberalism was out of step with the rest of the administration, but Hartmann also saw Cheney and Rumsfeld as too conservative for his tastes, contributing to the tension among them. The process challenges were a problem, too, as Hartmann's inbox spelunking, as well as the various wildcat speechwriting operations, created a sense of administration-wide chaos. While Ford did not exactly tolerate in-fighting, his indulgence of his friend Hartmann allowed some problems to fester beyond the points that they should have.

Ford was a decent man, and a better president than he was judged at the time. His decision to bring in Rumsfeld and Cheney would shape both the trajectory of the Ford administration as well as those of Republican administrations for a generation. The two of them would continue to hold leadership positions in both Congress and administrations for decades after. Their presence alone, however, was insufficient. Ford presided over a toxic White House staff that he ultimately could not control, and it contributed to his failure at getting the people's blessing to serve a full term in the 1976 election.

CHAPTER 6

# JIMMY CARTER
## Overlearning the Lessons of His Predecessors

Jimmy Carter came to the American people as something of a blank slate. A peanut farmer who became governor of Georgia, he was an upset winner over better-known Democratic rivals such as segregationist George Wallace, California governor Jerry Brown, Congressman Morris Udall, and Senator Scoop Jackson, among other Democratic heavyweights. In the general election of 1976, Carter barely defeated an unelected Gerald Ford, who was weakened by his chaotic White House and by his unpopular pardon of Richard Nixon in 1974. It was unclear exactly how the lesser-known Carter would structure his government. This lack of clarity flummoxed the D.C. establishment. As the *Washington Post*'s Ed Walsh wrote shortly after Carter's inauguration, "The manner in which the Carter White House will function remains largely unknown and is likely to evolve slowly over the first several months of the new administration."[1] The lack of clarity would challenge both reporters covering the administration and staff navigating the Carter White House.

The confusion began with the structure of Carter's White House staff. As with many transitions, battle lines appeared between the campaign people close to the candidate and the so-called "establishment" people. Political strategist Hamilton Jordan and press aide Jody Powell were the leaders of the so-called "Georgia Mafia," who stuck with Carter as the establishment cast skepticism at the unknown governor's presidential bid. Leading the establishment aides was Jack Watson, a Harvard-educated partner at an Atlanta law firm whom Carter had put in charge of transition planning. Watson soon learned, however, that securing this illustrious appointment was no favor. As he later said, "The president named me director of the transition—and that was awful."[2]

The campaign aides quickly started worrying that the transition aides were selecting the plum assignments for themselves. Jordan, who was frantically working to get Carter elected, had a personal staff of one assigned to him at the transition. Watson, in contrast, had fifty people reporting to him, with added responsibility for doling out jobs should Carter win. Mistakenly, Watson did not foresee this as a problem: "I sort of conceived that Hamilton would not get involved in the planning—that he was a political strategic planner but that he wouldn't be involved in the overall transition planning. And that was deadly." The experience scarred Watson, who vowed, "Never again, as long as I live, under any circumstance, will I have anything to do with directing a transition."[3]

Watson met both personal and structural obstacles in his efforts. On the personal side, Watson found Powell and Jordan were extremely close to Carter, in a way that Watson never would be. As Watson put it, "The bond that developed between Carter and Ham and Jody, those two very young men, from when they were just barely out of college, became almost filial." Watson was not ready for the level of animosity he faced from Jordan, which was plainly made worse by Jordan's closeness to Carter. According to Watson, "My limited experience in that rarefied realm did not prepare me for the turf consciousness, the long knives." Things were so bad, he later joked, that "it was two months into the transition before I felt safe starting my own car."[4]

Watson may not have had to worry about his physical safety, but Jordan was still after him in another way. Jordan worked with communications guru Gerald Rafshoon, another member of the Georgia Mafia, to undercut Watson and make sure he did not become chief of staff. Rafshoon in fact later told an interviewer that "Ham and I told Jimmy that Jack Watson would be a bad choice as chief of staff."[5]

On the structural side, Carter's vision of how to run the White House served as an obstacle to Watson—or anyone else, for that matter—getting the chief of staff job. In the wake of Ford's recent experiences with Haldeman, Haig, Rumsfeld, and Cheney, Carter was leery of having someone in the *primus inter pares* role. The anti–chief of staff animus was so great that one senior administration official joked that "the only thing I know about Dick Cheney is that he has a nice wife."[6]

Jordan himself could have had the job in the beginning if he had wanted it. Yet he did not pursue it at the outset of the administration, in part because of his bias against the role, but also in part because he knew that the role did not match his skill set. As Stuart Eizenstat, another member of the Georgia Mafia, recalled, "Hamilton—who was the logical candidate because of his closeness to the staff, and the power and influence he had, and the deference with which he was treated by other members of staff, and who was therefore the logical candidate for it— didn't want it either. Probably because he realized that administration was not his forte."[7] Jordan remained aware of this as well, calling himself in later years more of a "coordinator": "I wasn't a chief of staff in a sense that you'd send domestic policy papers through me. You'd come to me when you had a problem that you wanted me to help you with politically or evaluate politically."[8]

The anti–chief of staff bias came from the top. As Eizenstat noted, "The president consciously decided that he was not going to have a chief of staff and that he was going to have a system which I described to reporters as the spokes on the wheel theory." According to Eizenstat, there were several reasons that Carter took this approach. Among them was a general revulsion towards both Nixon and how he had run things. As Eizenstat recalled Carter's view, "the centralization of authority and power in a chief of staff during the Nixon era had been one of the things he had run against and one of the mistakes of the Nixon era." Another reason was Carter's professed interest in a cabinet government when he entered office.[9]

Going hand in hand with the elevation of cabinet government was an attempt to "to denigrate the importance of the White House staff." Eizenstat characterized this effort as "a series of self-defeating actions in reducing the White House staff in size and influence, but without bothering to consult the staffers themselves." Leading this endeavor to squeeze savings out of White House operations was Carter's cousin Hugh Carter. For his trouble, Jody Powell tagged Hugh as "Cousin Cheap." One of the most unpopular steps Hugh and his cousin considered was to get rid of the White House cars that took senior staffers around Washington. Stephen Hess of the Brookings Institution mocked the suggestion for its shortsightedness, asking, "Do you want them to hitchhike? Catch a bus?"[10]

The White House wisely passed on getting rid of the cars for business meetings during the day. Carter did, however, end the "portal to portal" service that ferried top staff to and from work. Eizenstat, who had young kids at home at the time, thought this was shortsighted as well: "Taking away the home-to-home limousine service—which had been enjoyed in the past…was a dramatic mistake. I lost an hour a day at work by not having that." Carter's decision clearly touched a nerve with Eizenstat. In addition to complaining about this decision in his oral history interview, he also mentioned it in his 2018 memoir, recalling that "the most ludicrous outcome occurred when gasoline lines emerged following the Iranian Revolution and I had to wait in line for more than half an hour so I could drive to the White House and try to end the shortage (and doing a pretty inadequate job at that)."[11]

The final element of the decision was presidential pride. Carter had no lack of ego and he wanted to be the one in charge of the White House. As Carter himself wrote, "From the beginning, my ability to govern well would depend on my mastery of the extremely important issues I faced."[12] Eizenstat, who like most aides was enormously deferential towards his boss, stated that "President Carter is a man of great pride—pride in his capacities and abilities and pride in his intellectual capacity." This pride led to a sense that he did not want anyone else to run the White House, as no one else could run it better than he could. As Eizenstat noted, "I think he prided himself on that intelligence and felt that perhaps it exceeded that of the people around him, and that therefore he should be the one to pull all these things together rather than having somebody else."[13]

This kind of pride is not unusual among occupants of the Oval Office. Presidents have usually defeated a host of worthy opponents and competitors to reach their lofty office. In fact, the sentiments that Eizenstat described are not that dissimilar to that of Barack Obama after his 2008 presidential election victory. According to Obama political director Patrick Gaspard, Obama had said that "I think that I'm a better speechwriter than my speechwriters. I know more about policies on any particular issue than my policy directors. And I'll tell you right now that I'm gonna think I'm a better political director than my political director."[14] The sentiment on the part of a president was not unusual. What was unusual was the decision by Carter, based on an oversized presidential ego, not to have a White House chief of staff.

If the decision not to appoint a chief of staff was based on a reaction to earlier administrations, the wrong lesson was taken from the wrong administration. Carter clearly did not like what he saw from the Haldeman model in the Nixon administration, but the constant infighting of the Ford administration should have proved instructive as well. Even with a chief of staff in place, Ford's spokes-on-the-wheel system led to endless strife and constant turf battles. Dick Cheney's welcome note warning to Jordan, "beware the spokes of the wheel," was an apt one, and advice Cheney had given Jack Watson as well.[15] It was also, Eizenstat recalled, "one piece of advice from Cheney we would have done well to follow."[16]

The decision to forgo a chief of staff would have immediate implications. For Watson, not getting the position was "a stunning blow," as his friend Robert Novak wrote.[17] Watson took a different job in the White House—managing intergovernmental relations—and would not attain the chief of staff role for another three plus years. As Watson complained to the *Washington Post*, "The instinct among government workers for turf is about 100 times what it is among gorillas."[18] But the experience also left him with the feeling that Carter's decision not to have a chief of staff and to diminish the power of the White House staff was an "overreaction." This overreaction fit in with the Carter campaign theme of being different from his predecessors, but it did not help the Carter team govern effectively. As Watson saw, the anti–chief of staff rhetoric "might have sounded pretty good in the campaign for the presidency, but it just doesn't work after the inauguration." Watson was adamant on the point, concluding that "it is an absolute necessity to have a chief of staff."[19]

Eizenstat would issue a similar complaint. He determined that "Our White House staff was operating without a fully engaged and experienced chief of staff to keep decisions in a proper order for their effect on diplomacy and domestic politics, and to sequence decisions so they did not conflict. Not only was the message muddled, but policy itself was often adrift." As a result, Eizenstat concluded, "Frankly, the president would have been far better off with a chief of staff from the start."[20]

For the White House more broadly, not having a chief of staff meant that no one on the staff was in charge. On the very first day of the Carter administration, the staff had no idea who should run meetings. Carter lawyer Robert Lipshutz, the group elder, tried to assert himself, saying, "I guess because I'm the oldest one here, I'll call this meeting to order." It did not work. While indeed older, he did not have the respect of the staff and was mostly ignored. Instead, Frank Moore, a Georgian, asked Jordan, "Ham, what do we do now?" He got no answer. After another staffer asked, "Should we have a staff meeting every day?" Jordan finally said, "We'll have a meeting when there's something to meet about." After they meandered on for a while, aide Mark Siegel wondered, "My God, what would the KGB think if they could see us now?"[21] Carter had not wanted a chief, and now that his administration was in place, he did not have one, with all of the implications that decision brought.

Having Carter serve as his own chief of staff created continual challenges. In fact, the whole first year of the Carter administration suffered from a lack of staff organization and management. James Fallows, a Carter speechwriter who would later write a bitter recollection of the administration in *The Atlantic*, wrote that "a year was wasted as we blindly groped for answers and did for ourselves what a staff coordinator could have done."[22]

With no chief, the detail-oriented Carter became more and more involved in both substantive and trivial matters, highly unusual for any president. Joe Califano, the former Johnson White House aide who served as Carter's Secretary of Health Education and Welfare, joked that Carter's deep involvement in welfare legislation made him "the highest paid assistant secretary for planning that ever put a reform proposal together."[23] On the less substantive side of things, Fallows recalled unhappily that Carter "would pore over budget tables to check the arithmetic, and…personally review all requests to use the White House tennis court."[24] The situation was untenable, but the president was set in his ways. Even when trusted aides tried to lighten his burdens, Carter would balk. National Security Advisor Zbigniew Brzezinski recalled that "Whenever I tried to relieve him of excessive detail, Carter would show real uneasiness, and even felt some suspicion, that I was usurping authority."[25]

Carter's inability to let go helped foster his legendary reputation as a president overly enmeshed in minutiae. As this view of him proliferated, it would have a political impact, negative for Carter but positive for his successor. As the *New York Times*' Hedrick Smith noted in his book *The Power Game*, "Reagan got away with his light routine partly because Jimmy Carter had slaved like an indentured servant and the public watched him sink in the morass of detail."[26]

## Zbig versus Cy: The Immigrant versus the WASP

Not having a chief of staff on board from the beginning allowed other problematic rivalries to develop. The result was that Carter's foreign policy team ended up resembling that of the one president he least wanted to emulate. Echoing Nixon, the Carter administration would also see a feuding national security advisor and secretary of state, but in this case the sides were more evenly matched, at least at the beginning.

Like Kissinger, Zbigniew Brzezinski was an intellectual and immigrant, but one who felt dismissed by the establishment. Born in Poland, he moved to Canada at age ten when his father accepted a diplomatic post. When the communists took over in Poland, Brzezinski's father was effectively exiled, and the Brzezinski family remained in Canada. Educated at McGill University in Montreal, Brzezinski also earned a doctorate from Harvard, where he and Kissinger were academic rivals. Later, when Harvard denied Brzezinski an academic appointment, he decamped for Columbia, where he made a name for himself as an expert on communism. It was a subject on which he had both academic and real-world experience, as well as strong views.

Brzezinski's family's exile made him a staunch anti-communist, albeit one in the liberal camp. When Harvard later made him an offer, in large part based on his work on communism, the prideful "Zbig" turned them down. He remained at Columbia until he joined the Carter administration, interrupted by a stint at the State Department under Lyndon Johnson. Despite the tumult in his academic career, Brzezinski was appreciative of America and what it had to offer. He rejected suggestions that he Americanize his name because, as he noted, "America is the only country where someone called 'Zbigniew Brzezinski' can make a name for himself without changing his name."[27]

As Carter's national security advisor, Brzezinski constantly fought with Secretary of State Cyrus Vance, a successful lawyer and long-time Democratic operative whom Zbig would dismiss as a member of the "once-dominant WASP elite."[28] The designation may have been harsh, but it was accurate. Vance was born in West Virginia to a prominent Democratic political family, attended an Episcopal prep school in Connecticut, and earned degrees from Yale College and Yale Law School. He then joined a

Zbigniew Brzezinski, Carter's national security advisor, feuded with Secretary of State Cyrus Vance from the very beginning of the administration. *Courtesy of the Library of Congress*

Wall Street firm, where he worked when he was not serving in government. In the Johnson administration, he served as deputy secretary of defense.

Although both men had sterling resumes, their appointments were not universally welcomed by other members of the Carter administration. Some staffers objected to such traditional or establishment picks, in keeping with the assertively anti-establishment Carter administration. Carter campaign aides saw picking insiders like Vance and Brzezinski as a turn back towards the old ways of doing things. Eizenstat, wary of what might happen with two such strong personalities inside the administration, was fine with hiring one of the two, but not both. Jordan summed up the internal opposition to Zbig and Cy when he said, "If Cyrus Vance is named secretary of state and Zbigniew Brzezinski head of national security in the Carter administration, then I would say we failed, and I would quit. But that's not going to happen." Both of those things did happen, but his promise to quit went unfulfilled.[29]

Eizenstat describes the promise more blandly, claiming that Jordan made the quitting vow "half-jokingly," and that the only implication of hiring "two certified members of the establishment" was that "the whole point of Carter's insurgent, anti-establishment campaign would be undercut"—no hat eating or quitting required. Watson made the key point that, despite the promise, "Vance was the president's first cabinet choice, and one strongly recommended." Despite his concerns, Eizenstat eventually justified the appointments of both men by making the case for experience, asking rhetorically, "How could the security of the United States be put in the hands of novices?"[30]

Beyond their establishment pedigrees, there was also the problem of their conflicting ideologies. Eizenstat remembers that when Carter told him about the proposed selections of Brzezinski and Vance, he warned him "that either one would be an excellent choice—but not both, because they held diametrically opposing views." Carter, however, was unmoved by the advice, blithely replying that "I like hearing different opinions. I can handle it." Unfortunately, Carter could do no such thing, and found that "their ideological differences were far more difficult to reconcile than he realized." The result, Eizenstat found, was that the palpable differences between the two men "often gave a Janus-like quality to the administration's stance toward the Soviet Union."[31]

Brzezinski and Vance disagreed on more than just the Soviet Union. In fact, they differed on nearly every major foreign policy issue. In addition to their policy differences, they also had divergent perspectives on their roles in the administration, as did their boss. Looking back, it is clear that the three men had very different views on each of their roles in the conduct of foreign policy. Carter's view that he could "handle it" turned out to be a significant miscalculation.

## Vance's Perspective

Of the three, Vance seems to have been the one most amenable to getting along in the beginning. More senior in experience and age, he had held a leading subcabinet post in the Johnson administration and was the first one asked to join Carter's cabinet. He also had other reasons to believe that he and Brzezinski would get along. Though Vance was older by a decade, the two men had birthdays one day apart (March 27 for Vance, March 28 for Brzezinski) and they spent election night 1976 together with their wives at the apartment of Columbia law professor Richard Gardner. Vance describes them all as being "thrilled" by Carter's victory, and Brzezinski and Vance walking together as they left the apartment. On the walk, he recalls, "Zbig and I speculated about what the future might bring and whether we both might be asked to play a role on the new president's team."[32] They didn't have to wait long.

Vance was initially optimistic about the arrangement. Ironically, he recommended Brzezinski for national security advisor, just as Brzezinski recommended Vance for secretary of state. He wrote in his memoir that "I did not know Brzezinski well, but I believed we could work well together." Brzezinski even had a signed picture of Vance on the wall of his White House office.[33] But Vance was also too experienced a bureaucratic player to put too much stock in external signs of allegiance, be they pre-election dinners, signed photos, or proximate birthdays. Vance wisely insisted on two things before agreeing to take the job: that he serve as the chief spokesperson on foreign policy for the administration, and that he be able to present his "own unfiltered views" to the president before he made key foreign policy decisions.[34] Both were promises made to Vance and violated by Carter.

Vance's view of the role of secretary of state was expansive. As he wrote in his memoir, "I favored a paramount role for the secretary of state on all foreign policy." He also wanted to put more power in the hands of the State Department bureaucracy, rather than the more political White House staff of the National Security Council. Unfortunately for him, Carter's approach, shaped in large part by Brzezinski, limited the role of the secretary of state in ways that Vance found increasingly unacceptable. Carter's structure, Vance found, granted the national security advisor "the power to interpret the thrust of discussion or frame the policy recommendations of department principals." On this point he was not shy, recalling that "I opposed this arrangement from the beginning, and I said so to the president."[35]

Still, while Vance was willing to stand up for his prerogatives in some areas, he held his tongue in others. In addition to Brzezinski's agenda-setting authority, he also had the final say on editing documents destined to top officials for discussion and review. Vance allowed granting Brzezinski this authority, and later regretted it. As he put it, "In retrospect, I made a serious mistake in not going to the mat on insisting that the draft memoranda be sent to the principals before they went to the president." Vance's regret stemmed from the fact that he often found the NSC memos overly simplistic and binary: "The summaries quite often did not reflect adequately the complexity of discussion or the full range of participants' views. The reports were too terse to convey the dimensions and interrelations of issues." Brzezinski did not deny that he had control of this process. In fact, he was quite proud of it, recalling that "any minutes from Vance's meeting were written up by my staff, sent in to the president by me, without Vance seeing them, with a cover note by me." He notes that Vance did try to change the process, but with little success.[36]

Vance also felt that the memos did not correspond to reality, or what the state of consensus—or lack thereof—was on a particular issue: "I found discrepancies, occasionally serious ones, from my own recollection of what had been said, agreed, or recommended." As a result, he had to spend too much time playing bureaucratic "fireman," working to correct or revise what should have been an accurate depiction of top advisor-level discussions. Given that the documents were "eyes only," meaning that he and he alone could see them, he was the only one able to work on correcting what he saw as inaccurate summaries or statements: "This meant that I had to go back to the president to clarify my views and to get the matter straightened out." Carter did offer to let Vance come to the White House to review drafts of memos before they were completed, that being the only choice before the advent of email. Given all the other things Vance had on his plate, it was unrealistic and Brzezinski kept control over the drafting process as well as the final copies.[37]

A larger problem was Vance's inability—or unwillingness—to recognize what was happening around him. Averell Harriman, one of the Wise Men of Democratic foreign policy gurus, did see what happened and tried to help. The octogenarian Harriman, who regularly peppered Carter, Brzezinski, and Vance with memos on his insights and conversations in D.C. and around the world, was concerned about the way Brzezinski dominated the foreign policy process. Harriman and Brzezinski had been close at one point—Brzezinski stayed in Harriman's Georgetown guest house for six months at the start of the administration—before Brzezinski froze him out. But Harriman—a former ambassador, governor of New York, and State Department official—remained close with his mentee Vance and tried to warn the secretary of state that he needed to be more assertive in the process. He even invited Vance to his estate in Middleburg, Virginia, for an intervention on the topic, where he explained how Brzezinski was taking advantage of Vance. The gentlemanly Vance was slow to believe it, despite nagging concerns, and continued to regard Brzezinski as ultimately a fair and above-board player, until shown evidence to the contrary during the Iran hostage crisis of 1979.[38]

On matters of structure and process, Vance, ever the lawyer, saw himself as willing to compromise, giving in on some issues, pushing back on others, and, in this desire to be a team player, did not weigh in on issues that he should have. As a State Department lawyer told the *Washington Post*'s Sally Quinn at the time, "Cy is a lawyer, he believes in adjudicating settlements between conflicting parties."[39] The result of this legalistic approach was that Vance was often on his back heels, playing defense in a bureaucratic structure and a process not of his creation. Without a chief of staff initially in place, and with a weak chief of staff following, he had nowhere to go to complain other than to the president. Unfortunately for Vance, Carter's White House and foreign policy apparatus from the beginning meant that the secretary of state was unlikely ever to be the top foreign policy person.

## Brzezinski's Approach

Brzezinski took a different approach going into the administration and into his relationship with Vance. From the beginning, he made it clear that he was in no way subordinate to the secretary of state. According to Eizenstat, on Brzezinski's first day, he was briefed on his phone set up, in which the president and the secretary of state each had telephone lines that allowed them to reach Brzezinski directly, without having to go through Brzezinski's secretary, as the other cabinet secretaries had to. Under the arrangement, Vance could ring directly to Brzezinski's desk. Brzezinski did not like that, insisting that Vance's direct line to him be terminated, yelling at his staff to "Yank it out. I'm working for the president, not for Vance."[40]

From Brzezinski's perspective, everything was set up his way. He had the status of a cabinet member, not a given for the national security advisor. His large West Wing office had a bathroom in it, something that even Vice President Walter Mondale had wanted but did not get. The bathroom door had been moved by Kissinger to open into the national security advisor's office, and Mondale's political advisor Michael Berman advised the vice president that "there's no way to change this bathroom back again!" Unlike other senior staff like Eizenstat, Brzezinski had access to a White House limousine and the coveted "portal to portal" service taking him to and from work. Brzezinski had the ability to drop in on Carter whenever he wanted, and with it came the ability to keep track of Carter's foreign policy meetings. And he also controlled the paper flow. To top all that off, Brzezinski played tennis on the White House tennis court with Carter more than any other staffer, and their families got together semi-regularly, with Carter's daughter Amy and Brzezinski's daughter Mika, of the same age, regularly coming together as playmates.[41]

Vance did have a weekly breakfast with Carter, but one which Brzezinski—and Defense Secretary Harold Brown—attended as well. Vance could send in a nightly report to the president, but it was more

President Jimmy Carter walks with Vice President Walter Mondale as Secretary of State Cyrus Vance and Secretary of Defense Harold Brown trail behind. *Courtesy of the Library of Congress*

of a summary of what was happening in the world rather than a policy guidance document. Brzezinski, in contrast, used Carter's marginal notes on his own weekly reports to Carter to obtain the presidential direction and authority needed to press forward with policy initiatives. While Brzezinski recognized that he and Carter did not share the same approach—Carter being more dovish and Brzezinski more hawkish— he used his access to get Carter to embrace his policies, if not his worldview. As he put it, "unlike Kissinger, who had in Nixon a clear ally in shaping a grand strategy for the country, I have to do it through indirection." Overall, though, things were set up from the very beginning in Brzezinski's favor, and he took full advantage of it.[42] Within six months of the administration's start, Washington insider columnists Rowland Evans and Robert Novak concluded that Brzezinski "has emerged the clear winner in his foreign policy struggle with the State Department."[43]

In addition to setting things up in his favor, there was also the fact that Brzezinski and his staff did not seem to think much of Vance. In an oral history interview, Brzezinski went out of his way to point out his superior loyalty to Carter, noting that "Vance supported Sargent Shriver for president, which I always thought showed a certain eccentricity of judgment." In Carter's world, as in many presidential administrations, highlighting that someone had not been a true believer in the early days could be a devastating dismissal. Despite this comment, Brzezinski felt that he was largely blameless—or at least not underhanded—in the dispute, recalling that "I know at least in my own conscience that seeing the president alone many times a day—and Carter will confirm this—that I never said anything about Vance that was personally derogatory."[44]

Brzezinski, who was coming out on top in the dispute between the two men, showed some schadenfreude over Vance's frustration. In an oral history interview, he mocked Vance over the times that Brzezinski's actions drove the older man to anger and showed that the outbursts did not really bother him. In one such incident, Vance did not appreciate the

*Washington Post's* declaration on U.S.-Soviet relations that read "Brzezinski Draws the Line." This was not just any headline, but "a huge headline." When Brzezinski came to his office, Vance "was sitting there with a big smile on his face and I could tell the big smile was the I'm really pissed off as hell kind of smile." Although angry, Vance did not raise his voice, instead saying, "'Well, you have really done it. I wonder whether you should have said it that way, put it that way,' all with a big smile." After they discussed matter for a bit, Vance left, but when they talked again the next day, Vance was contrite, saying, "I thought about it further, I think you were right."[45]

On another occasion, Vance got so angry at Brzezinski over a dispute about the Shah of Iran visiting Egypt that "he slammed the receiver on me." Despite Vance's anger, Brzezinski recalled, "even then he didn't really hit me." Brzezinski further makes the incredible claim that "In the four years I never had one unpleasant exchange with him." He recognized that this was surprising, especially given the fact that the newspapers were full of stories about the Vance-Brzezinski feud. Brzezinski even gave an explanation, albeit a self-serving one, for the "somewhat unusual" fact of their positive interpersonal relations: "that I was the only peer he had." Vance had nowhere else to go, Brzezinski thought: "Everybody else, Stu Eizenstat, Ham, Jody, Moore, were not really peers, and the Cabinet members were always at a distance."[46]

At the same time, Brzezinski took pains to point out that while he had heard Carter "really get mad at Vance.... He never once was nasty to me, never said anything unpleasant." The worst that happened, was that Carter once "wrote me a note which is slightly unpleasant, but that was the most he ever did, and that was actually something to do with handling the papers on his desk." Overall, Brzezinski "was struck by that, that in the four years he never once either raised his voice or growled at me."[47]

Brzezinski's military aide General William Odom recalled that Brzezinski was much more skilled than Vance at running Security Council meetings. Noting that "complete confusion could arise in those meetings," Odom appreciated how Brzezinski "could come in and structure the discussion, pick out the two or three key points with lightning-like speed, drive the meeting to a conclusion, get some actionable recommendations, and get them to the president." With Vance, in contrast, things would not go as well: "You put Vance in the chair, he'd drift about, and provide much less focus."[48]

If Brzezinski's staff disliked Vance, then Vance's staff disliked Brzezinski even more. NSC aide Gary Sick recalled that the level of Brzezinski loathing at the State Department was of "nearly pathological proportions."[49] Carter put it somewhat more diplomatically, noting that "Whenever Zbig went anywhere or said anything, it created tremors in the State Department."[50] This anti-Brzezinski attitude at the State Department was unsurprising, given the ways in which Brzezinski seized the initiative on foreign policy from Vance and from State. Yet even at the State Department, there was a grudging appreciation of the role Brzezinski could play as a needed tough guy, something Vance was seemingly incapable of doing. As one senior State Department staffer told the *New York Times*'s Richard Burt, sometimes "The Soviets do deserve to be told off, and I guess Zbig's the guy to do it."[51]

Just because Brzezinski had the edge on Vance, that did not mean that he had unfettered reign over policy in the White House. He faced his own challenges as someone who had not been part of the Georgia Mafia. As one Carter aide told the *Washington Post*, "Inside the White House I don't think Zbig could win a major battle with Ham or Jody. There's no question that if Jody wanted to take Zbig on, Zbig would get his a** handed to him. Just look at all the nicknames they call him. If he messes with Ham or Jody he'll get his legs cut off."[52]

The long-standing Carter staff not only had more power than Brzezinski, but they also viewed him as odd and overly aggressive. The nickname "Woody Woodpecker," bestowed on him by Jordan, stemmed from his reddish hair and angular features. He was so competitive that he once sent fellow aides scrambling out of his path while playing a supposedly friendly soccer game at a White House picnic.[53] On another occasion, when Brzezinski was playing chess against Israeli Prime Minister Menachem Begin during the Camp David negotiations between Egypt and Israel, Jordan said to the Israelis: "Do me a favor and make sure Begin wins. Otherwise Zbig will be insufferable." According to the author Lawrence Wright, Begin won three of four matches, but Eizenstat recalls Brzezinski being "diplomatic" about things: "In his memoirs he maintains there were two matches, which ended in a one-one tie."[54]

It wasn't just the staff that had issues with Brzezinski and his aggressive approach. Charlie Kirbo, a close friend and advisor to Carter, noted that "Brzezinski just kicked up dust everywhere he went." Carter himself said after the administration that Brzezinski was "feisty and provocative." When asked about the Carter plans for a second term, Eizenstat acknowledged that Brzezinski was rumored not to have been under consideration: "It was not my sort of decision to make, and I wasn't a participant in any sessions, but that's something that one heard."[55]

In addition to his challenges from within, Brzezinski also felt pressured by the specter of his old rival from Harvard, Henry Kissinger, widely regarded as America's top foreign policy mind. At one dinner with reporters, Brzezinski even vocalized his feelings of inadequacy *vis-a-vis* Kissinger, asking plaintively, "Tell me, what has Kissinger got that I haven't got?" But he made no apologies about his primacy within the foreign policy apparatus, rhetorically asking a reporter, "Can you imagine, or would you prefer, that a president's assistant for national security affairs was widely seen as soft and weak, fearful of the use of power?"[56]

## Carter's Approach

As for Carter himself, he was uncharacteristically disengaged from the daily fighting, even as headlines about the feud proliferated. In his diary, he acknowledged that Brzezinski was "too competitive and incisive," while Vance was "too easy on his subordinates." But in the same sentence, he puts the blame for the headlines on the press, complaining that "the news media aggravate the inevitable differences."[57]

Carter would have been better off placing at least some blame on himself. In one instance, Carter reported that "Zbig told me that Cy became almost emotional about his stopping by to see King Hassan, and this really aggravated me. Cy's so extremely jealous, it's ridiculous." And yet, Carter noted, "I didn't interfere." On another occasion, he reported that "Cy Vance was philosophically closest to me, but his first loyalty was to the State Department bureaucracy." What's worse, Carter reported that Vance "threatened to resign on numerous occasions when he felt that Harold Brown, Bob Strauss, Sol Linowitz, Zbig Brzezinski, Warren Christopher or anyone else might be given too significant a part to play in foreign affairs." This was an extensive list of people for a Secretary of State to be worried about, including his own deputy, Christopher. What's worse, Carter recalled, was that "It was almost impossible for me to get an innovative idea from State, and its primary role seemed to be to put brakes on any proposal that originated elsewhere."[58]

These comments from Carter showed that there was clearly something wrong with the Carter foreign policy team, something that he as president should have addressed. He failed to do so, and as a result his administration appeared disorganized as allies and foes alike received mixed messages. One key area of disagreement with real world implications came in the question of who would serve as the administration's voice on foreign policy. Vance complained that Brzezinski's efforts to make himself the spokesperson "became a political liability, leaving the Congress and foreign governments with the impression that the administration did not know its own mind." Brzezinski, for his part, explained that he felt the need to assert himself since "Vance, for all of his many gifts and personal qualities, was not an effective communicator, and the president started encouraging me to speak up more." *New York Times* reporter Bernard Gwertzman weighed in on these competing accounts and determined that "in practice it turned out that Mr. Carter, in his own book of memoirs, supports Mr. Brzezinski completely on this point."[59]

Post-administration memoirs aside, for most of the administration Carter could not decide between the two men, or between their competing visions of how things were to be structured. This indecision led both to confusion within the Carter administration and a worrisome lack of clarity on American intentions and resolve. Little wonder that it was a period of adventurism by America's opponents, including the Soviet invasion of Afghanistan and the embarrassing takeover of the U.S. embassy in Iran.

Brzezinski and Vance disagreed on virtually every key issue that came their way: on the Soviets, on Iran policy, on China, and even on the national security process. Yet even during all this disagreement, they did agree, along with Carter, in one area. All three favored a tough stance on Israel, coupled with a policy more tilted towards the Arabs in the Arab-Israeli dispute. As Eizenstat (himself more favorably disposed towards Israel) wrote, both Vance and Brzezinski, "and usually the president himself" were "aggressively pushing forward a peace process in ways that often alienated Israel and American Jewish leaders." Eizenstat further recalled, with frustration, that "Vance was very pro-Arab. Vance was impossible on this issue."[60] Eizenstat was not the only one frustrated with the negative take on Israel. Vice President Walter Mondale also did not like it. According to Mondale, the administration's Israel policies "made my life miserable.... Just another gratuitous show across my bow, and I think it was Zbig." The vice president also disliked the way that Brzezinski did not allow for a fair process to discuss things and went directly to Carter to get his way. As Eizenstat wrote, "Mondale concluded that that was how Brzezinski avoided debates and got his way on an issue." At another point, Eizenstat recalled that Mondale "exploded" when he was interrupted at a Georgetown dinner at the home of socialite Pamela Harriman to learn that Vance proposed to impose new concessions on Israel to placate the Palestinians. Beyond Mondale, the Israelis, as expected, did not like the administration's tilt, either. At one point, Simcha Dinitz, Israel's ambassador to Washington, complained to Eizenstat, "I would like to take away [Carter's] anger at Israel. He is dealing with an ally."[61]

Regardless of the complaints, Brzezinski and Vance remained united in their stance against Israel. Furthermore, they could be unforgiving towards those outside the fold on this issue. Eizenstat tells the story of

Ham Jordan's political aide, Mark Siegel, who had the difficult role of White House liaison to an understandably discomfited American Jewish community. When Siegel reported back that the Jewish community was unhappy with the U.S. selling F-15 fighter jets to Saudi Arabia—then a staunch enemy of Israel—he offered to resign his position. While Jordan, his direct boss, recommended that Siegel drop the Jewish liaison role but remain as a White House aide, Siegel decided it was best to go through with the resignation. The Carter team was unhappy with his decision. As Eizenstat recalled, "No one spoke to him during the few days he was packing up his things."[62]

Unfortunately, for Siegel, things would get worse. He complained to Carter on his departure that Brzezinski had been rude and borderline anti-Semitic to the head of the Los Angeles Jewish Federation, telling him, "You people better learn that you don't dictate foreign policy." After leaving, a reporter friend of Siegel's, the *Dallas Morning News'* Carl Luebsdorf, told him that Brzezinski was saying about him, "You're not going to meddle in foreign policy anymore." Even worse, the White House spread the inaccurate story that Siegel had not resigned but was fired. As Eizenstat ruefully wrote, "Welcome to the world of Washington and the brutal domestic politics of Middle East policy making."[63]

Vance would learn a similar lesson after he resigned in April of 1980, unhappy with the military decision to rescue the hostages in Iran. The effort would fail, giving the Carter administration another foreign policy humiliation. On Vance's resignation, the columnists Evans and Novak reported that Vance's departing shot was to make disparaging remarks about "those pygmies in the White House." As Evans and Novak wrote, Vance "specifically included the president" among the pygmies.[64] Carter was displeased and would remain so for a long time. When Carter published his diary years after leaving the White House, he expressed his disenchantment with Vance. According to Energy Secretary James Schlesinger, "By that time he was quite angry with Cy Vance, by the time he writes his memoirs. He takes, I think, unkind cuts at Cy that are unnecessary."[65]

## Conclusion

Presidents need to study and learn from predecessors, including on the subject of managing the White House. Looking to the mistakes of the past can help one avoid pitfalls in the future. Jimmy Carter, however, looked a bit too hard. He overreacted to the Ford and Nixon experiences and was determined, for example, to avoid having a chief of staff. In doing so, Carter initially left no one in charge of the day-to-day management of his administration other than himself. This created a poor first impression—something that could never be undone—overburdened the president, and took his focus away from loftier presidential duties, and also created pathways for staff mischief among aides like Brzezinski and Vance, which further hurt his administration.

On the three-part test of ideology, process, and presidential tolerance, Carter and his team score poorly. The central battle of the administration, the one between Brzezinski and Vance, took place between two antagonists with well-known ideological disagreements over foreign policy. The process challenge was worsened by the lack of a chief of staff to mediate disputes in the administration's early days, followed by the appointment of a self-admitted ineffective chief of staff in Ham Jordan. While Carter did not like the disagreements taking place between his subordinates, his "I like hearing different opinions. I can handle it" attitude was the wrong approach given his White House. As a result of failures on all three of these fronts, the Carter administration descended into ineffectuality and constant fighting.

Unfortunately for the nation, the fights played out in the context of, and contributed to, a worsening global situation, which included the Arab oil crisis, the Iran hostage crisis, and growing Soviet adventurism in the Cold War. The result was unnecessary confusion at a time when the world needed resolve and unerring leadership from the president.

# CHAPTER 7

# RIVALRIES UNDER REAGAN

## Baker versus Meese, and Regan versus Nancy

R onald Reagan was the first president to complete two terms since Dwight Eisenhower. The preceding presidencies, dating back to Kennedy, were all truncated: Kennedy was assassinated; Johnson withdrew his candidacy; Nixon resigned in disgrace; and Ford and Carter lost campaigns as incumbents. Reagan's ability to earn and expand the support of the American people rested in large part on his own political talent, but also on his successful management of his staff. He brought in a smart group of aides led by a chief of staff, Jim Baker, who is considered by many to be the most successful White House chief of staff in history. But the Reagan staff, while skillful, was not without its conflicts. In fact, as Reagan speechwriter Peter Robinson said, "there was a lot more in-fighting going on in the Reagan White House than anybody was aware of because there was no such thing as Tweeter, Twitter, Twotter in those days."[1]

Robinson raises a key point. As media have become more pervasive, not to mention less deferential, the outside world has learned far more about internal disputes within administrations. Today, reporters and commentators are on high alert, eager to exploit every new dispute, real or imagined. In addition to the media's appetite, individuals now have many more ways to alert the wider world about internal White House developments. In short, it is now possible for staff conflict to escalate more quickly—and more publicly—than ever.

The Reagan team may have been spared the modern electronic media, but old-style journalists were quite prepared to report plenty on tensions in the Reagan camp. The tensions began early, during the presidential campaign. At the center of the infighting in the early days was Reagan's campaign manager, John Sears. Sears knew the bitter course that personal battles could take. He had learned that it was time to leave the Nixon White House after relegation to an unfavorable attic office in the Old Executive Office Building. During Reagan's 1976 primary campaign, Sears had adopted the grandiose title of "executive vice chair." In 1980, he demanded the same imperial honorific. This time, however, rivals challenged him. One challenger was a conservative San Diego lawyer named Edwin Meese III. Meese knew Reagan well. He had served as Governor Reagan's chief of staff, so when the presidential run started, he called himself chief of staff once again with Reagan's approval. Another challenger to Sears was Michael Deaver. Deaver was a gifted spin doctor who had started working for Governor Reagan in 1966, while still in his late twenties.[2]

Sears saw what he called "the Westerners"—including Meese and Deaver, but also Lyn Nofziger and Martin Anderson—as a threat to his power. Meese's conservativism was in line with Reagan's ideological approach, and Deaver developed a close, quasi-familial bond with both Reagan and his influential wife, Nancy. Sears even complained that Deaver served as Nancy's "eyes and ears," which made him a threat to Sears. As David Keane recalled, "Sears had undisguised disdain for them." He resolved to get rid of both Deaver and Meese. In November 1979, Sears made his move against Deaver. The effort came in the wake of what long-time Reagan aide—and former Nixon White House aide—Martin Anderson called "an especially vicious round of internal campaign politics," which included the departures of old Reagan hands Lyn

Nofziger and Anderson himself. Joined by Press Secretary Jim Lake and political director Charlie Black, Sears had Deaver called to the Reagans' Los Angeles residence. Mrs. Reagan asked Deaver to wait, leaving him to sit for twenty minutes. Deaver lost patience, and went on his own to the living room, where he found both Reagans with Black, Lake, and Sears. The Reagans confronted Deaver with accusations from the three aides about Deaver bilking the campaign with excessive charges. The charges infuriated Deaver, who quit on the spot, saying, "You need to put somebody in charge, and if these gentlemen have convinced you that I am ripping you off, after all these years, then I'm out. I'm leaving." This was clearly not Reagan's intent, as he tried to stop Deaver, telling him, "No, this is not what I want." Regardless of Reagan's desire, Deaver stormed out, only to return sheepishly a moment later, saying, "I forgot that Carolyn dropped me off. Can I borrow Nancy's station wagon to get home?" With the transportation issues sorted out, he left again. The story did not end there. After Deaver left, Reagan, typically slow to anger, expressed his displeasure to the three conspirators with uncharacteristic sharpness, "Well, you sons of bitches, the best guy we had just left." Sears and his compatriots had succeeded at getting rid of Deaver but doubly angered Reagan by forcing out Deaver and by getting Reagan involved in interpersonal squabbles. Anderson called Deaver's departure "one of the biggest mistakes Ronald Reagan ever made," but it would end up hurting Sears more than Deaver. [3]

With Deaver gone, an emboldened Sears continued to assert his dominance on the personnel front by hiring favorites and dropping those he saw as rivals. Eventually, he moved against Meese, recommending marginalizing his role in the campaign. This was a step too far. As Meese described it, rather mildly, "At this, the Governor, I am glad to say, balked." The real incident was more tumultuous. When Sears tried to put in another layer above Meese, Reagan once again got angry, saying, "I know what you're doing. You're after Ed [Meese]." Reagan's face turned red, and Lake thought Reagan might throw a punch at Sears. His frustration plain to see, Reagan yelled at Sears: "You got Lyn Nofziger. You got Mike Deaver. You're not getting Ed Meese!"

It was the beginning of Sears's end, as Reagan lost confidence in him. At two o'clock on the day of Reagan's New Hampshire primary victory, Reagan fired Sears, along with Black and Lake, and put William J. Casey, the future director of central intelligence, in charge. To outsiders, the victory turned out to have been an opportune moment, but win or lose, Sears was going to be gone after New Hampshire. [4]

Getting rid of Sears was a relief for Reagan. He had long chafed under Sears's direction, and he did not trust Sears's manner. As Reagan complained to Nofziger about Sears, "He won't look me in the eye; he looks me in the tie." Overall, Reagan reporter Lou Cannon wrote in the *Washington Post*, "Reagan is a far happier man with Sears out of the way." The move showed that Reagan, not any of the staff, was in charge, and helped pave the way for smoother internal dynamics on the way to Reagan's 1980 primary and election victories. [5]

## Baker: The Enemy Within Takes Charge

In running for the GOP nomination, the Reagan team saw George H. W. Bush as by far Reagan's biggest rival. It wasn't just a matter of Bush's stature and impressive resume. The two men had a history. In 1978, Bush's son George W. ran for congress in Texas. Reagan endorsed the younger Bush's opponent, forcing a runoff in the race. Bush won, but the move did not endear Reagan to the elder Bush. When Bush and Reagan squared off more directly in the 1980 primaries, Bush made an explicit point of highlighting his own age—fifty-six—as the ideal age for running for president. Implicit in this argument was the fact that Reagan, Bush's chief opponent, was much older at sixty-nine. In addition, the Bush campaign's use of the jibe "voodoo economics" to describe Reagan's successful economic plan, which stuck with its critics, would continue to plague Reagan long after the campaign ended.

The primaries were a bitter battle, as a crowded GOP field quickly turned into a two-man race between Reagan and Bush. Reagan eventually prevailed, but Bush, helped by campaign manager James A. Baker III, put on an impressive show, which should have placed him in immediate contention for the vice-presidential slot. Unfortunately, the bitterness of the primary campaign counted against Bush, and Reagan went into the 1980 Republican convention leaning towards making former president Gerald Ford his number two.

In the end, despite the tensions, Reagan and Bush formed an alliance. In July 1980, Reagan offered, and Bush accepted, a spot on the ticket at the GOP convention in Detroit. Part of this alliance included the merging of staffs, including veterans of the rough-and-tumble primary campaign that had just taken place. This meant that Baker, the Houston lawyer who had also served as Gerald Ford's campaign manager in 1976, became manager of the Reagan-Bush campaign. Baker, Bush's longtime doubles partner in tennis, was chosen because of his political skills but remained an outsider to the Reagan operation.

At the end of the successful campaign, Reagan had to build his governing team. Ed Meese, who had held senior roles with both Reagan's gubernatorial staff and his campaign staff, was seen by himself and the outside world as the presumptive candidate to serve as Reagan's chief of staff. Some of his fellow Reagan insiders, however, did not see the disorganized Meese as the right person to serve in the top management job in the White House. Leading the charge against Meese was Deaver—whom Reagan asked to come back after Sears left—and Stu Spencer, another long-time Reagan political advisor. Spencer was particularly adamant on the point, telling Reagan a week before the election, "Ed cannot be chief of staff. He's not organized."[6]

Unlike the outsider Sears, who had tried, and failed, to take out Meese, Spencer was an insider. In addition, Spencer wasn't trying to exile Meese but wanted to ensure that Meese did not get a job that multiple people in the Reagan circle, including members of the Reagan family, thought he could not handle. Meese's disorganization was so legendary that his briefcase had its own nicknames—the "Meesecase," "a briefcase without a bottom" and "the black hole"—from which briefing papers entered never to reemerge. Spencer also had a pithy way of describing

Meese's shortcomings on the organizational front: "Ed couldn't organize a two-car funeral."[7]

Reagan was surprised but amenable to the idea of denying Meese the chief of staff role. Still, someone needed to fill it, as the more business-oriented Reagan team did not share Carter's disdain toward having a chief of staff. In fact, Reagan had even praised Jack Watson, Carter's last chief of staff, suggesting that had Watson started sooner, Reagan would not have won the 1980 election. Given the need and desire for a chief of staff, the Meese critics needed to present an alternative to succeed. The only realistic choice was Baker. As a veteran White House aide later told Reagan speech-writer Peggy Noonan, "They picked Baker because he was smart, because he had a sense of organization, and because he knew something about Washington." Reagan was uncertain, but deferred, as he often did, to his staff's recommendation, saying, "Well, fellas, if you think so...."[8]

While Baker was an obvious choice from a skills perspective, picking him had its challenges. According to Congressman David Stockman, who had helped the Reagan campaign debate preparation efforts, inner circle Reaganites saw Baker as "tainted goods." In addition to serving as campaign manager for two moderates, Gerald Ford and George Bush, Baker was also "a bright neon light that blinked: 'Voodoo Economics!'"[9]

For these reasons, Baker's appointment came as "an utter shock to the true blue Reaganauts."[10] Beyond the lingering campaign bitterness, there was also a concern among the inner circle from an ideological perspective. Baker was pragmatic, moderate, and seen as too different from the more conservative Reagan team. As Lou Cannon wrote, longtime Reagan hands found it "inconceivable" that "Reagan would want a political pragmatist as his top aide."

Beyond the Reagan circle itself, there was also Meese's understandable personal reaction. According to Baker, Meese, feeling slighted, took the news of Baker's appointment badly: "Meese was down. Meese was very down." Spencer, who set matters in motion, went further, recalling that Meese "went *ape sh\*t*" over the move.[11]

President Reagan horseback riding with James A. Baker III. Baker made an unexpected but successful transition from campaign manager for Reagan rival George H. W. Bush to chief of staff to Reagan. *Courtesy of the Ronald Reagan Presidential Library and Museum*

All this internal drama had an impact on Baker as well. As he put it, "You could have knocked me over with a feather when he asked me to do this." Baker was sure his previous roles had made him a nonstarter: "Coming from where I'd come from, I mean I'd been Ford's campaign manager, I'd been Bush's campaign manager, so obviously I had to be flattered by it."[12]

Surprise or no, Baker took the job. Still, he was coming into a high-profile position, and lacked allies on the Reagan team. Baker was effectively a *persona non grata* to many of them, for ideological and personal reasons. Unsurprisingly, his introduction to the Reagan staff was touchy. As Baker recalled, "That was a traumatic thing for me." As he approached his new team members, he noted that "there are all the people I've been fightin'! *All* of 'em!"[13]

Reagan, astutely recognizing the blow to Meese's ego, had even asked Baker to "Make it right with Ed."[14] Baker being Baker, he had a plan for coopting Meese, while also calming him down from his "ape sh*t" state. First, he planned to keep a low profile as chief of staff. As the *Christian Science Monitor*'s Louis Sweeney wrote in a puff piece on Baker shortly after his appointment, "You won't see his Stetson showing over the rim of the hill too often." For this reason, Baker aide Margaret Tutwiler, who saw how isolated he felt initially, labelled him "Mr. Cautious." Furthermore, while the Reagan people disliked the moderate Baker, he did have a powerful ally in the sitting vice president. When Bush was asked what Baker's weakness might be, he only offered a trivial one: "He's an excellent tennis player, but his service is not known for its blinding speed."[15]

For Meese, Baker gave him clear areas of responsibility. While Baker got the chief of staff title, Meese became "Counselor to the President for Policy." Baker also granted Meese cabinet rank, which Meese considered vital. Under the terms of their arrangement, sketched out in a famous chart, Meese ran the policy councils and could take part in cabinet meetings, while Baker took control of legislation, press, and paperwork. Baker's responsibilities encompassed "Coordination and supervision of White House Staff functions," "Hiring and firing authority over all elements of White House Staff," "Coordination and control of all in and out paper flow to the President and of presidential schedule and appointments," and the ability to "Preside over meetings of White House Staff." Overall, he told Meese, "You've got the policy; I'll just make the trains run on time." The arrangement flattered Meese, but what it really did was leave Baker in charge.[16]

## The Third Man: Mike Deaver

The third man in what became known as the White House troika was Deaver. As a longtime trusted Reagan aide, Deaver's title was deputy chief of staff, but his job was really keeper of Reagan's image and soother of Nancy Reagan. His regular reports to her about staff goings on were called "the Mommy watch." Another pragmatist like Baker, Deaver did not really care about the ideology. He did not care much about his long-standing ties to Meese or the Californians, either, as he was happy to ally with Baker in the troika when it suited him. Because he didn't seem to care about ideology, and for his alliance with Baker, the California circle labeled Deaver "a renegade."[17]

Those who crossed Deaver would find that he could use all manner of tactics against them. Deaver and Baker both disliked Secretary of State Al Haig and were determined to get rid of him. As George Shultz, Haig's successor, recalled of the former Nixon chief of staff, "Haig's bristling manner did not suit the Meese-Baker-Deaver circle, and bureaucratic turf battles were constantly being waged between the White House and the State Department."[18]

Deaver, who controlled White House operations, had the power to make Haig's life miserable, and he did. On one presidential trip to London, Deaver not only made sure that Haig did not ride with the president on Marine One but also made sure that the chopper Haig was on was noisy and uncomfortable. In response to his distance from the president, Haig asked, "What am I, a leper?" Haig would also find himself having difficulty getting on Air Force One or into presidential hotels and motorcades on foreign trips. Worse for him, Mrs. Reagan noticed his constant complaining—and bristled.[19]

Deaver also micromanaged Haig's hiring of an assistant, leading to a blowup in which Haig screamed, "How dare you talk to me like that? I have served six presidents." When asked about these perceived oversights, Baker disingenuously said, "I don't blame him for being pissed off. I had nothing to do with it." Haig complained that a White House aide was running a *guerilla* campaign" to get him. In addition, Haig had called the troika of Baker, Deaver, and Meese "the gorillas in the White House." In response, Deaver even dressed up in a gorilla suit in the White House, saying, "I'm Baker's gorilla"—mocking Haig's noticeable paranoia. The shenanigans worked, or at least contributed to Haig's misery, for in June of Reagan's first year in office, he fired Haig. George

Shultz concluded that "Haig's resignation was the result of clashes with the White House staff over both style and substance."[20]

Deaver was protective of Reagan, but since being ousted during the campaign, he was more protective of himself. When Judge William Clark, who became Reagan's second national security advisor early on, suggested that they expand the troika to a foursome, Deaver would not hear of it. He told Reagan, "it won't work. If you do this, I'll have to leave." Deaver got his way, but he also made an enemy out of Clark, who stopped speaking to him.[21] Evidently, it was worth it to keep his closeness to Reagan.

When Deaver was not flummoxing rivals, he focused on his main duty: making Reagan look good. This often involved beguiling the press, a group manifestly determined to make the handsome, amiable Reagan look bad. Deaver was a master of message discipline and good visuals. The White House would feed the press a message of the day and a video of Reagan to bolster the message. The press might try to undercut the message with negative reporting, but Deaver understood that visuals for Reagan were more important than voiceovers. CBS reporter Leslie Stahl learned this when she ran a piece criticizing the Reagan administration for budget cuts, using White House–provided footage of the president at the Special Olympics. Stahl was convinced she had nailed the administration and was surprised when White House officials told her they "loved it." Stahl was surprised, recalling that she had done "a piece that was— where I was quite negative, to be honest with you, about Reagan. And yet the pictures were terrific, and I thought they'd be mad at me, but they weren't." Deaver later explained Stahl's miscalculation to PBS's Bill Moyers: "The problem with it was that she had to put on during her piece all these wonderful visuals that we created. And if you really believe that the visuals are going to outlast the spoken word in the person's mind, then we were delighted with it."[22]

Not everyone was eager to view Deaver as the administration's savior when it came to the press. White House political aide Lyn Nofziger wondered whether Deaver got too much credit for something for which

Reagan really deserved the credit. As Nofziger said, "You could have put the Reagan stuff in there with Jimmy Carter and Jimmy Carter still wouldn't have come out good. You can't make a silk purse out of a sow's ear." Nofziger was sure it wasn't Deaver, and he was willing to double down on his critique, saying, "my mother could have run [Reagan's] campaign and he'd still have been elected president...I don't mean to belittle Mike Deaver, he did a fine job, but I would like to have seen him working with Ford or Carter or Nixon and then come back and tell me."[23] Deaver felt just the opposite, telling fellow Californian Martin Anderson, "You know, I am Ronald Reagan. Where do you think he got most of those ideas over the years? Every morning after I get up I make believe I am him and ask what should he do and where should he go."[24]

## Baker and Deaver: Leak Central

Looking at the two Californians, Baker shrewdly picked Deaver as his ally. It made sense: Deaver was close to the Reagans and had a long history with them, which gave him staying power. He was a political streetfighter. And, most importantly for Baker, unlike the conservative Meese, Deaver cared less about movement conservatism and policy outcomes. Deaver's two main concerns were promoting Reagan and protecting his own turf.

There was one more significant reason that made Deaver a better friend and worse enemy than Meese: Deaver was a master of the press. Baker constantly leaked to make himself look good and to make his rivals look bad. Whether Baker learned from Deaver or just recognized a kindred spirit, they both saw the press as a deployable asset. This contrasts with the typical conservative viewpoint, espoused by Ed Meese. He saw the press as an enemy to avoid. In his memoir, Meese complained of the "backstabbing by leak" that "had a corrosive effect on the president's staff and particularly infuriated the many people inside and outside the White House who supported me and the policies I stood for." Despite Meese's obvious anger, he made a conscious decision not to respond in kind. He "made it a rule not to leak, and not to allow my staff to do so." This kind of unilateral disarmament required some fortitude, and Meese got some criticism for this approach. As Meese recalled, *The New Republic*'s Fred Barnes "publicly criticized me for refusing to leak— saying I was foolish not to." Nonetheless, Meese stuck to his principles. Baker, in contrast, had no such self-imposed limitations. This one-sided leaking led, Meese said, to press stories in which "My supposed failings were contrasted with the merits of 'super efficient White House chief of staff James Baker, a smooth and gregarious doer.'"[25]

Baker did not get his "super efficient" reputation just by making the White House run smoothly. He was good, to be sure. William Niskanen, who served on Reagan's Council of Economic Advisers, saw that "Baker earned his influence because he was decisive, well organized, and politically skilled, in particular contrast to Meese." David Stockman concluded that "Baker was clearly the most competent of the inner circle."

But Baker also made sure other White House aides knew who was in charge. On one occasion, Baker was talking to CBS's Lesley Stahl when he suddenly got up and rushed off to see a departing Marine One. He returned after a while, and Stahl asked him, "Well, tell me, what was so urgent?" Baker's response was telling: "Oh, I didn't have anything special to tell them. I just wanted them to see me standing there as they left for the weekend."[26]

Baker's personal brand management extended far beyond the walls of the West Wing. Columnist Robert Novak wrote that "Nobody in my long experience was more skillful in manipulating reporters than Baker, who devoted the equivalent of one full working day each week to massaging the important news media." Amazingly, even Baker's enemies spoke of him in superlative—if negative—terms. Al Haig, forced out by Baker with Deaver's help, said of Baker that "that son of a bitch is the worst influence I have ever seen in the federal government."[27]

To Meese's chagrin, Baker did not just apply his considerable skills to advancing himself. He made Meese a target to be diminished and neutralized. In this effort, Baker was relentless and implacable. According to Nofziger, "Anything [Baker] could do to move Meese to one side or cut him down, he would do. I don't think there was much in the way of policy. It was just Jim Baker wanting to control the place, and Ed Meese there as the guy who'd been closest to Reagan."[28]

Meese certainly gave Baker ample ammunition in this regard. In addition to Meese's unilateral decision not to use the press to his benefit, there was also his sloppy appearance and manner. As David Stockman recalled, "Ed Meese came across as almost the opposite of Baker. He was heavyset, rumpled, and jowled."[29] His disorganization stood in stark contrast to the smooth Baker with his slicked-back hair. Whenever Meese stumbled, Baker—and Deaver—were there to take advantage. In 1981, for example, two U.S. F-14 Tomcats shot down two Libyan MiG fighters. Reagan's staff, directed by Meese, chose not to wake Reagan while they held a staff meeting at three o'clock in the morning to assess the situation. One reason for Meese's decision was Nancy Reagan's constant insistence that Reagan get enough sleep. Although Meese did wake Reagan at four o'clock once they had more information, the press seized on the fact that Meese did not initially wake the president, making for a story, which, according to Meese, critics of the administration used to "discredit" the president and himself.[30] Worse, Nancy would blame Meese for the fallout, bolstering her view of him as too disorganized for more responsibility. Baker and Deaver would use Meese's mistake as an opportunity to take foreign policy issues out of his portfolio.[31]

## Fighting beyond the Troika

With characters like these roaming the halls of the West Wing, it's not surprising that the Reagan White House became known as a contentious place. When the speechwriter—and future *Wall Street Journal* columnist—Peggy Noonan joined the team, Richard Darman greeted her by saying, "I'm sure you've heard all about this White House. That there is a great deal of infighting, and we're splitting into separate warring groups which leak unpleasant things about each other to the amusement and delight of the media, which are not slow in passing it on." After a pause, Darman told her, "It's all true of course."[32]

White House Communications Director David Gergen was another sharp-elbowed character in the Reagan White House. Press aide Larry Speakes saw Gergen as a Baker spy who would try to undermine the press operation in his reports to the chief of staff. In response, Speakes and his team "retaliated with tactics of our own." One of those tactics was trying to ridicule the six-feet-four Gergen. Speakes nicknamed him "The Tall Man," which later was shortened to just plain "Tall"—and it stuck. Speakes also told jokes about Gergen's height like "Gergen had been kidnapped as a child and raised by giraffes"—with a version of that joke appearing in the *New York Times*. More cruelly, Speakes would have press assistant Mark Weinberg set and tighten the adjustable White House podium to its lowest height before Gergen would speak. The result, Speakes wrote, was that "Gergen would go in and tower over it like Ichabod Crane. He never was able to figure out why the podium struck him well below the waist." Speakes was not the only one skeptical of Gergen. Reagan National Security Advisor Richard Allen called Gergen "Professor Leaky," and even thought that Gergen was slipping in and out of the Situation Room during the fraught period after Reagan's attempted assassination to give surreptitious updates to the press.[33]

Relations among the troika and their staff stemmed from a basic management challenge. In its first term, the Reagan White House was dominated by three men who each felt he should be the primary person advising the president. As a result, none of them would allow Reagan to be in the presence of the others alone. This also created opportunities for staff who wanted to operate without troika oversight. David Stockman recorded that he knew that none of the troika would attend his Budget Working Group meetings, since they were all "busy keeping their eyes on each other, making sure no one was whispering in the president's ear about the other." According to Stockman, "It was a phenomenon peculiar to inner circles, but it suited me well. They wouldn't attend a meeting unless the president did."[34] The three men were so joined at the hip that when all

President Reagan with staff members Michael Deaver, James Baker, Ed Meese, James Brady, and Richard Allen. Deaver, Baker, and Meese constituted the troika, which ran the White House for most of Reagan's first term. *Courtesy of the Ronald Reagan Presidential Library and Museum*

three went to visit Reagan at the hospital after he was shot, Reagan joked, "I should've known I wasn't going to avoid a staff meeting."[35]

Beyond the fighting, the men of the troika had an understanding not always understood by others. Noonan recalled an old Reagan hand explaining to her that more junior staff members had a misleading view of the Baker-Meese relationship, which they then spread to colleagues as well as the press. Someone might attend a meeting in which Baker and Meese disagreed over a policy, but "They never see Meese and Baker calmly and amicably working it out. They just saw them letting off steam at the meeting." In other words, the fighting captured the attention of reporters, historians, and memoirists, but the periods of cooperation and collective action garnered less interest, even if they were equally a part of the same reality.[36]

The troika also worked to keep the equilibrium they had created. In 1983, a group including Baker, Deaver, Mrs. Reagan, and George Shultz all worked to force Judge William Clark out of the position of national security advisor. They succeeded but failed in their larger effort to get Baker enthroned as his replacement. Here, Baker's relationships with the press did him in. William Casey, Reagan's 1980 campaign manager and director of central intelligence, could not abide the idea of the Baker move, saying, "I know he's the biggest leaker in town. He can't go to NSC!" When Reagan arrived at the Oval Office to talk to Baker and Deaver, he told them, "I've run into a real firestorm of opposition from some of the boys downstairs. I don't think I can move forward right now. I want to think about this over the weekend." Deaver, who stood to be chief of staff if the move went through, quickly grew exasperated with Reagan's hesitation, saying loudly, "Oh, Jesus." Worse, he even yelled at the president, shouting, "You don't have enough confidence in me to make me chief of staff." Deaver claimed that his frustration "wasn't a question of confidence in me" but instead "the fact that [Reagan] couldn't make a choice." Deaver's long-standing ties to Reagan enabled him to recognize what the delay meant. Baker at NSC and Deaver as chief of staff was not going to happen. In the end, Reagan tapped Robert "Bud" McFarlane to replace Clark at NSC.[37]

A key lesson of the Reagan administration is that infighting and the leaking do not doom an administration to failure. The right approach is to learn to manage them. Even through the fighting, policy was able to advance through this troika system. The Reagan administration became known not for the dysfunction—although there certainly was some—but for turning around the economy and giving America its mojo back following the foreign policy failures of the Carter administration. Reagan cut taxes, introduced cost benefit analysis in regulatory policy, rebuilt the military, reformed the immigration system, and passed a bipartisan tax reform bill. These successes could not have taken place without a way to get effective performances from the White House staff. Meese would later reflect on those days and say that "the White House staffing arrangement that we worked out functioned well." He admitted that "There were problems, of course." But in his eyes, "The troika and other staff elements of the Reagan presidency did an effective job."[38] Other White House staffers agreed. David Gergen, who had seen staff dysfunction up close in the Ford White House, openly acknowledged that "On paper, the troika was a lousy idea." And yet, he felt that, "What saved it was the emergence of a pecking order among the three," by which he meant that Baker emerged on top.[39] For the rest of Reagan's first term, the troika remained unchanged, and however imperfect and, at times, petty, it was effective.

## Worst Staff Trade Ever

Despite, or perhaps because of, their successes, all three troika members were gone from the White House in Reagan's second term. With their departures, new tensions arose. Replacing Baker as chief of staff was the gruff, former World War II Marine Lieutenant Colonel and Merrill Lynch head Donald Regan, who had served as secretary of the treasury in the first term. In an unusual job swap in the White House staff era, Baker replaced Regan at the Treasury Department, while Regan took Baker's slot running the White House staff.

The way the trade came about was in some ways emblematic of the Reagan White House. It developed after a disagreement over a leak. On November 16, 1984, there was a *Washington Post* story about White House worries that the economy was slowing down. Treasury Secretary Regan accused Baker of leaking the story to the *Post* and told Baker to "f*ck yourself and the horse you rode in on." Regan also threatened to resign over the story, but Reagan sweet-talked him into withdrawing his resignation. In the wake of the blowup, Baker and Regan had a reconciliation lunch at which Regan proposed they switch jobs. Surprisingly, the plan went forward, and they let Reagan know of the switch on January 7, 1985. The youthful Deaver cracked about the sixty-six-year-old Regan, "Mr. President, I finally brought you someone your own age to play with."[40]

The idea had surface appeal. Regan had real management experience from both the Marines and Merrill, and he wanted to be at the center of action in the White House. For all of Baker's talents as a political operator, he longed to be taken seriously, and a cabinet slot was a perfect way to earn that respect.

As perfect as it sounded in theory, the plan proved to have serious drawbacks and unintended consequences to the Reagan presidency. The loss of Baker from the White House meant Reagan lost some of Baker's valuable political instincts. Regan was a sharp contrast on this point because he was largely politically tone deaf. While Baker was obsessive about returning calls from members of Congress, Regan refused to do so, a fact that angered allies and opponents alike. Furthermore, Regan was not that close to the president, acknowledging that "In the four years that I served as Secretary of the Treasury I never saw President Reagan alone."[41] He was also imperious, insisting on all kinds of pomp and circumstance. When traveling with the president, Regan demanded that he get his own introduction, as White House chief of staff. Baker and Deaver were mortified when they found out—a bad sign for Regan.[42] When Baker took the job as chief of staff, he had intentionally looked to endear himself to Deaver, knowing that Deaver was close to Nancy. Regan was not so wise. A joke went around the White House about the possibility of Regan becoming a Catholic cardinal and why that would be an improvement: "that's good, now," the joke went, "we'll only have to kiss his ring."[43]

To be fair to Regan, he had to deal with some hostile staffers who predated him in the White House. Mark Weinberg wrote cattily in his memoir that Regan "seemed to forget that he was on the staff and that it was the Reagan administration, not the Regan administration." Weinberg also leaked negative stories about Regan, acknowledging that he "made some unflattering observations about his imperial style to reporters." Amazingly, Weinberg was surprised and hurt to learn that he would be moved out of the White House shortly after Regan's ascension, guessing that some of his comments "got back" to Regan. Yet, on the same

President Reagan walking through the Old Executive Office building with Donald Regan and James Baker holding a "Tax Reform" football. The job swap between the two men would play out badly for the Reagan administration. *Courtesy of the Ronald Reagan Presidential Library and Museum*

page of the memoir in which he acknowledges leaking about Regan, he writes, indignantly, that "I was loyal to the Reagans, knew that I had done nothing wrong, and that Donald Regan's firing me was undeserved."[44] To most observers, but obviously not to Weinberg, telling reporters embarrassing stories about one's boss would fall in the category of something very wrong.

Another point in Regan's favor is that not all the stories about him were true. One oft-repeated yet false story, which both the *Washington Post* and CBS's Lesley Stahl dutifully reported, was that Regan insisted on being called "Chief" by the White House staff. Peter Wallison, who served under Regan at both Treasury and the White House, knew the story was false. He also knew that Stahl "couldn't have checked it with anyone either." According to Wallison, "The senior staff at the White House called him Don, as had the staff at Treasury."[45] Even if many of the stories were untrue, enough were true to be a problem for Regan. As even he acknowledged to the journalist Lou Cannon, he had a bad case of "Potomac fever"—letting temporary power get to one's head—during that period.[46]

Worse than his "affliction" was Regan's feuding. He quickly got off on the wrong foot with McFarlane, the national security advisor. On March 24, 1985, Soviet troops murdered a U.S. Army major in East Germany. McFarlane awakened Reagan to alert him, but without telling Regan. The new chief of staff yelled, "I'm in charge of running this place and I need to be kept informed." McFarlane acknowledged he was wrong, but also defended himself, replying, "You're right you should've been informed, but I'm not gonna stand here and put up with abuse of this kind." Regan, a former Marine Corps officer, not a diplomat, escalated matters, saying, "Well, I'll run the place the way I want and you'll goddamn do it the way I say to do it." This response did not recognize the traditional authority of the national security advisor. McFarlane ended the conversation with a flat refusal of "No, I won't."[47]

Regan later apologized to McFarlane, but relations between them never recovered. McFarlane would eventually leave because of Regan's insistence that McFarlane report to the chief of staff, and not directly to the president.[48] The bitterness between them continued even after McFarlane left. When McFarlane unsuccessfully attempted suicide in the aftermath of the Iran-Contra scandal, a rumor went around the White House that Regan muttered: "That poor son of a bitch can't do anything right."[49] Peggy Noonan tried but could not verify the rumor. She did, however, speak about the incident to a reporter, who concluded: "It sounds like him."[50]

In the Reagan White House, much worse than butting heads with the national security advisor was running afoul of the first lady. And Regan ran straight into Nancy at full speed. Regan did not know what Clark and other staffers called "the Sacramento rule: 'A Happy Nancy means happy governor.'"[51] A corollary to the rule was political aide Ed Rollins's observation that "Your chances of survival were always better if Nancy Reagan didn't know who you were."[52] In the first term, Haig ignored both the rule and the corollary, alienating Nancy with his grandiose behavior and protocol violations. In the second term, the worst violator would be Regan, whom Nancy described as liking the sound of "chief"—not "of staff."[53]

The Regan-Nancy relationship collapsed because of the Iran-Contra scandal. The administration stood accused of negotiating for the release of U.S. hostages by selling arms to a hostile regime in Iran and using the proceeds from those sales to support the Nicaraguan contras, something that Congress had expressly prohibited. The scandal highlighted some of the downsides of Reagan's light touch management approach. There was also a sense that it was poor management of the White House staff chart that had enabled national security aides like Lieutenant Colonel Oliver North to run an unsanctioned and unsupervised operation. Ironically, many believed the experienced manager Regan fell asleep at the switch. As long-time Reaganite Martin Anderson wrote in his memoir, "the Iran-Contra fiasco" was "something that almost certainly never would have happened if Jim Baker, Ed Meese, Michael Deaver, and Dick Allen had remained close by the president, advising him in the White House."[54]

Once the scandal began, in November of 1986, relations deteriorated as Nancy started keeping a scorecard of Regan's various offenses. She did not like his November crack that he was running a "shovel brigade," responsible for cleaning up the president's messes. In January, she was angry that Regan insisted on Reagan giving the State of the Union Address only three weeks after he had undergone prostate surgery. They had multiple arguments about Iran-Contra over the phone, including several in which Regan hung up on Nancy. When Jim Baker heard about the hang-ups, he cracked—"That's not just a firing offense. That may be a hanging offense." Nancy complained about these and other Regan episodes with her informal kitchen cabinet of Deaver, Spencer, columnist George Will, and pal Nancy Reynolds.[55] Regan did apologize to Nancy for hanging up, but Nancy felt that his jokey excuse—"my wife made me do it"—was a jibe at her influence over her husband. As a result, the apology did not improve Regan's situation.

Things came to a head with a late February call in which Regan insisted that the president hold a press conference to address the scandal. Nancy did not much like the idea, but Regan kept insisting. This time it was Nancy who hung up, telling him, "Have your damned press conference." She did not apologize for the hang-up.[56]

By this point, Nancy was determined to get rid of Regan. She nagged her husband to do it, but he was reluctant to do so. Nancy then asked Vice President Bush to demand that the president fire Regan, but he said, "It's not my role." Nancy shot back: "It's exactly your role."[57]

What finally finished Regan was not Iran-Contra, but a now mostly forgotten scandal. On February 15, the White House announced the hiring of a new communications director, John Koehler, who had an impressive record at the Associated Press and the United States Information Agency. Unfortunately, Koehler had something else on his record that was troubling and needed explaining: he participated in a Nazi youth group as a ten-year-old in his native Germany. The *Washington Post* reported this fact on February 20, and on February 21 Don Regan said that Koehler's name had come "directly from the East Wing." Everyone knew that "East Wing" meant Nancy, and in throwing Nancy under the bus, Regan had sealed his own fate. Reagan's diary entry the next day read, "That does it. Nancy had never met Koehler and had nothing to do with his appointment." Regan was gone within the week. Koehler was gone quickly as well. He started on March 1 and left on March 7, making his six-day tenure as White House communications director even shorter than Anthony Scaramucci's eleven-day tenure in 2017.[58]

Even with Regan gone, however, things did not come to an immediate end. At the Gridiron Dinner at the end of March, Reagan joked that "Nancy and Don tried to patch things up the other day. They met privately over lunch—just the two of them and their food tasters."[59] But it was Regan who would have the last laugh. In his bitter memoir, he revealed to the world that Nancy used an astrologer to help determine the president's schedule, something that still shadows Nancy's reputation, even after her death. Serving as Reagan's chief of staff did not enhance Regan's reputation—but his timebomb of a book had a lasting and harmful impact on Nancy's historical image.

## Conclusion

Ronald Reagan had singular political gifts and a unique management style for a politician. He preferred to devolve and decentralize power, trust his cabinet and staff, and avoid open conflict. He wanted staff to resolve disagreements without involving him and would reinforce all these preferences with, "Well, fellas, if you think so...." Stockman recalled that in the face of disagreements, Meese aimed to ensure that "Reagan never had to make a disagreeable choice in front of his contending factions." His method was simple: Whenever there was an argument, Meese would step in and tell us to take our arguments to some other *ad hoc* forum. The president would smile and say, "Okay, you fellas work it out."[60]

At the same time, Reagan had a stubborn side and disliked being pushed. During the 1980 campaign, when Deaver was continually pressing Reagan not to talk to the media, Reagan pushed back, saying, "If you're so damned smart, why aren't you the one running for president?" He later felt bad and gave Deaver a gold pen, but he had made his point.[61] His resistance to such pressure even applied to his wife. When pushed too hard, Reagan would say, "That's enough, Nancy, I understand." If she continued to nag, as was the case with her campaign against Don Regan, he'd even say, "Get off my goddamn back!" He would also occasionally secretly turn off his hearing aids during dinner with Nancy so that he could eat in peace.[62]

These incidents reflect Reagan's personal style and professional approach. He was amiable and agreeable, but he also had well-formed ideological principles, and knew what he wanted. The public quickly figured this out about him. This unique combination of temperament and deep conviction contributed to the first successful two-term presidency in thirty years, and one of the most consequential presidencies of the twentieth century. Reagan's management style even earned a backhanded compliment on *Saturday Night Live*, with Phil Hartman playing Reagan as a doddering fool for the photo ops, but a hard-charging and all-knowing executive behind closed doors. In the skit, Reagan is slow and amiable with a reporter, a visiting Girl Scout, and his Hollywood pal Jimmy Stewart, but aggressively runs rings around his top staff, speaking foreign languages with leaders of other countries and doing complex financial calculations in his head.

More seriously, in 1986, *Fortune* magazine featured him in a famous cover story, "What Managers Can Learn from Manager Reagan." In the article, Reagan shared his management tips, saying things like, "I believe that you surround yourself with the best people you can find, delegate authority, and don't interfere as long as the overall policy that you've decided upon is being carried out." This certainly reflected Reagan's approach, as did his observation that "I make the decision, then I expect every one of [my staff], whether their views have carried the day or not, to go forward together in carrying out the policy." He even addressed the leak issue, blaming it on his propensity to ask aides to express their views honestly behind closed doors. According to Reagan, "this has led to some of those press stories, since the walls of the building leak profusely, saying that we're torn with dissension or something." Although the piece had more than a touch of puffery, it accurately reflected the hands-off, but keep driving, Reagan approach to managing.[63]

The amiable Reagan with his actor's training also had a secret weapon: his ideology. His aides may have had ideological disagreements, but there was less doubt about where Reagan himself stood. Reagan's well-defined conservatism meant that even aides who had no contact with Reagan had a keen sense of what he wanted and where he wanted the administration to go. As Reagan aide Peter Wallison wrote, "The interest in ideas and principles sets Reagan apart from other presidents." Reagan's ideology served as a successful management tool. As Wallison put it, "Because of the firmness with which he held his ideas, and the single-mindedness with which he communicated and pursued them, it was not necessary for him to take personal command of everything his administration did." Reagan's principles let him take a more hands-off approach and allow his team to advance his policies. With another president, Reagan's light touch could have led to chaos. But Reagan's ideological clarity allowed for just enough dynamic interchange and discussion to foster a consequential presidency.[64]

# CHAPTER 8

# GEORGE H. W. BUSH
## Darman and Sununu versus All

Few presidents can compare to George H. W. Bush when it comes to resume and experience in government. Bush had been a congressman from Texas, director of the CIA, head of the Republican National Committee, chief of the U.S. Liaison Office in the People's Republic of China, ambassador to the United Nations, and vice president of the United States under Ronald Reagan. Then, in 1988, Bush won the presidency and the opportunity to put this vast array of experience to use in the highest office in the land.

Yet, despite following conservative hero Reagan into the Oval Office, what distinguished Bush was his non-ideological nature. Most agree Bush served in what was effectively Ronald Reagan's third term, but Bush knew he was different. This fact came as a surprise to many Reaganites when told they would not be keeping their presidentially appointed positions in the new administration. One anonymous Bush transition official explained how this new administration would be different from the earlier one: "Our people don't have agendas—they have mortgages." This attitude should not have come as a surprise. Bush had long said he was no conservative ideologue. After he lost the nomination fight against

Reagan in 1980, he picked up a copy of William F. Buckley's conservative *National Review* and joked, "I guess we can put this away now."[1]

With the successful 1988 election behind him, Bush was also no longer a deputy, aide, or appointee: now he was in charge. During the Reagan years, Bush was studiously deferential and distanced; for example, he told Nancy Reagan that weighing in to have Don Regan fired was not his place. Even beyond that issue, he often kept his own counsel when serving as vice president. As Reagan press aide Larry Speakes said of Bush, "Seldom did I hear him speak up, either in Cabinet meetings or in private sessions like our issues luncheons on Monday. Almost never did he weigh in except to say he had heard something from the Texas oilmen or he would say he had just been in Iowa and he had heard such and such." Direct advice from Vice President Bush was not forthcoming in the Reagan White House. As Speakes noted, "I never heard him say, 'Mr. President my advice to you would be, this is the wrong thing to do.' Or, for that matter, 'This is the right thing to do.'"[2]

Bush's non-ideological approach led to a vastly different White House staff. Instead of having a troika at the top, Bush merged power in the hands of his chief of staff, former New Hampshire Governor John Sununu. In the Bush administration, the era of presidential schizophrenia on the question of a chief of staff was officially over. Truman had a *primus inter pares* assistant to the president named John Steelman; Steelman is considered by many the first chief of staff although he did not officially have that label. Eisenhower, with his military background, had started the practice of having a chief of staff with Sherman Adams, but Adams's imperious nature and ethical problems stemming from the infamous vicuna coat scandal contributed to Kennedy's decision not to have one. Instead, Kennedy relied on the spokes-on-the-wheel system. Johnson had provided aides like Walter Jenkins and Marvin Watson with chief of staff–like powers but eschewed granting them the actual title. Nixon gave H. R. Haldeman and Al Haig enormous powers and employed the chief of staff title but was also criticized for creating an "imperial presidency." Ford called his chiefs of staff "staff coordinators" and employed a version of the spokes-on-the-wheel-system, but the title was just a cover, and he was plagued by near constant infighting among aides who saw themselves as having equal authority and equivalent titles. Carter initially refused to name a chief of staff, then gave the title to Hamilton Jordan, who was ill-suited to the role. He then granted the title and the responsibilities to the effective Jack Watson, but by that point, it was too late to save his sinking presidency. Reagan started and finished with a chief of staff, and Bush did the same, making it the first time that two consecutive administrations had taken the same approach. So, by ratifying Reagan, Bush in effect solidified an uneven tradition of having a top aide as chief of staff. With the decision to have a chief of staff made, the question turned to whom it would be.

## Sununu as Chief

New Hampshire Governor John Sununu made sense for Bush. He had been an indispensable part of Bush's 1988 campaign effort, especially in the crucial primary state of New Hampshire, which Bush won after coming in third in the Iowa caucuses. That victory revivified the campaign, giving Bush, as he described it, "The Big Mo." Even Sununu's critics admitted his importance. "As much as I dislike Sununu," admitted campaign staffer and White House aide Jim Pinkerton, "I would have to say he got Bush elected."[3] Bush agreed, writing in 2013 about Sununu that "The former governor of New Hampshire is one of the brightest men I know, and his all out support was critical in helping me win the New Hampshire primary in 1988." Consequently, Bush wrote, Sununu "was a logical choice to be my White House Chief of Staff."[4] Sununu was attractive as a close political ally for another reason: He was well known as a conservative, and could thereby help Bush shore up his perpetually rocky relations with the right.

Even before Sununu took command, his weaknesses were well established and widely known. He was by his own, and just about everyone else's admission, an abrasive colleague and headstrong leader. He could

President Bush, Legislative Affairs head Fred McClure, Reagan Chief of Staff Ken Duberstein, Chief of Staff John Sununu, and Deputy Chief of Staff Andy Card. Sununu once bragged to Card that yelling at the staff would make them say, "That Sununu is a tough son of a bitch." Card responded, saying, "No, they're not. They're going to go back to their offices and tell everyone, 'That Sununu is a f*cking a$$hole!'" *Courtesy of the George H. W. Bush Presidential Library and Museum*

be funny, and often made light of his reputation, saying that he was "just a warm, fuzzy pussycat." But he also wore his abrasiveness proudly, claiming it was part of the job of making the president look good. He once described it this way: "If people don't like you—and love your boss—then you've done your job." Sununu also had a temper and was apt to yell at staff, members of Congress, even journalists. He tried to explain it away, arguing that "I guarantee you that contrary to the legend, any strong statements on my part are both controlled, deliberate and designed to achieve an effect." Like so many in Washington, enviable intelligence was soon put in service of rationalizing imperious behavior: "There is no random outburst. It is all designed for a purpose."[5] His critics, and of greater concern, his colleagues, did not agree.

Sununu's fury became infamous, but married to his territoriality, it created serious problems. Before the administration even started, rumors circulated that Sununu did not want Bob Teeter as deputy chief of staff because of Teeter's closeness to both Bush and his secretary of state–designate (and best friend) Jim Baker. Teeter, who, unlike Sununu, had long-standing ties to Bush, could potentially have served as a counterbalance to Sununu. But Sununu, the story went, objected to Teeter having direct Oval Office access to Bush and vetoed Teeter's appointment. Sununu pushed back against this story, and columnists Rowland Evans and Robert Novak defended Sununu against the charges. Evans and Novak argued that it was untrue that Sununu objected to Teeter getting the title of counselor in addition to deputy chief; or that Sununu refused to let Teeter have a hand in domestic policy; or that Sununu did not want to allow Teeter unfettered access to Bush. Evans and Novak even quoted Teeter himself as saying, "There can only be one White House chief of staff, and it is Sununu." Evans and Novak's source was, as usual, anonymous, but it is not a stretch to imagine that it was Sununu. Novak's memoir admits that he and Sununu saw each other as allies, even if he did not reveal the source of that story. In the end, Teeter did not get the job, and the incident showed both that the knives were out for Sununu even before the administration started, but also that Sununu was willing to push back in the press against those coming after him.[6] Without a check in the form of Teeter, Sununu managed the White House in his abrasive way, with serious consequences for the Bush White House.

## Dick Darman: Sununu's Partner in Crime

Joining Sununu at the top of the administration was Richard Darman. Like Sununu, he was very bright, but while Sununu was known to let his 180 IQ score slip—a fact that regularly appeared in Sununu profiles—Darman was known to tout his perfect math SAT score. Former Reagan speechwriter Ken Khachigian archly recalled Darman's propensity to advertise his SAT success, joking, "just ask him."[7] Another Reagan-era colleague, Ed Rollins, agreed that Darman was smart, but noted that his intelligence came with a cost: "Certainly Dick was probably the most brilliant guy in there, but he had an ego to match his IQ."[8]

Darman had played a key role in the Reagan White House, as a top aide to Jim Baker. As talented as Baker was, he needed help in running the operational side of the White House and Darman was indispensable in that regard. A graduate of Harvard College and Harvard Business School, Darman was hard-charging, ruthless, and knew the federal government inside and out. As the *New York Times*'s Hedrick Smith wrote of him, "Darman is brilliant, if arrogant. A former professor of government, he simply knew more, studied more than the others."[9] He had served in a variety of agency jobs in the Nixon and Ford administration, at Defense, Justice, and Health, Education and Welfare, and worked as an assistant secretary of commerce when Baker was undersecretary there. He managed to score a high-level slot in the Reagan White House without having worked on the Reagan campaign, something that did not go unnoticed by campaign veterans. As Reagan loyalist Martin Anderson noted, Darman "was the only senior White House staff member working for Reagan who did not help elect him. Darman alone stood by and did not lift a finger to help Reagan during the five long years he ran for president."[10]

Darman may not have worked for the Reagan campaign, but there was no doubt he was willing to work hard once he got in the administration. Darman would soon distinguish himself as one of the hardest working people in the Reagan White House. As Anderson recalled, "Many a night I left my White House office at 9 or 10 p.m. feeling somewhat virtuous that I was the last one to leave. But I never had that satisfaction for long. It seems that no matter how late I left, there is always one lighted office in the basement of the West Wing that I could see if I walked away from the White House and looked back— Dick Darman's."[11]

Darman's hard work and knowledge did not earn him the trust of his colleagues, however. Beyond his lack of service in the campaign was the fact that his ideology was suspect as well. Darman not only worked for the pragmatic Baker, but he had also worked for the liberal Republican Elliott Richardson while at the Nixon Justice Department.[12] Like his mentor Baker, Darman was also a legendary leaker and manipulator. As the *Washington Post*'s Marjorie Williams wrote in a lengthy profile of Darman, he and Baker "would form an almost perfect symbiosis. And it was with Baker that Darman's political, short-term, game-playing skills—his more cynical side—reached full flower." In the Reagan White House, Darman was known for both overseeing and tormenting the speechwriting operation, which was a conservative hotbed in the Reagan years. Darman's skepticism of conservatives, his relationship with the powerful Baker, and his own Machiavellian tendencies helped make him, Williams concluded, "the White House aide conservatives most loved to hate."[13]

Conservatives were hardly alone in their distaste for Darman. According to Anderson, the "abrasive" Darman "was easily the most disliked man in the White House. Even his boss, Baker, didn't seem to like him very much."[14] Darman's unpopularity—and his thin skin—made him a ripe target for practical jokes. Darman was particularly sensitive to the notion that he was a deputy to Baker and not a principal in his own right. After Reagan's reelection, Deaver had a second inaugural license plate made up that read "BAKER AIDE" and gave it to Darman as a gag gift at the White House senior staff meeting. The assembled staff laughed—all except for Darman. Reagan aide William Niskanen described Darman's reaction as "visibly irritated." Afterwards, Darman showed his disgust by folding the offending gift in half.[15]

By the time he took a position in President Bush's White House, Darman wasn't going to be anyone's aide. He started and finished as a "principal," the director of the Office of Management and Budget, a cabinet-level position. Unlike what happened with Teeter, Sununu was comfortable having Darman as a colleague. In his memoir of the Bush administration, Sununu wrote that Darman "was a budget manager who understood the financial implications and imperative of what Bush wanted to accomplish and the complex ins and outs of how to weave those together in a way that worked."[16] Sununu was even willing to acknowledge that Darman was in his intellectual stratosphere, admitting that "Darman is a very smart guy." Beyond his intelligence, though, Darman was also knowledgeable about the federal government, having worked in Republican administrations dating back to Nixon. As a result, Sununu recalled, "Darman understands the Washington process as well as anybody around." He further acknowledged that he found Darman worthy, comparing himself and Darman to two baseball greats, "Ted Williams would love to play in the same outfield as Joe DiMaggio." This was classic Sununu. Most people would have been wary of comparing themselves to baseball legends like Williams and Dimaggio. Sununu barely gave it a second thought.[17]

Bush's team would soon discover that the same Darman characteristics that had proved a challenge in the Reagan administration appeared in the Bush administration as well. First was Darman's ideological opportunism and malleability. Darman was well known for fighting Bush's famous line at the 1988 GOP convention: "Read my lips, no new taxes." As Sununu put it, "Darman was livid that Peggy Noonan put 'Read my lips, no new taxes' in there. He thought it bound the President."[18] Noonan insisted on the line, but Darman kept trying to remove it. Noonan later recalled that unnamed Bush aides tried to remove her signature line "on the grounds, I believe, that lips are organs [and] there is no history of presidential candidates making personal-organ references in acceptance speeches." In the end, the image guru Roger Ailes resolved the issue, declaring, "Boys, here's your sound bite." He was right. The line was Bush's most memorable line of the campaign and helped get Bush elected.[19] (Violating the promise also helped Bush lose in 1992.)

Darman admitted to Sununu that "I may be less conservative than you or Reagan or Bush." At the same time, he claimed that their ideological differences would not matter, since "I don't have an agenda. Get me a decision for the president and that's the track I ride."[20] This promise was not quite true. Once the administration began, Darman sought to undo the tax pledge and would eventually succeed in doing so at the 1990 Budget Summit. But the concern about Darman went beyond his being a moderate or a liberal. It was that he lacked any ideological predisposition at all. It was all about Darman. As one anonymous colleague said of him, "If the cavalry is winning, he's for Custer. And if the Indians are winning, he's for Sitting Bull."[21]

Despite his own ability to morph when needed, Darman was merciless to staff. As Tom Scully, who served under Darman at OMB, recalled, "He would come to staff meetings and rip me to shreds every day." Despite the regular shreddings, Scully still admired Darman's talent. As Scully put it, "he knew the workings of government better than anyone I ever knew."[22]

Beyond his smarts, Darman also had some ability to charm when he wanted to. He had a wicked sense of humor and was an excellent ping-pong player. He had exacting standards and hired the best people, proving that he was unthreatened by having talented people around him. He was acutely aware of the importance of the press, and in a pre-Google era, had his staff keep an archive of his press mentions. He tried to show his regular guy side—and took some heat in the process—by comparing federal entitlements to the insatiable yellow muncher in the game Pac-Man. He also enjoyed a good practical joke, when he was not the butt of it. On Bush's birthday in June of 1989, Darman dressed up in a gorilla suit to deliver birthday balloons to a surprised president. Bush had no idea it was Darman, admitting afterwards that "I thought it was Marlin," referring to Press Secretary Marlin Fitzwater.[23]

Darman's attempt at playfulness was considered phony and inappropriate by many observers. According to Bush domestic aide Jim Pinkerton, "Darman is a smart guy but go back and look at it, now-now and Pac Man, like he was deliberately trying to play faux-dumb, like some intellectual running around with a score card just to sort of prove he is a regular guy; like George Will being a baseball fan." Pinkerton had particular disdain for Darman's gorilla suit stunt, saying, "This is a true story, it was on TV, Bush got off the helicopter and there's Darman in an ape suit, you wouldn't even know it was him until you read it later. You remember this? It was on TV. Ask him about it. He was out there sort of frolicking with Bush." According to Pinkerton, Bush did not think much of the stunt, either: "This was not what Bush wanted to do as president, to have somebody in a gorilla suit."[24]

Darman and Sununu were both complicated individuals. Both were smart, abrasive, and territorial. With their hard-edged personalities and differing ideologies, the expectation might have been that they would have been at each other's throats. Such a dynamic would have been in keeping with the typical kind of rivalries found in earlier White Houses. An unexpected development took place, though, as Darman and Sununu became close allies. Darman actively pursued an alliance with Sununu, and Sununu saw in Darman a kindred spirit from a management, if not an ideological, perspective. Darman's understanding of government operations, coupled with his lack of a clear ideology, can explain his partnership with Sununu. Sununu had the ideology credentials but not the knowledge of the federal government, while Darman had the knowledge and coherent vision for the role of government and our unique federal system. In this way, each man got something from the other beyond just an intellectual sparring partner.

The Darman-Sununu alliance was slow to appear. Vice President Dan Quayle recalled that "Sununu, at first, clashed with Darman." The two staffers, however, thought better of this early adversarial relationship and became allies. Quayle recalled finding this "surprising," especially given their ideological differences. Quayle, who liked both men, attributed the alliance to the fact that "Darman was just so good at the internal debate that he just tended to dominate all these meetings."[25] Pinkerton, had a less charitable, more ideologically-based take on the origins of the Darman-Sununu alliance, in line with how many conservatives viewed it: "Sununu got seduced by Darman and went over to the dark side… Darman just totally conned him, I believe."[26]

Whatever the origins behind it, the Darman-Sununu alliance placed a chokehold on the policy process, dominating decision making and restricting the development and flow of innovative ideas. In fact, the Darman-Sununu alliance, improbable as it may have seemed in the beginning, poised them for rivalry with the rest of the White House domestic policy team.

## Darman and Sununu: Shutting Down Other Voices

Once together, Darman and Sununu did their best to make sure no one else challenged their primacy. As Quayle has said, "The dominant figures were Darman and Sununu. They ran the show. They had the intellect, they had the personality. Nobody else really had much of a voice."[27] The unanimity on this concept of the Darman-Sununu dominance among Bush aides was remarkable. Pinkerton called the two men the "co-regents of domestic policy together," adding somewhat snarkily that "there's nothing wrong with that, from their point of view."[28] John Podhoretz, who had served as a speechwriter in both the Reagan and Bush administrations, recalled in his book *Hell of a Ride* that when it came to domestic policy, "Sununu and Darman and their trusted aides were the loop."[29] Vin Weber, an influential young congressman at the time, dropped Darman from the equation but observed that "When you ask how to influence decision-making in the Bush White House, it's always the same answer: Sununu."[30]

The specifics of how they kept their dominance were often uncomfortable. Press Secretary Marlin Fitzwater said that "Sununu's staff meetings were a farce in which no one said anything for fear of being publicly humiliated by Sununu or Dick Darman."[31] Quayle, who felt that Darman and Sununu had "not contempt, but disdain for a lot of the other White House staff," went so far as to ask them "Do you guys ever listen to these others?" Darman and Sununu had so little regard for other staffers that Quayle observed, "That 7:30 meeting Sununu had—I mean, they might as well not even have had it."[32] The real decisions were made between the two men in direct conversation—the two of them installed "drop lines" that connected their desk phones directly to one another, an unusual arrangement between staffers. As for the input of other staff, Podhoretz felt that Darman and Sununu "turned the staff meeting into their own private comedy competition, since both men considered themselves wits and punsters." Podhoretz, a long-standing and talented entertainment critic, didn't think much of their abilities in this regard, pointing out on humor and puns that "the latter is the lowest form of the former."[33]

The problems of the Darman-Sununu method went beyond just not listening to staff. Darman and Sununu used staff meetings as opportunities to embarrass staffers thought unworthy. There was even a phrase for such humiliations: "being Darmanized." Darman, sitting on the opposite end of the room from Sununu, would remain silent at the beginning of a meeting, letting others speak at first. Then he would seize on one staffer's remarks and belittle the staffer. Few if any staffers would stand up to defend the staffer in the hot seat for fear of being Darmanized themselves. The chastised staffer would retreat, far less likely to pop his head up again to argue for a non–Sununu-Darman policy initiative.

In one instance of Darmanization, domestic policy chief Roger Porter gave a standard update on a trade speech he had given. Afterwards, Darman said, "I would like to call everyone's attention to one of the *stupidest* things I have ever read," then read from Porter's speech, without naming Porter as the author. Upon finishing his reading, Darman said, "Whoever wrote this is a complete moron." Porter of course knew at the time that Darman was reading from his trade speech, and everyone else who didn't know already figured it out quickly.[34]

Porter was a regular victim of these kinds of humiliations and reacted to them. He was heavily involved in the negotiations over the Clean Air Act, a major environmental endeavor passed in a bipartisan effort in 1990. In fact, White House lawyer John Schmitz even joked about Porter's high-level discussions with the Democratic congressional leadership, complaining that "each time George Mitchell smiled at or complimented Porter, it cost the American taxpayers an additional $25 million." Given the importance of the Act, not to mention all the time and effort Porter had put into it, Porter understandably wanted passage of the bill to be feted in a White House signing ceremony. This is how presidents show their ownership of legislative accomplishments on their watch. At the same time, Porter knew that Sununu was opposed to such a ceremony, in part because he was less invested in it than Porter, but he may also have been concerned about reaction on the right to such an expansive environmental package.[35]

Porter went to White House staff secretary James Cicconi to make the case for the ceremony. Cicconi agreed with Porter about the importance of the legislation to the administration and raised the idea and his support for it at a senior staff meeting. For his troubles, he was yelled at by both Darman and Sununu. Cicconi pushed back and continued to make his case. He looked to Porter, who had brought him the idea, for help, but Porter remained silent, head down and assiduously taking notes as was his wont. Sununu and Darman piled on Cicconi. Sununu called it a "dumb idea" that "wasn't going to happen." As Charles Kolb, Porter's deputy, described it, Darman "heaped scorn" on the idea as well. In the end, the White House did have a signing ceremony for the bill, on November 15, 1990, but the incident revealed a great deal about process in the Bush White House, as well as the impact of the Sununu-Darman duo on aides like Porter. As Kolb, who wrote a memoir that is quite harsh on Porter, put it, "Porter avoided all responsibility if it meant getting yelled at by Sununu or Darman."[36]

These incidents with Porter were quite telling about life in the Bush White House. Porter was assistant to the president for economic and domestic policy, one of the most senior aides in the West Wing. He earned a Ph.D. from Harvard and was a professor of government at the Kennedy School, and he had also served in both the Ford and Reagan White Houses. An excellent tennis player, he also played regularly with the tennis-loving Bush. Pinkerton even joked that Porter's "ambition in life is to be domestic policy adviser to every Republican president in the latter years of the 20th century."[37] If he could be treated—and cowed—in that way by Darman and Sununu, everyone would be fair game. If his intellect was in question, then no one else had any chance of being thought worthy by the two "Deputy Presidents." Little wonder that a popular joke that circled around the administration in those days was that the White House was staffed by "John Sununu and a thousand interns."[38]

Porter was not the only victim of the Sununu-Darman alliance. Michael Boskin, a Stanford economist serving as chairman of the Council of Economic Advisers, often found himself at odds with Darman. Kolb reported that Darman "elbowed [Boskin] aside" at the outset of the administration.[39] But even with his primacy over policy proved early on, Darman continued to press Boskin for what he saw as Boskin's overly dour view of the economy. In the end, Darman and Sununu were complacent as the economy worsened during the latter part of Bush's term, while Boskin was trying to sound a warning about the economy and its political implications. He resented Darman's attacks and told him that "he won't cook the books or lie to the president." As it turned out, Boskin was right, and the souring of the economy helped lead to Bush's electoral undoing in 1992. For the rest of the staff, though, the message of Darman's attacks—and Sununu's silence in the face of those attacks—was clear. As Podhoretz put it, "West Wingers understood that Darman was acting either at the behest of Sununu or with at least his tacit approval. They took the hint, and shut up."[40]

Sununu did not limit his attacks to the White House staff. He also had contentious relationships with cabinet secretaries like EPA Administrator William Reilly, Health Secretary Louis Sullivan, and Treasury Secretary Nicholas Brady, who complained to friends about Sununu's disparagement. Sununu alienated members of Congress so much that Senator Robert Byrd told him: "I have had thirty years in the U.S. Senate, and I have participated in many such summits, and I have never in my life observed such outrageous conduct as that displayed by the representatives of the president of the United States. Your conduct is arrogant. It is rude. It is intolerable." Sununu also had a famously difficult relationship with the *Washington Post*'s Ann Devroy. He upbraided her publicly at one White House event, shouting at her, "You're a liar. Your stories are all lies. Everything you write is a lie."[41]

Even after Devroy died tragically of cancer in 1997, Sununu kept his grudge against her. The animus stemmed from Devroy's reporting on Sununu's use of White House cars for non-official business, which would contribute to his ouster as chief of staff. Years later, Sununu made a cruel joke about Devroy *vis-a-vis* her *Post* colleague, David Hoffman. Sununu jokingly claimed that "My favorite *Washington Post* reporter, I think it was Ann Devroy, is on the plane, it was either she or [David] Hoffman, they're twins, they're virtually indistinguishable. Hoffman didn't shave as often as she did." When reminded, after his uncharitable remark about Devroy's perceived masculinity, that Devroy had died at forty-nine, Sununu said he "almost" felt guilty about it, "occasionally, but not really."[42]

## Nature Finds a Way: The Search for Alternative Policy Pathways

The Darman and Sununu clampdown had a stifling effect on domestic policy development in the Bush administration. Roger Porter took some of the blame for this, especially from Kolb. Yet the insights Kolb shares are quite telling. According to Kolb, "sending a memorandum to Porter with a suggestion was the kiss of death." He also notes that Porter, an incredibly hard-working individual by every account—John Sununu said Porter "seemed to work 24 hours a day"—had six inboxes to handle all the material and information in his purview. The problem, Kolb joked, is that for all the inboxes he lacked an outbox. If Porter wrote on a memo, "Interesting. Let's discuss," that was code for "Interesting. Forget it." Porter's endless insistence on the formatting and reformatting of documents led one of his staffers—Princeton and Chicago graduate Hanns Kuttner—to earn the nickname "the Fontmeister." Porter's frustrated staff made buttons reading "Born to process."[43]

The impression one gets from this is that whatever was going on, staff dysfunction was a problem in the Bush White House: Either Porter was a massive roadblock, or Kolb was using his memoir to exact revenge on a boss with whom he did not get along—or both. Whatever the case may be, reading the Kolb memoir paints a disturbing picture of interpersonal relations and domestic policy processes in the Bush White House.

Porter aside, at the heart of the problem stood Darman and Sununu. Without the traditional pathways for moving domestic policy forward, Bush staffers looked for alternative approaches to policy development or to expressing their frustrations. This is a standard response. The most common method of expressing frustration with a process, something that we have seen with multiple administrations, is leaking. Leakers leak for a variety of reasons: to undercut rivals, for self-aggrandizement, or to scotch a policy one disagrees with, among others. This would particularly be the case in the first Bush White House. While leaking is endemic to White Houses, the Bush White House brought new tactics to an old habit. The *Washington Post*'s Joel Achenbach revealed that Bush staffers used to leak about one another using the diction and speech patterns of other staffers to deflect blame from themselves. As Achenbach wrote, "If someone wanted to sound like Budget Director Richard Darman, for example, the secret would be to use an absurdly big word, a word from the hoary depths of the dictionary, like 'inchoate.' People would read an anonymous quote in the paper with 'inchoate' in it and at once think: 'That Darman! What a leaker!'" Bill Kristol, who served as Dan Quayle's chief of staff, would call these misdirection efforts "carom shots": "X would leak something and make it look like Y leaked it so Z would get mad at Y."[44] Kristol himself was also believed to be a notorious leaker. One Bush staffer recalled that Marlin Fitzwater would cease talking when Kristol came into meetings as he believed Kristol would leak to the media what he said. In one meeting, Fitzwater went silent when Kristol entered the room, and just stared at Kristol with arms folded until Kristol got up and left the room. Only then did Fitzwater resume speaking and the meeting continued.[45]

Leaking had repercussions beyond the silent treatment. Sununu would have his aides review anonymous staff quotes in the press and attempt to name the culprits. Armed with his staff's best guesses, Sununu would then go and yell at the accused leaker.[46] Little wonder that staffers would try to disguise their speaking styles in leaking to the press, and do their best in the way of "carom shots" to deflect the blame upon others.

Beyond leaking, though, there were process violations. Leaking is a method for circumventing or undercutting a decision already made. In the Bush White House, the problem was often the lack of decision-making itself. At one point, when Bush was pleased with an apparent slowdown in the appearance of leaks, Pinkerton was sardonic about the cause: "the reason there are no leaks is easy to understand: there's nothing to leak."[47] As this comment indicates, Pinkerton and others felt considerable frustration about the slow-down of domestic policy development in the Bush White House.

When the policy development pathways do not work, staffers often feel justified in violating policy norms and committing a variety of what are known as "process fouls." Process fouls include not going through the normal channels, not inviting the right people to meetings, not sticking to your lane, and the like. These process fouls began happening with regularity in the Bush White House. People would avoid the Darman-Sununu-Porter blockages and try to press forward with allies wherever they could find them. With the administration's legal reform initiative, for example, Porter's inaction was an obstacle, so Kolb asked Al Hubbard, an aide on the Council of Competitiveness, to take the lead on the issue. Kolb would also extensively "bcc" individuals in other parts of the White House on his memos to Porter to get things moving. He called his bcc group recipients "the usual suspects," and it included Pinkerton, Hubbard, Kristol, communications aide Tony Snow, and John Schall in Cabinet Affairs. This last office, Cabinet Affairs, is not supposed to be a policymaking entity, but when policy does not come from the normal channels, different policymaking bodies appear. Cabinet Affairs also happened to have been a repository of young talent in the Bush administration, including Dan Casse and Jay Lefkowitz.[48]

Lefkowitz, a gifted attorney who would return to the White House in the next Bush administration, was involved in one legendary incident of policy circumvention. According to the story, Lefkowitz was walking through the White House and he ran into Sam Skinner, who had by then replaced Sununu as chief of staff. Skinner asked, "What are you working on?" Lefkowitz replied, "Trying to get the *Beck* decision implemented," referring to a Supreme Court decision that said that a union could not compel federal workers to give contributions to political causes with which they disagreed. Skinner liked the idea, and at once set up an April 13 Rose Garden event on the issue, breaking a policy logjam that had persisted since the previous summer. The story of Lefkowitz's policy coup would appear in a piece by Fred Barnes in *The New Republic*, which was eagerly read in Washington at the time. A wicked parody of the Barnes piece would also circulate around the White House, with Thomas Jefferson asked what he was working on? He answered, "the Declaration of Independence."[49]

## Brother, Can You Paradigm?

The biggest challenge to the Sununu-Darman logjam would come from a lower level staffer who may have done more than any other White House staffer to get Bush elected: Jim Pinkerton. Pinkerton, a Stanford grad who worked in the Reagan White House, served on what Bush 1988 Campaign Manager Lee Atwater called the "nerd patrol" of the Bush presidential campaign staff. Pinkerton was the one who highlighted the issue of Willie Horton to campaign manager Lee Atwater. Horton was an African-American convict who raped a woman while out on furlough from the state of Massachusetts while Michael Dukakis, Bush's opponent, was governor. Dukakis opponent Al Gore initially raised the issue of Horton during the Democratic contest, but the Bush team saw in Gore's discovery an opportunity. The ads highlighting Dukakis's poor decision were effective in Bush's comeback from a seventeen-point deficit in the summer of 1988 to his convincing election day victory.

Pinkerton's reward for his discovery was a job as deputy assistant to the president in the Bush White House. Pinkerton's frustration with the Darman-Sununu blockages led him and a group of allied staffers calling themselves "the Perestroika group" to try to goose the process with a collection of policies Pinkerton labelled "the New Paradigm." The idea behind the New Paradigm was twofold: first, to highlight pro-market, pro-empowerment, anti-bureaucratic, choice-based policies that were a stark contrast to both the collapsing Soviet Union and the sclerotic Washington-based welfare state. Second was an attempt to create some coherence behind a Bush administration domestic policy that clearly was secondary in importance to foreign policy. The specifics of the policies were less important than the existence of them. As Bush attorney general—and future Trump attorney general—Bill Barr later recalled, or didn't, to be more precise, "I know Pinkerton was the guy on the new paradigm, but I can't remember what the new paradigm consisted of."[50]

In addition to the process challenges Pinkerton met, he was unhappy with Bush's June 1990 decision to abandon the tax pledge that had helped get him elected. As Pinkerton recalled, "I spent two or three years working the tax pledge thing and it had all sort of been booted away for nothing and that did irk me some." Then Pinkerton gave an interview in a minor publication in which he said Bush was receiving a "spectrum of opinion." The point seemed innocuous. As Pinkerton explained, he had not said, "Darman says it's great and Pinkerton says it stinks," only that there was a "spectrum of opinion." Nevertheless, that comment alienated the top brass, especially Sununu, who yelled at him over the article. As a result of these incidents, Pinkerton recalled that he "was sort of deeply alienated from the process."[51]

Pinkerton had worked on the New Paradigm for some time. He gave a little-noticed speech outlining it to the World for Future Society in March of 1990. In September of 1990, he mentioned the concept at one of the dreaded Sununu-Darman staff meetings. Darman, in his typical comedy club way, told an old joke, "All I can think of when I hear that is 'Brother, Can You Paradigm?'"[52] Nevertheless, Pinkerton's concept began gaining attention. Both Washington and the administration were awakening to the fact that someone other than Darman and Sununu was pushing a programmatic agenda in the Bush White House. That someone was Pinkerton, and Darman did not appear to like Pinkerton's newfound notoriety. On November 16, Darman gave a legendary speech, reusing the "Brother, can you" line—which as a punster he particularly liked—and a whole lot more. He dismissed Pinkerton's idea as "neo-neo-ism" and little more than rhetoric.[53]

Pinkerton initially responded to this shot across the bow with sarcasm. He told the *Washington Post*'s Dan Balz, "After the success of the budget agreement, it's good to see Dick rejoining the intellectual dialogue," prompting Balz to "howl" with laughter.[54] But Pinkerton quieted down quickly after Sununu's deputy, Andrew Card, told Pinkerton, but not Darman, not to respond any further. Pinkerton defenders such as House Minority Whip Newt Gingrich criticized Darman in the press, while former Bush Education Secretary William Bennett called Darman to suggest he knock it off.[55]

Darman did not listen to Bennett. Five days after Darman's November 16 speech, he came to a Roosevelt Room meeting of the Empowerment Working Group, a band of aides who sided with Pinkerton's approach to things. Jack Kemp was the guest speaker at that event, but after Darman came in, the group asked if Darman wanted to speak. He did, speaking for fifteen minutes, telling the group he was okay with empowerment but not "The New Paradigm." Darman also got a little intimidating, if not creepy, telling participants, "I'm going to come to all your meetings and keep an eye on you." His bragging about how he had forsaken private sector opportunities for public service led one unimpressed participant to joke that he was pulling his "St. Dick" act.[56]

Pinkerton, however, remained silent throughout Darman's performance. During the tirade, he was thinking that if he engaged with Darman, it would be misinterpreted in the *Washington Post* the next day, where Pinkerton was sure the story would leak. As Pinkerton said, "If this emerges that we had a shouting match between us, I'm a peon, he's a big shot. I can't afford to be in a shouting match with him." Pinkerton's solution was to "say nothing, zero, zilch. So I just sat there and kind of wrote it all down." He was not the only one to remain quiet. Pinkerton recalled that "Porter being Porter never said a word in response. He'd sit there and listen." As for Public Liaison head Bobbie Kilberg, Pinkerton remembered "her sort of gasping." This being the Bush White House, Pinkerton later called *New York Times* White House correspondent Maureen Dowd and gave her his side of the story.[57]

Pinkerton's leak presented Darman in a bad light. Overall, Pinkerton "was perfectly satisfied after twenty minutes of him just ranting that everyone in the room thought he was a jerk and that I had just held my fire, played rope-a-dope with him for twenty minutes." Even so, Darman was the more senior official, and therefore, Pinkerton's group was forevermore exiled in their meetings to the Indian Treaty Room, on the fourth floor of the Old Executive Office Building. This shift in real estate had real impact within the cloistered world of the White House. As Pinkerton ruefully said, "You know you're a loser when you're having your meetings on the fourth floor of the EOB as opposed to the West Wing."[58]

Meanwhile the story about a senior official mocking a junior aide rocketed around Washington. In those pre-email days, Pinkerton "got like forty-two voicemail messages on my machine." While Pinkerton did remain silent publicly, he also felt the need to push back. As Pinkerton put it, "I can't for my own sake and for the sake of sort of this empowerment, Jack Kemp, no tax increase kind of pledge torch, I can't let myself just get squashed like a bug. I can't just be some laughing stock where Dick Darman gets the last word on this." In the time-honored but oft-denied White House tradition, he enlisted allies like White House counsel Boyden Gray and Gingrich to defend him. Pinkerton particularly enjoyed it when Gingrich used the kerfuffle to call for Darman's resignation.[59]

Allies or no, White House status differentials required that Pinkerton be the one to apologize. After a month or so of the story remaining alive, especially in the *Washington Times*, Pinkerton wrote Darman a note: "Dear Dick, we've had our differences but we must unite to help the president." He went over to Darman's office on a Saturday and placed the note on the table in the conference room where the always press-friendly Darman was sitting in conversation with *Time*'s Michael Duffy.

Pinkerton left, but half an hour later he got a call from Darman. The two men then met and had what Pinkerton described as "a correct meeting" in which neither party accepted blame but they agreed to move on. The two were not friends, but at least Pinkerton felt that he would not be fired because of the disagreement. While the New Paradigm never went anywhere in the Bush administration, many of its ideas would later see light in Gingrich's *Contract with America* that helped the GOP take over the House of Representatives in the 1994 election.[60]

The story died down after the apology note, but it remains a telling incident. The revolt of junior aides against a stifling system, followed by the public rebuke, private threats, and retribution by a cabinet member, was certainly abnormal. Sununu's reaction, however, was typical and telling. The chief of staff felt that the "'New Paradigm' was second and third rate staffers like Kristol and Pinkerton wanting to get a little bit of publicity and claiming that they had been shut out of the process." He did fault Darman somewhat, claiming that "Dick took the bait and wrote that silly speech of his, or inserted that silly line in the speech of his." Overall, though, Sununu was pleased with what Darman had done, saying "The speech was pretty good actually, and took them on publicly."[61]

Darman won the fight in the short term. In the long term, though, the incident highlighted the unsuitability of the Darman-Sununu alliance running the Bush domestic policy apparatus. At the end of the next year, Bush would have Transportation Secretary Sam Skinner—who often clashed with Sununu—replace the cantankerous chief of staff. No one, including Bush, wanted to do the actual firing, and Bush had to enlist his son—future president George W. Bush—to talk to Sununu. Even then, according to some accounts, Sununu still would not leave and had to be told even more starkly that the time had come.

With Sununu gone, things changed for Darman. According to Vice President Quayle, "when Skinner came in, there was just a total implosion because of Darman. Skinner was trying to contain Darman or control Darman." One of the ways Skinner did this was by bringing in new aides to limit the former's influence. He also took out the "drop line" between his office and Darman's. Unsurprisingly, Darman was unhappy with Skinner. One White House aide told the *New York Times* that "the tension between Darman and Skinner was so obvious you can see it."[62]

Changing the dynamic at the top was no panacea. A stilted process and demoralized staff cannot be miraculously cured by replacing the chief of staff. The shift also had some unintended consequences in empowering voices who should have remained quieter. As Podhoretz wrote, "one of the unfortunate consequences was that [Darman] and everyone else descended into morning staff meeting purgatory. Suddenly people who had been silent in the Sununu years would start talking and never stop. Minor White House aides were dominating the meeting while the genuinely powerful ones (Darman especially) would sit in silence."[63]

The change at the top also came too late to help Bush. The Bush administration never gained its domestic policy footing. As the economy worsened with the recession of 1991 and the election neared, an administration that never had been able to master domestic policy still could not do so, even when faced with the existential threat of a reelection campaign. Bush's "veto strategy," designed to deal with an activist Democratic Congress, meant that the administration could point to more things it had stopped than things it had passed. Furthermore, 1988 campaign manager Lee Atwater's brain cancer diagnosis meant that no one in the inner circle had the political instincts that Bush needed to correct the ship's course.

The domestic policy weaknesses stood in stark contrast to Bush's success on the foreign policy front. Bush successfully managed the end of the Cold War with the Soviet Union and skillfully built a coalition that helped expel Saddam Hussein from Kuwait. Bush was able to accomplish these things because he had more expertise and passion about foreign than domestic policy, but also because of his cooperative foreign policy team. As Peter Rodman wrote in his indispensable look at presidential foreign policy management styles, "From a management point of view, the administration of our forty-first president was the most collegial and smoothest-run of the presidencies we are considering." Secretary of State James Baker, who knew something about running a White House from his days as Reagan's chief of staff, wrote that "We made the national security apparatus work the way it is supposed to."[64]

Bush's excellent foreign policy team had a line-up of experienced professionals like Baker, Defense Secretary Dick Cheney, Chairman of the Joint Chiefs of Staff Colin Powell, and National Security Advisor Brent Scowcroft. All had served in earlier Republican administrations in senior roles. Scowcroft, for example, had served as national security advisor, and was assigned the difficult task of replacing Kissinger when Ford took away that portfolio while Kissinger was also serving as secretary of state. Together, this talented team successfully managed the end of the Cold War and the collapse of the Soviet Union. They removed the drug-dealing dictator Manuel Noriega from power in Panama. And they turned back Iraqi despot Saddam Hussein's invasion of Kuwait with a large and effective coalition of nations.

The success of Bush's foreign policy team made the failures of the Sununu and Darman–run domestic policy team appear difficult to explain. But there are understandable historical reasons for this break. At the core was the ideological revolution taking place in the GOP. The Republican Party was becoming a conservative party, and Darman's moderating efforts were a last gasp of a northeastern establishment that would soon be nonexistent as a credible and effective force within the GOP. In the formulation of domestic policy, the fitful process of discussing and moving initiatives led to leaks and freelancing. Of course, as is always the case, the climate for work is shaped and set by the top. Presidents rarely overtly stoke bitter conflict, but Bush's prioritization of foreign policy came with the cost of indirectly tolerating the control and counter-productive bullying of Sununu and Darman. That fact, coupled with the administration's domestic policy ideological confusion and the sclerotic policy process, made for a deeply divisive administration and a one-term presidency.

# CHAPTER 9

# THE CLINTON ADMINISTRATION
## Semi-Controlled Chaos

**B**ill Clinton's administration seemed destined for conflict. The very existence of the Clinton administration stemmed from an inner conflict within the Democratic party. From 1980 to 1992, the Democrats had lost three consecutive presidential elections, and five out of six dating back to 1968. As governor of Arkansas, Bill Clinton accurately diagnosed the Democrats' problem as excessive liberalism. He ran his 1992 campaign as a corrective to that overly leftward drift. Clinton summarized his critique by saying, "No matter how popular your programs may be, you must be considered in the mainstream on the shared values of the American people, the ability to defend the nation and the strength to enforce its laws."[1]

Clinton did not engage in this moderating effort alone. He worked closely with other centrist Democrats such as Georgia senator Sam Nunn and Virginia senator Chuck Robb in the Democratic Leadership Council, on which Clinton served as chair. But in addition to allies, the effort also had significant and committed detractors. Civil rights activist Jesse Jackson—a multi-time candidate for the Democratic presidential nomination—denounced the DLC as "Democrats for the Leisure Class."[2] Even within Clinton's campaign and later his administration, these ideological tensions manifested as both liberals and DLCers maneuvered for dominance. As *New York Times* reporter Thomas Friedman wrote at the start of the Clinton administration, Clinton's team was "a political Noah's ark, with veteran Washington and Wall Street insiders, newcomers from the left wing of the Democratic Party and the academic world, appointees placed both by his wife Hillary and the Vice President–elect, Al Gore."[3]

As examinations of earlier administrations reveal, ideological divisions are one of the three key causes of internal dissension within an administration. The Clinton administration scored high on the other two indicators as well, in the form of a principal willing to tolerate disagreement, as well as a messy internal process. The Clinton administration also revealed another lesson. While these three factors indeed predict the level of internal disagreement, external opposition can serve as a uniting factor. The first Clinton term had more than its share of rivalries. And the second term was dominated by Clinton's impeachment by the Republican-led House of Representatives, which saw these first-term rivalries quiet down as Democrats across the party rallied behind their embattled president.

All of this would come later. First, Clinton had to get elected. By most accounts, Clinton ran a remarkably disciplined campaign in 1992. There were two major features of that successful 1992 effort. One was a relentless focus on the economy. Campaign strategist James Carville became known for his singular guidance: "It's the economy, stupid." The second Clinton campaign innovation was its high-tech and ever-churning "War Room," driven by the then-groundbreaking concept of refusing to let any charge go unanswered.

In stark contrast to the campaign's message discipline stood the candidate's lack of personal discipline. In Arkansas circles, Clinton was already infamous for his "zipper problem." But in those days before the internet, Clinton's appetites for extramarital affairs as well as sexually aggressive overtures remained largely secret or simply ignored in his small state. With the presidential campaign, the potential for emergence of these stories grew.

The campaign team and other key Democrats had to deal with these facts to protect their candidate. They knew the stories, if they became public, could pose an existential threat to Clinton's candidacy. Donna Shalala, a Carter administration official who would later go on to serve as Clinton's secretary of Health and Human Services, went so far as to tell fellow Democrat Alice Rivlin, "Well, I know Bill Clinton, and he's terrific, and everything you say is right, but he's never going to be president of the United States." When Rivlin understandably asked, "Why not?" Shalala's answer was stark: "He's got a woman problem." Concerns about Clinton's extramarital activities led campaign aide and longstanding Clinton friend Susan Thomases to issue a tough warning directly to the candidate: "You're stupid enough to blow this whole presidential thing over your d\*\*k. And if that turns out to be true, buddy, I'm going home, and I'm taking people with me. If you don't have enough self-control to keep yourself straight, then it's just dumb."[4]

Clinton's women issues would haunt the campaign. One of Clinton's longer-term relationships was with lounge singer Gennifer Flowers. She would eventually sell tapes of her phone conversations with Clinton to the *Star*, a tabloid paper. The news exploded in late January of 1992, leading to Clinton's January 26, 1992, appearance on *60 Minutes*, with a dutiful Hillary Clinton by his side. Although Hillary famously "stood by her man," others in the campaign wavered. George Stephanopoulos, for example, was a talented young Columbia grad and former Dick Gephardt staffer who became a key policy and communications aide on the 1992 effort. Yet Clinton loyalists, particularly the Arkansas team, saw Stephanopoulos as panicked by both the Flowers revelations and stories about Clinton's machinations to avoid the Vietnam War draft.

According to campaign lore, Stephanopoulos reacted to the Flowers story by going into the fetal position and crying, "It's over." Dee Dee Myers remembered a similar reaction to the blockbuster story about Clinton "forgetting" his Vietnam draft induction notice, recalling "George in his classic darkness, 'It's over, it's over, it's over. The campaign's over.'" Myers then tellingly added, "But it wasn't over, you know." Stephanopoulos's fears and emotions at the time were remembered in Clintonland. As late as the 2016 presidential campaign, Hillary Clinton still saw Stephanopoulos as soft because of his internal wavering and complaints over the Flowers revelations.[5]

Draft avoidance and extramarital shenanigans aside, the 1992 Clinton campaign was remarkably effective. Clinton came from nowhere to defeat a heavily favored incumbent in George H. W. Bush. Bush had an almost unheard of 83 percent approval rating in the aftermath of the 1991 Iraq war, but lost popularity in the wake of a short, painful recession and the Clinton campaign's relentless hammering of Bush as out of touch.

While Clinton the campaigner was a marvel to behold, governing—and transitioning to governing—was a different matter. Once Clinton won the 1992 election, many of the papered-over ideological divisions in the Democratic party reemerged, and the disciplined Clinton team became more disorganized. Having a transition in Little Rock, the home of the Clinton campaign, proved a challenge. Prospects for top administration jobs had to come through Little Rock's tiny airport, making it easy for reporters to stake out the airport and speculate on appointments. The selection-process took too long, and the transition lacked a central team authorized to make key decisions. Twelve years out of power had left the Democrats rusty when it came to vetting potential nominees. Clinton—who had promised to appoint a female attorney general—had two prospects flame out because of "nanny tax" problems. In the end, Clinton would appoint Janet Reno, someone whom he did not know and with whom he did not develop a close relationship. She stayed for all eight years. And of course there was the constant backbiting and jockeying for position, so intense that it led healthcare advisor Chris Jennings to observe, "I guess I should say that if anybody ever have the opportunity to do a transition, you should just not do it." Carville, as is his wont, made a similar observation in a more evocative way: "A campaign is about screwing your enemies, and the transition is about screwing your friends." Presidential expert and former White House aide Stephen Hess judged the Clinton transition to be "downright chaotic."[6]

Once appointments were made, insiders and outsiders analyzed them through the lens of old-line liberal Democrats versus DLC New Democrats. Labor Secretary Robert Reich and Council of Economic Advisers Chair Laura D'Andrea Tyson were on the liberal side of things, while Treasury Secretary Lloyd Bentsen and National Economic Council head Robert Rubin were more on the new Democrat wing.

Another big distinction among appointees was age. Clinton was remarkably young—forty-six—when elected, and some top aides like Stephanopoulos were even younger. Because of the long streak of Democratic losses, the only experienced candidates with Democratic administration experience were former Jimmy Carter aides. The Carter folks were not only getting up in years, but they were associated with an administration widely seen as a failure. As a result, youth predominated at the Clinton White House, bringing its own baggage. As Myers recalled,

President Bill Clinton, with Secretary of Education Richard Riley, Tipper Gore, Vice President Al Gore, First Lady Hillary Rodham Clinton, and Secretary of Labor Robert Reich. *Courtesy of the William J. Clinton Presidential Library and Museum*

"Well, you know, the kids got blamed for a lot of things that went wrong in the early months of the campaign."[7]

The big problem, however, was discipline. The White House, in the early days, was a disorganized mess. People did not stay in their lanes, meetings did not begin on time, and there was a general sense that Clinton was not running things well. According to Bob Woodward, White House Deputy Chief of Staff Mark Gearan—a relatively seasoned thirty-six in 1992—felt that Clinton's White House staff "was too often like a soccer league of 10-year-olds. No one stuck to his part of the field during a game. The ball—any ball—would come on the field, and everyone would go chasing it down the field."[8]

Part of the problem in the early days was the chief of staff, Thomas G. "Mack" McLarty. A childhood friend of Clinton and successful business executive, he was universally liked by those who knew him. Therefore, many seasoned Washington observers saw McLarty as not chief of staff material. *Time* called him "Mack the Nice" and asked, "Is Thomas McLarty, Bill Clinton's kindergarten classmate, just too nice a guy to be White House chief of staff?"[9]

McLarty had wanted to bring on board Carter domestic policy advisor Stu Eizenstat, another old Washington hand, but Clintonites vetoed Eizenstat for a White House gig because of his previous work for Carter.[10] Not being able to pick his own deputy contributed to McLarty's ineffectiveness. Clinton himself acknowledged in his memoir that McLarty was "an unusual choice" and "hardly a Washington insider." Furthermore, according to Clinton, "In the first months of our tenure, both he and I would suffer from some of our tone deafness about Washington's political and press culture."[11]

As critical as this Clinton self-assessment may have been, the reality was worse. The Clinton administration got off to a truly terrible start. Incidents like Hair Force One, in which Clinton allegedly held up traffic at Los Angeles International Airport while getting a $200 haircut, or Travelgate, in which the Clintons appeared vindictive in firing the career officials in the White House travel office—both of which happened in

May of 1993—were certainly contributors to the problem. But there was a larger problem as well. The administration just did not seem to function correctly. Domestic policy advisor Bruce Reed described that initial period as "just chaotic. There wasn't anybody in charge." Media consultant Frank Greer had a similar view, but also noted McLarty's lack of a coherent process. As Greer put it, Clinton's "first White House staff, and the way they constantly went around Mack McLarty—it was destructive." As a result, "everybody was freelancing, everybody was promoting themselves, everybody was looking out for themselves."[12] Myers recalled that things were so bad that "There was a piece in I believe the *New York Times* that basically said this would be a failed presidency. You know, ten days into Bill Clinton's first term."[13]

McLarty may not have been suited to the job, but the problems were not all his fault. Stephanopoulos, for example, liked McLarty, whom he describes as "a good man, a successful business executive, and a close Clinton friend." Stephanopoulos blamed Clinton for the failure of the selection, noting that in addition to McLarty's lack of D.C. experience, "Clinton never gave him real authority."[14] Reed not only blamed Clinton but thought he encouraged the chaos. As Reed described Clinton's approach, "I think he kind of liked it that way. He knew he was his own best strategist; he liked being able to make the decisions. So he didn't worry too much about the fact that his advisers couldn't agree."[15]

The chaos would have consequences in the form of staff upheavals. Stephanopoulos was a victim of sorts in one of the first major staff changes. On Memorial Day weekend in 1993, a scant four months into the administration, Clinton and McLarty decided that they needed an "old hand" to help stabilize the troubled administration. To do this, they brought in David Gergen, a former White House aide in three Republican administrations, to replace Stephanopoulos as communications director. Some old Clinton campaign hands did not take this well. Myers reported that she "was stunned. Gergen certainly had a lot of experience, but he was a Republican. And I assumed he hadn't even voted for Bill Clinton. Didn't share his philosophy." In addition to the philosophical concerns, she had practical ones was well. While Myers acknowledged that Gergen "had many good relationships with reporters," she also noted that he "had some not so good" as well. Beyond the competence and ideological questions, there was also one of culture. As Myers put it, Gergen "represented a lot of the things that we thought we were riding in to save the world from, you know."[16]

Myers and others were also worried about Stephanopoulos's reaction. Myers complained that "You know, George was one of the architects of this campaign and a loyal staffer, and there he was just toilet paper, Kleenex, tossed out."[17] Carville, who opted not to join the administration, but consulted from the outside, was a Stephanopoulos defender as well. As he put it, "George has more gray matter than gray hair, and he came to a place [Washington] that had a lot more gray hair than gray matter."[18]

The Gergen move also accentuated the feeling of the old/young split in the administration. In her book on the Clinton White House, journalist Elizabeth Drew wrote about older White House staffers who were giving background statements making the case that the Stephanopoulos-Gergen move was based on "the idea that we need some adults here."[19] The *Washington Post*'s Lloyd Grove, clearly the recipient of these types of background statements—also known as leaks—wrote an article called "The White House Kiddie Corps." In the piece, Grove wrote of speculation that Stephanopoulos's loss of the communications portfolio may have been a "harbinger of a general shakeup of twentysomething staffers, some of them males who sport earrings in the Oval Office and dress like the host of 'Sprockets.'"[20]

Understandably, Stephanopoulos had his concerns as well. The night before the announcement, Stephanopoulos recalls being worried that the next day he was going to be "publicly humiliated." Clinton himself allayed Stephanopoulos's worries, calling him at one thirty the night before the announcement to say, "I think it's the best thing. I need you by my side." Clinton's personal touch solved the problem for Stephanopoulos, who called it the "Perfect thing to say."[21] Other Stephanopoulos defenders took this line as well. Paul Begala, another campaign aide turned outside consultant, told the *Washington Post* that "Only in Washington are people so arrogant—or ignorant—as to construe a move in which someone goes from spending all his time with the press, to spending all his time with the president, as a demotion."[22]

While this spin solved the problem of Stephanopoulos worrying about a loss of status, it did not stop Stephanopoulos's larger problem with Gergen. Gergen was not only older, more experienced, and a Republican, but he was also a skilled practitioner of the dark arts of undercutting White House rivals. He was a rare aide who had already served in three White Houses and had been involved in aide versus aide dueling in all of them.

Gergen continued his sharp-elbowed ways in the Clinton White House. One of his timeworn tactics was to circumvent the process. A veteran of multiple White House operations, Gergen believed that Democratic White Houses tended to be more chaotic and less buttoned down than Republican ones. Whether the observation is true or not, in the Clinton White House, things were even worse than normal for a Democratic administration. As Gergen put it, "in this case, it was totally chaotic." Gergen described the speechwriting process as "suddenly, ten minutes before the event, people would pour into the office, to give him advice." This was even more frenzied than the Ford administration, in which the president would occasionally not have important remarks such as the State of the Union ready the night before the speech.[23]

Gergen may have complained about the chaos, but he also knew how to exploit it. In one instance, he took advantage of facetime with the president to give Clinton a new Gergen-authored version of a speech, effectively supplanting the speech that had been making its way through the process. Gergen had learned this tactic from Donald Rumsfeld back in the Ford administration, as a way of displacing Robert Hartmann's "laundry list" State of the Union speech draft. The trick failed then, but it worked here, infuriating Begala. Begala chased down Gergen after the meeting ended, calling Gergen's act a "chicken***t double cross" and adapting a line from the *Godfather* film, saying, "I'm going to work with you, I'm going to respect you, but I'm not going to trust you." Gergen apologized for the ploy, but he got his way on the speech.[24]

Gergen also alienated Clinton staff in the way he gave advice. Stephanopoulos thought Gergen's Republican perspective colored the advice he gave to the president in an infuriating way. In Stephanopoulos's view, Gergen framed issues in a left-right way that favored the Republican position. This meant that choosing the Republican position earned Clinton praise from Gergen for being principled. In contrast, Gergen saw taking sides with the Democrats as surrendering to his base. To Stephanopoulos, a dedicated member of the liberal wing, Gergen's framing was "intolerable."[25]

Another favorite Gergen tactic was the leak. He had obviously seen the leak at work in the Reagan—recall his Professor Leaky sobriquet—Ford, and Nixon administrations, but here he was in an even more senior position, with access to even more inside information. And he had a larger goal in mind: moving to a position at the State Department. The urgency of this ambitious, devious move became even greater once McLarty, Gergen's patron, left the White House. Stephanopoulos estimated that as many as 25 percent of the "Clinton foreign policy is in chaos" articles emanated from Gergen.[26]

Understandably, Gergen's critical drumbeat did not endear Gergen to Tony Lake, Clinton's national security advisor. Lake did not want Gergen underfoot at the White House, and McLarty's departure left Gergen exposed without a protector. When Gergen did leave to go to the State Department as an advisor to Secretary of State Warren Christopher, Lake said he "supported it right from the moment the president told him about it." The State Department, however, had its own concerns. In an interview with the *New York Times* before Gergen started, State spokesman Mike McCurry likened the arrival of Gergen at State to that of "a 1,000 pound gorilla."[27] Stephanopoulos and other White House aides did not like Gergen and were pleased to see him go. But their dislike of Gergen paled before their reaction to an even more conservative advisor who would mysteriously appear in the White House in 1995.

## Charlie Appears

In November 1994, the Democrats lost control of both Houses of Congress for the first time in four decades. This, more than anything else, was the defining event of the Clinton administration. More than Hillary-care, more than impeachment, more than Whitewater and the related scandals, more than the 1996 reelection, more than any foreign event including the Israeli-Palestinian peace deal, the 1994 election shaped the Clinton White House years. Coming just two years after a groundbreaking election that brought Clinton to power and the Democrats to the White House for the first time in a dozen years, the 1994 Newt Gingrich–led Republican Revolution was an embarrassing rebuke to Clinton and the Democratic Party as a whole. The election loss reflected the country's discomfort with the administration's chaotic first two years, and it would shape how Clinton handled his remaining six. The debacle justified Clinton's core instinct to tack to the center, just as it forced him to find common ground with the party's liberals to face down the conservative challenge.

It also brought "Charlie" to the White House.

Charlie was the code name for Dick Morris, a New York–based political consultant and pollster. Morris had a contentious relationship with Clinton dating back to his time in Arkansas and had not worked on the 1992 effort. When advice from Charlie started appearing after the 1994 election, White House aides, even Chief of Staff Leon Panetta, did not know who the mysterious Charlie was. What they did know, however, was that Clinton was getting outside advice from somewhere. As Myers recalled, "Things started to happen, like he would get a draft of a speech and it would come back completely rewritten. And, you know, like where'd this come from?" The changes were not just random, but they were pushing Clinton in a direction unpopular with the liberal White House staff. Specifically, Myers complained, "all of a sudden the president wanted to announce this middle-class tax cut and a middle-class bill of rights. And it was like, well, you know, he's jumping on the Republican bandwagon. Where's this coming from?"[28]

The changes were coming from "Charlie." Morris had been a Clinton advisor before, helping Clinton navigate Southern politics as governor of Arkansas. Clinton was a wunderkind governor of Arkansas, first elected as a thirty-two-year-old in 1978, with Morris's help. The voters rejected Clinton in 1982, but he recalibrated and was successfully reelected in 1986, again with the assistance of Morris. But the Clinton-Morris relationship was a brittle one. Morris had been drifting right and advising Republicans, including conservative Southern Republicans like Mississippi's Trent Lott. There was even a physical altercation between Clinton and Morris in 1990. As Morris recalled, "Bill ran after me, tackled me, threw me to the floor of the kitchen in the mansion and cocked his fist back to punch me." Morris cited this fight as the reason for his refusal to work for Clinton's 1992 election effort.[29]

The incident damaged but did not end the relationship. When Clinton got into political trouble in 1994, he reached out to Morris to do some polling. Initially, they were working together on what Morris called a "trial basis." For this reason, as well as Morris's increasing Republican ties, they kept the relationship secret. To maintain secrecy, they decided not to use Morris's name when they talked. Instead, Morris created a code name: "Charlie." According to Morris, the name derived from his "favorite Republican political consultant, Charlie Black." Morris found his use of a Republican amusing, recalling that "I just thought it was kind of funny that I'd use a Republican name, working for Clinton."[30]

Other White House aides would fail to see the humor. Secretary Bettie Currie would interrupt Clinton in meetings with staff by telling him "Charlie's on the phone." Clinton would leave the room, telling his staff, "Excuse me, that's a call I have to take." This led to staff speculation and befuddlement over who Charlie might be. As Morris recalled, "they'd all be wondering, 'Is this some head of state? Is this some CIA agent or something?' And they had no idea who it was. It was kind of funny."[31]

In addition to the mystery phone calls, there were unexpected changes to agreed materials. These changes raised suspicions among the staff. As Morris put it, "At some point, the staff realizes that something is going on. They're submitting drafts in the daytime, and the next morning these drafts are coming back with significant, even radical, changes." Erskine Bowles, the deputy chief of staff, wondered if he was missing meetings: "Where was the real meeting taking place? And it became clear that the real meeting was taking place over in the East Wing with this guy who I had never heard of!"[32] White House staff started wondering what happened between the evening agreement and the changes that appeared the next morning, leading to speculation that "there's a day Clinton, and there's a night Clinton."[33]

The document changes and the mysterious calls piqued staff curiosity. Most curious was Harold Ickes, the liberal stalwart and son of a Franklin Roosevelt aide of the same name. Ickes's longstanding willingness to take on unsavory tasks for Clinton led to his being nicknamed "the garbage man" and "director of the sanitation department" in the Clinton White House.[34] When polls continued to come in that were not generated by official Clinton pollster Stan Greenberg, Ickes asked Panetta a direct and reasonable question about the pollster: "Who the hell is this?"[35]

It is astounding that Panetta, who was White House chief of staff, did not know the answer. Morris, in his furtive phone calls and visits to the White House residence, was directing the Clinton administration in a way that was an obvious challenge to the authority of the chief of staff. A mortified Erskine Bowles, Panetta's proper and buttoned-down deputy, said, "It was amazing to see something planned in Leon's office—and then literally the next day none of that happened."[36]

Clinton had managed to keep the secret from Panetta and the rest of the team. The cost, however, was high, in the form of a suspicious staff. Still, he was enjoying his conspiracy of three—First Lady Hillary Clinton was in on it—with Morris. When Morris and he worked together on the 1995 State of the Union address, Morris told the president, "You know, this is what I've wanted to do since I'm eight years old." Clinton, like Morris a political junkie, responded, "Me, too."[37]

The secrecy of the arrangement appealed to Clinton as well. He even told Morris, "I like subterfuge, that's why I like you." But keeping a secret like this was impossible. Things had to end at some point. Ickes's "Who the hell is this?" question prompted Panetta to confront the president directly. Clinton told Panetta about Morris, and Panetta passed on the information to an unhappy Ickes. Ickes had hated Morris for a long time. As Stephanopoulos, who at this point did not know about Morris, described the relationship: Ickes was "Dick's mortal enemy since like 1966.... They used to run against each other in these Upper West Side city council races in Manhattan on different sides, and they just despise each other...."[38] Given this history, Ickes's reaction was unsurprising: "Oh, no, this is crazy, you can't get this guy into it."[39]

Panetta called together a small group to tell them about Morris. Panetta recognized that Clinton, still smarting from the 1994 election, needed Morris. But as chief of staff, Panetta also needed to impose order in the White House. From Panetta's perspective, what "he could not tolerate as chief of staff was to have somebody who was planting political advice with the president and then trying to implement it through the staff of the White House." To address this problem, Panetta "drew the line and told the president, 'Look, this is unacceptable. I can't have any political person trying to deal with the staff.'" In Panetta's view, this solved the problem, as Clinton "to his credit respected that, and we told Morris that he's got to present the information to the president and to me, and then we'll decide what does or does not get done." As Panetta saw it, "Morris understood that he was going to have to play by my rules."[40]

Others disagreed with Panetta's assessment. As Stephanopoulos would later write, "From December 1994 through August 1996, Leon Panetta managed the official White House staff, the Joint Chiefs commanded the military, the cabinet ministered the government, but no single person influenced the president of the United States more than Dick Morris."[41] Ickes, now brought into the circle, was quick to reveal the secret. As Morris recalled, four months into the renewed relationship,

Clinton brought Morris to meet Ickes, Panetta, and Bowles for weekly strategy sessions. Morris asked that his presence remain a secret, but Ickes was dismissive of his request, telling Morris, "Well, the one thing I can guarantee you is you won't be anonymous." Ickes was right. As Morris recalled, "Sure enough, about a week later, Jane Mayer of the *New Yorker* magazine called me and said, 'I understand you've been attending strategy meetings with the president every week. Can we talk about it?' And then I was outed."[42]

## Exit Charlie, Enter Dick Morris

The Charlie incident brought all three factors of White House staff contentiousness into play. There was significant ideological disparity, with the liberal White House staff objecting to the more conservative guidance from Morris. The process was not a fair and open one, as decisions made one day were mysteriously overturned overnight, with no explanation given of why or what had happened. And there was presidential tolerance for the dysfunction, as Clinton enjoyed the clandestine relationship with Morris, and got a kick out of both the secrecy and the seeming frustration of his staff. Unsurprisingly, this confluence of the three dysfunction factors led to internal dissension, most prominently between Morris and his newly designated minder, George Stephanopoulos.

*All Too Human*, Stephanopoulos's 1999 White House memoir, is a remarkable document on multiple levels. It is a revealing book, easily one of the best of the many White House staff memoirs. It came out while the Clinton administration was still in office, which angered many in Clinton world. The book's publication led to his former colleagues calling him a "backstabber" and an "ingrate," and dubbing the rookie TV pundit Stephanopoulos with the nickname "commen*traitor*."[43] But most of all, the Stephanopoulos book is one of the closest we have to a diary of a White House rivalry playing out in real time. Stephanopoulos, who devotes a sizeable portion of the book to his fraught relationship with Morris, even includes his inner thoughts in italics throughout his details of their interactions. These thought bubbles do not paint Morris favorably.

Stephanopoulos first noticed something unusual going on shortly after the 1994 election. As he recounted in an oral history, "The first time I ever saw the word 'Charlie' was on a little yellow post-it note on the president's desk next to his phone saying, 'Charlie called.' I thought, 'Hmm, that's odd.'"[44] Stephanopoulos was used to Clinton getting advice from outside advisors. He had learned long ago that "monitoring Clinton's phone calls was nearly impossible. He called all sorts of people at all hours of the day and night, and would often pass on new thoughts without revealing his sources—kind of blind market testing."[45]

"Charlie" was different, however, as he was changing Clinton rhetoric and policies. In preparing for Clinton's December 15, 1994, Oval Office address, Stephanopoulos noticed one new draft with completely different language in it. The language referred to an Economic Bill of Rights—it would be changed to a Middle Class Bill of Rights in the final version. Stephanopoulos liked the language and asked Hillary where it had come from. Hillary smiled, which Stephanopoulos incorrectly took to mean she had written it. She had not; the language, and the idea, came from Morris. The smile meant that she was read into the mystery of Charlie, but Stephanopoulos was not.[46]

Eventually, Stephanopoulos would learn who Charlie was. As Stephanopoulos wrote, "It was never announced, really. It just happened." Even with the new language and the new revelation, it still did not strike Stephanopoulos as a big deal: "a lot of us who had been around were used to things like this happening." Stephanopoulos initially thought of Morris as Clinton's "flavor of the month." But things were more complicated. Looking back, Stephanopoulos didn't "think any of us realized how deep and tangled this tie was."

For the next twenty months, Morris would be Clinton's most powerful advisor. He constantly pushed Clinton to the right of the Democratic congress, calling his theory of gaining popularity in the space between the party extremes as "triangulation." To Stephanopoulos, as well as other Clintonistas, this was a betrayal of the liberal values they thought they had run on.

Triangulation or no, once Stephanopoulos learned about Morris, he would have to find some way to work with him. It would not be easy. The two men had obvious ideological disagreements. Morris was trying to pull Clinton to the right, and Stephanopoulos was from the party's liberal wing. Beyond the ideology, though, Stephanopoulos just did not like Morris's whole approach. His description of Morris upon their initial meeting just drips with disdain: "He was a small sausage of a man encased in a green suit with wide lapels, a wide floral tie, and a wide-collared shirt. His blow-dried pompadour and shiny leather briefcase gave him the look of a B-movie mob lawyer, circa 1975—the kind of guy who gets brained with a baseball bat for double-crossing the boss."[47]

Looks aside, there was also the fact that Morris was a confrontational guy. On one of their first meetings, Morris accused Stephanopoulos of leaking bad stories about Morris to the press: "Now listen, George, I know you leaked those stories on me in April. Don't say you didn't. I don't care what you say. I know you did."[48] This was a fairly direct approach, guaranteed to make Stephanopoulos defensive. So, the parameters of their relationship were laid out at the beginning. Morris thought Stephanopoulos was a leaker—"ambassador to the *Washington Post*," as he put it—and Stephanopoulos thought Morris was an obnoxious right-wing clown.[49]

On another occasion, Morris leaked an internal Clinton polling memo to Bob Dole's campaign. Dole's campaign promptly leaked the polls to the *Washington Post*, which called the White House for comment. Press Secretary Mike McCurry asked Morris about it, and Morris blamed Stephanopoulos. According to Morris's version, Stephanopoulos gave the memo to his pal James Carville, who then shared it with his wife, the Republican operative Mary Matalin. Matalin then supposedly leaked the memo to the *Post*'s Ann Devroy to embarrass Morris. This implausible story did not convince anyone, and even prompted Clinton to chide Morris, saying, "whenever something goes wrong around here, you blame it on George." Moved by Clinton's defense, Stephanopoulos's eyes welled with tears. More importantly, Morris apologized—Stephanopoulos did not accept it—and Stephanopoulos received a form of immunization from future attacks. As Stephanopoulos wrote in his memoir, "from now on, no Dick attack on me will stick."[50]

Still, they did try to work together. Sensing Stephanopoulos's neediness, Morris proposed a deal: Morris would give access and Stephanopoulos would cut back on the backbiting. Stephanopoulos agreed but even so, it was a marriage of convenience at best. Stephanopoulos wanted access because he was frozen out and wanted to try to block whatever conservative-to-moderate advice Morris was giving Clinton. From Morris's perspective, cooperating with Stephanopoulos was a better choice than the available alternatives. Panetta could not bear to be in the same room as Morris and referred to him as "little campaign sh*t from Arkansas." Harold Ickes was even worse. Morris, who could be obtuse, understood how much Ickes disliked him, telling Stephanopoulos that "I have a list of twenty-three times Harold has f*cked me over."[51]

Stephanopoulos may have been marginally more pleasant to Morris than Ickes or Panetta, but that did not make him a Morris fan. As Stephanopoulos freely admitted, "We all despised him, and more than that." Morris recognized this, and even called the Panetta-Ickes-Stephanopoulos axis and their aides a "thugocracy." They, in turn, called Morris "the Unabomber." When Morris installed his own aide, Bill Curry, in the White House, hazing activities against Curry by the thugocrats included denying him a desk, giving him false information about meeting times and locations, and laughing at his resulting tardiness.[52]

The Clintonites were also happy to mock Morris for his oddities, of which there were many. In the summer of 1996, Stephanopoulos called Morris with the news that a meteorite from Mars had fallen to earth and an administration response was expected. Morris got excited, more perhaps than an adult should get about something like this. Calling the news "huge," he began to suggest policy proposals to allow Clinton to capitalize on the news. His favorite? A manned mission to Mars. Morris saw the Mars news as an opportunity to highlight the extent to which Clinton was a candidate of the future while his opponent, the septuagenarian Senator Bob Dole, was a man of the past. To Morris, this contrast represented the "ultimate triangulation."[53]

To the Clinton staff, however, this incident was just another opportunity to make jokes at Morris's expense. Morris jokes flew around the White House faster than the manned flight could have. In one, Morris was told: "The good news is that we've agreed to go ahead with the manned mission you proposed. The bad news is: you're the man. How soon can you be ready?" Another one, attributed to Stephanopoulos, went, "There's life on Mars. Dick's proof."[54]

Soon after, Morris's political career imploded. In August of 1996, the *Star* reported that the married Morris had regular assignations with a prostitute at the Jefferson Hotel in Washington. Ickes was downright gleeful when he reported the news, chomping on a pear and laughing as he told Stephanopoulos, "You've got to see the tabloids tomorrow. Dick with a prostitute is coming out. He's gone." Ickes contributed to the revelations, which would constitute the twenty-fourth time he had done Morris ill. He was responsible for telling reporters about Morris's exorbitant hotel bills at the Jefferson, where he charged the Democratic National Committee for video rentals and minibar charges.[55]

Stephanopoulos confessed: "I was enjoying it as well. I'm not claiming any superiority here." But he also had some ambivalence about the situation. After telling Morris he was sorry, his "thought bubble" revealed his true feelings: "I didn't like Dick—hell, I hated him. I wanted him gone. But to face such a public disgrace on a day of such personal triumph seemed too cruel, too unusual, too Greek." On the record, he was compassionate, saying: "On a human level, we're all sorry for Dick and his family. At the same time, we have work to do and we're going to move on. It's a speed bump and not a pothole." Paul Begala, another 1992 campaign alum, was more cheeky about Morris's ignominious departure, telling Rick Berke of the *New York Times*, "I've been dealing with the press for thirteen years, and I've always wanted to say this, and I never was able to until this moment: No comment."[56]

The Morris episode was a curious one. There is little doubt that Clinton wanted Morris there, even with the attendant backbiting he brought. In bringing in Morris, Clinton ramped up the three factors leading to internal dissension. Morris highlighted ideological disagreements, bringing in a more conservative perspective, one disliked by the liberal White House staff. Having a secret advisor wreaked havoc on the White House process, such as it was. As Stephanopoulos said of the process in the Morris period, "To use the word 'process' is to imply a kind of organization that wasn't there. It really was parallel universes, both somewhat chaotic." As for the question of presidential tolerance for the disagreements, Clinton knew what he was doing when he brought in Morris. On this, both Morris and Stephanopoulos agreed. Morris recalled that "in the last analysis, the channel that Clinton wanted me to pursue was the direct, private channel that we had with each other." Stephanopoulos, for his part, felt that "Clinton was just being Clinton. For months, he'd been playing me off against Morris, taking the best from both of us and turning it into something better."[57]

The feuding around Morris was Clinton's fault. He enabled it and was happy to reap the benefits of it. Clinton's staff mocked and despised Morris, and they unceremoniously ushered him out the door, but there is little doubt that Morris was essential to getting Clinton's presidency back on track. He maneuvered Clinton to sign the welfare reform bill of 1996, which burnished his reformer bona fides. He got a post-1994 Clinton to connect with middle of the road voters in a way that the pre-1994 Clinton of the failed Hillary-care health plan and the excesses of the midnight basketball crime bill could not. As columnist Robert Novak wrote in late August of 1996, after Morris's humiliation and departure, the Democratic party was "now Dick Morris' party."[58] Morris may not have made friends in the White House, and he may have left in disgrace, but Clinton did owe Morris a debt of gratitude for rescuing Clinton's teetering presidency.

## Second Term: Unity in the Face of a More Hated Enemy

Clinton's second term is best known for one thing: the Monica Lewinsky affair and attendant impeachment trial. In January of 1998, a story leaked out that Independent Counsel Ken Starr had learned about a recurring intimate relationship between President Clinton and White House intern Monica Lewinsky. The president had lied about the existence of the relationship to Starr's team, making him vulnerable to perjury. Some commentators predicted that this would spell the end of the Clinton presidency.

Erskine Bowles, who had replaced Panetta as chief of staff, found the story appalling. Clinton assured Bowles that the story was untrue, and Bowles believed him because he felt there was no other alternative if he was going to remain as chief. When United Nations ambassador Bill Richardson called Bowles to explain why he had offered a job to Lewinsky, Bowles cut him off, saying, "I don't want to know a f*cking thing about it! Don't tell me about it!" Further discussions of the situation disgusted Bowles, to the point where he left a meeting with the words, "I think I'm going to throw up." He did not return to the meeting and would be gone from the chief of staff position before the end of the year.[59]

Health and Human Services secretary Donna Shalala, who had predicted years earlier that Clinton could not become president because of his affairs, had misgivings as well. In September, after Clinton publicly admitted to the nation that he had indeed had an inappropriate relationship with Lewinsky, Clinton went to his cabinet to apologize. Shalala and Small Business administrator Aida Alvarez pushed back at Clinton, with Shalala questioning the sincerity of his apology. She said to Clinton, "To say it is one thing, to demonstrate it is another."[60]

These minor insurrections aside, the Lewinsky scandal and investigation became a unifying event for the administration. In the face of the Starr inquiry, followed by impeachment proceedings in the House of Representatives in the fall of 1998, the Clinton team closed ranks behind the president. James Carville, the guru of the 1992 campaign, remained loyal as well. As Carville explained matters, "Look, I wish he wouldn't have done it. It was a silly, stupid thing to do to fool around with a young woman like that, okay? But I am not going to abandon a guy over something like this. No way." Among some aides, like White House communications director Ann Lewis, the prevailing attitude was that Clinton's behavior was bad, but the policy goals of the Republicans were worse. To Lewis, the choice was obvious, "Ken Starr? Newt Gingrich? Henry Hyde? Were these the people I should have allied with instead?"[61]

The Lewinsky episode led Democrats, especially those inside the administration, to circle the wagons. Even Sidney Blumenthal, the divisive figure nicknamed "Sid Vicious," after the 1970s punk rocker charged with murder, seemed less polarizing within the White House while everyone was coming together to protect the president. Blumenthal came to the White House from the world of opinion journalism, where he was known as a sharp-penned practitioner of the dark arts of politics. In the White House, he was so prone to conspiracy theories that he was called GK, for the Grassy Knoll theory of a second shooter favored by Kennedy assassination conspiracy theorists.[62]

In the scandal-plagued second term, Blumenthal became a powerful asset to Clinton. The *Washington Post*'s Michael Powell described him as "the first to urge aides to man the ramparts." As a result of Blumenthal's eagerness to defend the president, his paranoid act, which had by some accounts been wearing thin, suddenly became more appealing. In fact, Powell even noted that talk of getting rid of Blumenthal "abated" as the Lewinsky matter became all-consuming. Blumenthal became a staunch Clinton ally, organizing a supportive letter by liberal intellectuals and helping Hillary Clinton both create and amplify her vast right-wing conspiracy allegation.[63]

The unifying nature of the Lewinsky debacle served as the ultimate irony of the Clinton White House. The president ran and won as a New Democrat, then got in trouble governing from the left and faced internal questions about his ideology throughout his presidency. These internal questions led to bitter staff rivalries such as those between Stephanopoulos and Gergen, or Morris and Stephanopoulos. Yet when the presidency was most in danger, the ideological issues fell aside, and partisan loyalty trumped other questions. When Democrats realized that whatever their policy differences, the prospect of Republican victories was worse to them, they came together in support of an embattled president. It may not be the best formula for success, but political crises can themselves serve as a potent way to resolve the nagging problem of internal White House dissension.

# CHAPTER 10

# GEORGE W. BUSH
## Domestic Calm, National Security Turmoil

I t is important to begin this chapter with full disclosure. In contrast to earlier chapters, in this one I am not just a student of history; I was, at times, a participant and witness. I served in the administration of President George W. Bush and part of that work was in the White House. When the invitation to work on the White House Domestic Policy Council came, I accepted at once. But as the honor came home to me, I began to reflect on it with some trepidation.

So, before starting, I called a friend who had served in the Clinton White House and I asked for his advice. His suggestion was quick and pointed: "Watch your back." I was thankful for his personal advice but was pleased to find it unneeded. In my experience, the disagreements, animosity, and rivalries that characterized earlier administrations did not show up in the same way. However, this experience did not extend to the Bush national security team, where my Clintonite friend's advice would have been right on target.

On the domestic side of the Bush White House, there did not seem to be the level of undercutting of one another seen in other administrations. As for leaking, reporters complained about the lack of leaks coming from the disciplined White House operation. As Bush communications aide Mary Matalin recalled, "Because we have a common agenda we're not trying to advance any position but the president's. So we don't use the vehicle of leaks to advance our own agenda."[1]

Bush had consciously set out to avoid the missteps and rancor that had undercut his father's administration. When Karl Rove, "the architect" of both of Bush's election victories, had initially balked at leaving Texas to join the administration, he had mentioned his concerns about the bitterness and backbiting for which the Beltway was legendary. "People told me before I went to Washington that the White House would be a snake pit," he recalled. "Leaking and backbiting just come with the territory." President Bush told him his administration would not be like that. Loyalty, clarity of command, and collegiality would be the watchwords. Rove found that Bush team members "can go to the Oval Office and advocate a perspective diametrically opposed to the point of view of the person on the sofa across from [them]," and, even if they lose, "you can link arms and go on, and be certain that your [losing] view won't appear in the paper."[2]

This overall comity dated back to the 2000 Bush presidential campaign. Tim Goeglein, a Washington veteran who served on that campaign and would go on to work in the Bush White House, wrote in his memoir that "I have never seen such unity and goodwill among a political team as we had on that team in 2000."[3] When there were tensions, staff members would downplay them and tended not to give details of any fights they may have had to the media. The 2000 campaign had three top dogs: Rove, communicator Karen Hughes, and campaign manager Joe Allbaugh. Collectively, the three were known as the Iron Triangle. Yet a year and a half into the administration's start, only one of the members of the triangle remained in the White House. Allbaugh never entered the White House, choosing instead to head FEMA. Hughes returned to Texas in July of 2002; rumors of tensions with Rove persisted during their period together, but few specifics appeared. When Hughes announced her departure, the *New York Times*'s Elizabeth Bumiller asked Rove whether the two had clashed. His response was both gener-ous and unrevealing: "I'll be the first to say that she and I disagreed, and 9 times out of 10 she was right." In addition to quoting Rove, Bumiller noted that other knowledgeable people said that reports of tensions had nothing to do with Hughes's departure, as well as the fact that Rove chose not "to specify the exact nature of the disputes." For her part, Hughes recounted that "unlike what I read and heard about infighting among previous White House staff, ours was remarkably collegial."[4]

Even staff members with less favorable experiences acknowledged that the Bush administration's domestic shop was loyal and tightly knit by White House standards. University of Pennsylvania professor John DiIulio, who joined the administration to head Bush's White House Office of Faith Based Initiatives, lasted less than a year in the White House. There were several reasons for this, including a brutal, multi-hour commute from Philadelphia each day. When DiIulio left, he gave a critical interview to Ron Suskind in *Esquire*, in which he infamously called some Bush staffers "Mayberry Machiavellis," by which he meant small-town, small-minded, yet treacherous, aides who focused on politics rather than policy. But even here, DiIulio was loathe to criticize his former colleagues by name and seemed to think the problem was groupthink rather than internal dissension. He might have preferred dissent, as his complaint was that the administration did not sufficiently debate policy alternatives. DiIulio also acknowledged the discipline of the Bush team when it came to the press—especially when compared to the press management of the Clinton team, who "were less disciplined about it and leaked more to the media and so on."[5]

Journalists saw this too and were unhappy about it. Richard Brookh-iser wrote in *The Atlantic* that "Bush's advisers do not rat each other out in public." Media maven Ken Auletta had a similar view, telling the *New Yorker*'s Daniel Capello that "from Bush on down, talking to the press off the record is generally frowned upon and equated with leaking, which is a deadly sin in the Bush White House." As Auletta saw it, the Bush team was "a cohesive White House staff, dominated by people whose first loyalty is to Team Bush." David Frum, a White House speechwriter who was also willing to be critical, observed that the Bush staffers "who control the channels of communication have their egos carefully under control. They have fewer psychodramas than any staff since the invention of staffs."[6]

Bush put together an ideologically cohesive White House staff who generally agreed with his concept of "compassionate conservatism." Many of them came from Texas as part of Bush's "Texas mafia." The conservative movement was strongly behind Bush, having backed him in the primaries against John McCain, and overwhelmingly so in the general election campaign against Al Gore. The battles between conservatives and moderates that had dominated disagreement in the Reagan and Bush 41 White Houses were in the past (and, as it would turn out, the future).

Bush was also the first MBA president. As such, he stressed strong management principles and discipline in the running of the White House staff. On the management side, Bush took the theory and practice of management seriously. As Rove put it, "I had read Peter Drucker, but I'd never *seen* Drucker until I saw Bush in action." Bush's 2000 campaign manager Joe Allbaugh agreed, saying that Bush "is the best one-minute manager I've ever been associated with."[7]

Bush's focus on both articulating common goals and on measurable external results echoed Drucker's famous principles.

Discipline was also a recurrent theme. Peter Rodman wrote that Bush's "concept of leadership as purposeful and resolute also put a premium on coherence of policy-making and discipline in execution." Andy Card used to tell staffers that "George W. Bush is the most disciplined person I know." This discipline, Card would explain, extended to his exercise, his religious worship, and his management of the White House staff. Others, like White House correspondent Peter Baker and outside advisor New Gingrich, also stressed discipline when discussing the Bush White House. Gingrich's comment was typical: "Bush has a very disciplined sense of himself as a team leader." Even his opponents remarked on his discipline. A staffer for Ann Richards, whom Bush had unseated as Texas governor, warned fellow Democrats that "Anyone who takes this man lightly and doesn't think he is a serious, extremely disciplined candidate would be making a very big miscalculation."[8]

One other factor in the way Bush ran things was his time as a close observer of his father's White House. As Frum noted, Bush's work with his father in the 1988 campaign and during that administration meant that he was "the only president with functional experience of being a White House staffer." That experience had a powerful effect on Bush 43, as the Bush 41 White House had significant management challenges. The fact that a young George W. Bush had had to step in and tell John Sununu, his father's chief of staff, that it was time to go showed the depth of the problems of that White House. So, when it came time to create his own White House, George W. intentionally selected a chief of staff with White House experience—Andy Card—who would not run roughshod and would consciously contrast himself with Sununu. In one incident, after Sununu had blistered his staff, he then bragged to Card that the staff would be thinking, "That Sununu is a tough son of a bitch." Card corrected him, saying, "No, they're not. They're going to go back to their offices and tell everyone, 'That Sununu is a f*cking a$$hole!'" That Card, who had an aversion to profanity, used such language suggests that he had significant disagreement with Sununu's management techniques.[9]

When Card served as chief of staff, he would take a decidedly different approach. He was much more soft-spoken, collaborative, and plainly averse to foul language. He was also wary of alternative power centers in the White House, something that he had seen in Bush's father's White House. Deputy Chief of Staff Josh Bolten had also worked in the Bush 41 White House and had similar concerns. The two men worked together to make sure that there was a coherent and consistent process governing policy development and decisions. There would be no domestic policy originating in Cabinet Affairs or the vice president's office in the Bush 43 White House. Process was everything, and woe betide the staffer who would commit the dreaded "process foul."[10]

## The Limits of a Domestic Policy Presidency

Bush's approach worked for him, especially at the beginning. He quite consciously wanted to be a domestic policy president, avoiding foreign entanglements. For the first nine months of the administration, the application of Bush's discipline and management principles in a domestically focused presidency led to some significant accomplishments, including the creation of his faith-based initiative, passage of a tax cut, and serious progress towards the No Child Left Behind education reform, which would pass in early 2002. All these initiatives passed with bipartisan support, an alien concept in today's Washington. But the Bush administration would not remain a domestic policy presidency.

Fate intervened on September 11, 2001, when terrorists from the Islamist group Al Qaeda hijacked four airliners and crashed three of them into the Twin Towers of New York and the Pentagon outside the nation's capital. An administration that had set its sights on domestic policy accomplishments suddenly had to protect America in a way not seen since the attack on Pearl Harbor in December 1941.

Unfortunately, Bush's domestic policy approach, focused on comity among low-profile aides adhering closely to a well-defined process, did not extend to the foreign policy operation. The White House that had seen a well-run domestic policy had a semi-dysfunctional foreign policy operation, one in which backbiting, undercutting, and leaking occurred as a matter of course.

There were several reasons for this strange dichotomy between foreign and domestic policy. First, while the Bush domestic team consisted of basically anonymous aides, where most of them were unknown before the 2000 campaign, the foreign policy team was dominated by well-known figures with long-standing public profiles. Recent history has shown that relatively unknown aides are often less territorial, and less prone to leaks than more famous aides who already have existing reputations and independent relationships with the press.[11] In the Bush administration, for example, Defense Secretary Don Rumsfeld had previously served in the same position in the 1970s under Ford, as well as chief of staff. He was a reliable conservative with decades of experience in Washington.

Facing off against Rumsfeld was Secretary of State Colin Powell, a moderate who would later go on to endorse Barack Obama for president. A Vietnam veteran, Powell had served as national security advisor under Reagan and chairman of the Joint Chiefs of Staff under both Bush 41 and Clinton. He, too, was famous in and outside of Washington, but his worldview differed markedly from that of Rumsfeld.

Rumsfeld and Powell were not the only antagonists in the dispute. Each had powerful allies within the administration who shared their views and had extensive Washington experience. Rumsfeld allied himself most closely with Vice President Dick Cheney, his old deputy from the Ford administration. Cheney had run the selection process for the vice presidency and ended up with the job himself. Often, he was referred to as the most powerful vice president in history—one who brought a keen interest in foreign affairs.

Powell had powerful allies as well. These included many fans in the press, but also Richard Armitage, his deputy secretary. A former naval officer, Armitage had held multiple roles in both the State and Defense Departments in the Reagan and Bush administrations. Armitage was dismissive of what he saw as the war hawks on the other side of the divide, saying "these guys never heard a bullet go by their ears in anger.... None of them ever served. They're a bunch of jerks."[12] On another occasion, he tore into a new assistant secretary of state who naïvely told Armitage that "I think with my contacts I'll really be able to fix the relationship and act as a bridge between Defense and State." Armitage's response was brutal and revealing: "You're on our team. You don't bridge sh*t. I've known all those f***ers for thirty years. You ain't bridging sh*t." The man got the message. Within three weeks, he reported back to Armitage about his run in with the "mother****ers" at Defense.[13]

These kinds of tensions made for a difficult internal dynamic. The job of corralling and controlling the players in an administration's national security team usually belongs to the national security advisor.

President George W. Bush meets with his National Security Council in the Situation Room on September 20, 2001. Participants from left include: Robert S. Mueller, director of the FBI; Lewis Libby, chief of staff to the vice president; George Tenet, director of the CIA; Attorney General John D. Ashcroft; Secretary of the Treasury Paul H. O'Neill; Vice President Dick Cheney; President Bush; Secretary of State Colin Powell; Secretary of Defense Donald Rumsfeld; and General Henry H. Shelton, chairman of the Joint Chiefs of Staff. The Bush team was faced with a challenging task in the wake of the 9/11 terrorist attacks, a task made more difficult because of internal strife. *Courtesy of the George W. Bush Presidential Library and Museum*

In the Bush administration, the person tasked with containing these large egos and potent personalities was Condoleezza Rice. Although she had worked on the National Security Council in the Bush 41 administration, she was the most junior member of the bunch, both in terms of age and previous government experience. As she would learn, controlling such a group would be beyond her—or anyone else's—capabilities. When she confronted Rumsfeld after one blow up on the swirling problems of the Bush national security apparatus, Rumsfeld's answer alienated her deeply. Rice asked Rumsfeld, "What's wrong between us?" Rumsfeld replied, "I don't know. We always got along. You're obviously bright and committed, but it just doesn't work." Rice's response came in the form of an unhappy internal monologue, "*Bright?* That, I thought to myself, is part of the problem." Rice, reading a lot into a single word, believed that Rumsfeld was only comfortable with her as a subordinate, and not as a colleague. Overall, Rice felt, "Don simply resented the role I had to play as national security advisor."[14]

Rumsfeld did indeed have issues with Rice. In his memoir, he made sure to point out their "differing backgrounds," noting that "Rice came from academia." He framed it as a compliment, albeit a backhanded one, describing her as "a polished, poised, and elegant presence." The message, however, was clear: she was a pointy-headed professor playing out academic theories in the national security realm, while he was a hard-headed man of action with decades of real-world experience. Rumsfeld was even more explicit about this point elsewhere, telling ABC's Diane Sawyer after the administration that Rice had "never served in a senior administration position" before the Bush administration and that "She'd been an academic. And, you know, a lot of academics like to have meetings. And they like to bridge differences and get people all to be happy." Rumsfeld also thought her lack of experience led to real weaknesses as a manager, complaining in his memoir that he often found NSC meetings "not well organized."[15]

Rumsfeld was not the only principal to cross swords with Rice. Cheney, Rumsfeld's deputy in the Ford administration and later secretary of defense in the George H. W. Bush administration, was integrally involved in the national security process. He often allied with Rumsfeld on substantive matters, and he used both his stature and his knowledge of the White House process to shape the policy outcomes in the administration. In one incident early on, he asked the president to name him as the chairman of the national security principals committee. This may sound like a minor bureaucratic matter, but the national security principals committee is a grouping of senior officials in national security who report directly to the president. In fact, the only difference between this group and the National Security Council itself is that the president is a member of the latter grouping. Rice was not happy with Cheney's request. As one colleague put it, "She threw a fit," arguing that "This is what national security advisers do." Bush, who was close to Rice and met with her seven or eight times a day, acceded to her request and put Rice in charge of the national security principals' meetings. As senior Pentagon aide Peter Rodman described the outcome, "Thus it came about that the supposedly all-powerful vice president sat at the table with cabinet secretaries at Principals meetings chaired by an assistant to the president." Rice won the day on this, but doing so did not endear her to the vice president.[16]

Unfortunately for Rice, she could not go to Bush for his intervention on every bureaucratic issue. She was indeed close to him and brought him up to speed on foreign policy issues while he was governor. Beginning in 1998, while Bush was thinking of running, Rice would come join Bush at the family compound in Kennebunkport, where they would play tennis and work out between briefings. Yet despite their close personal relationship, Bush—the disciplined manager—did not see it as his job to serve as an on-field referee. As Rodman wrote, "He did not want to referee every dispute."[17]

Bush's preference on matters of staff disagreements was reminiscent of Reagan's "you fellas work it out" mantra. Reagan took this approach because he did not want to deal with staff conflict. Bush did not mind conflict *per se*, but he thought it better from a management perspective for staff to seek consensus, an approach that had served him well as governor. According to Rodman, Bush's repeated instruction to the NSC staff was to get things worked out, and Rice dutifully pursued her friend and boss's desired approach: "At Principals or Deputies meetings, Rice and her deputy Stephen Hadley repeatedly conveyed the president's injunction to reconcile disagreements, to 'merge' or 'blend' or 'bridge' competing proposals, to split the differences, to come up with compromises." Bush's general reluctance to intervene made sense from a management standpoint. But it also made things more challenging for Rice as a junior player among national security heavyweights such as Powell, Rumsfeld, and Cheney.[18]

Rice's relative inexperience was only part of the issue. The group of advisors she had to corral—the national security principals—were at odds with one another. There was a lack of trust among the top advisors, especially Powell and Rumsfeld. Bush did not really know either of them well before the administration. The dislike went beyond the principals and extended to the staffs as well.[19] This meant that the rivalries were particularly difficult to manage and controlling them proved impossible.

The consensus approach is a challenging one when it comes to national security policy. Compromising on domestic policy can mean splitting the dollars spent on a program or moderating the impact of a proposed rule or bill. But issues in the national security realm are often binary. There is no real compromise between "invade Iraq" and "don't invade Iraq." Furthermore, national security issues are viewed as, and often are, existential ones, hardening positions and making compromise more difficult. This was especially true after the 9/11 attacks, with every issue seen through the lens of whether a position would make a terrorist attack more or less likely. This perspective, coupled with the difficulty of compromising over binary issues, tended to favor harder line views. As White House lawyer Brad Berenson put it, the "raw" feelings after 9/11 had a potent impact on policy deliberations. In that environment, if there were a question about whether a policy could prevent another attack from taking place, "if you have to err on the side of being too aggressive or not aggressive enough, you'd err by being too aggressive."[20]

The rawness Berenson described had an impact on interpersonal relations. The most prominent rivalry on the national security team was between Rumsfeld and Powell, but it was a strange antagonism. The two men had known each other a long time and had been friendly, but not friends. Even as they staked out distinct positions in the administration—Rumsfeld more hawkish, Powell more dovish—there was little direct confrontation between the two men, unlike that between Vance and Brzezinski, for example. As Rice put it, "The two did not confront each other face-to-face, let alone in front of the president."[21]

The stakes were high. Rumsfeld, along with Cheney, supported an invasion of Iraq to deal with the rumors of Iraqi dictator Saddam Hussein's program and accumulation of weapons of mass destruction. The intelligence community had confirmed the existence of these weapons and, the argument went, America could ill afford to have a ruthless dictator who supported terrorism get a hold of WMD. Powell was more skeptical and argued for the United Nations to handle things via resolutions and sanctions, a request that Bush granted, even though there was internal dissent over the approach. As Powell later recalled, both Cheney and Rumsfeld "weren't happy about" going to the United Nations before invading Iraq. But, Powell argued, "they saw the wisdom of doing it, and so they all agreed to my recommendation to take the issue to the United Nations." At the U.N., Powell famously made the case that Iraq had weapons of mass destruction, which was an important precursor to the U.S. invasion.[22]

Powell was wary of going to war, especially given that the U.S. would be inevitably responsible for the post-invasion aftermath. Powell called this the Pottery Barn rule, "You break it, you own it." After the U.S. did invade, the disagreements got worse, as each man—and their respective teams—differed on how to handle the post-invasion Iraq. Here the aversion to confrontation began to play a role. Neither man would address each other's disagreements directly, although they had their unique ways of dealing with them. According to Rice, Rumsfeld "would ask Socratic questions rather than take a position," which irked and frustrated Powell.[23]

Powell, in contrast, would remain quiet, even on issues where he had qualms. Rumsfeld noted that Powell did not speak up in internal meetings to express concerns, if he had them, on the wisdom of invading Iraq. In discussing the war, Rumsfeld later said, "There's a lot of stuff [in] the press that say Colin Powell was against it. But I never saw even the slightest hint of that." Rumsfeld also expressed a level of frustration when discussing Powell's non-confrontational method. "My Lord, he's the guy who had more experience than anyone else. He worked hard with George Tenet, with Condi Rice. He prepared his speech. He went up to the U.N. He made his case. And he wasn't lying. The idea that he was lying or duped is nonsense."[24]

Just as Rumsfeld and Powell had differing internal takes on disagreement, they also had differing external strategies. Rumsfeld would issue "snowflakes," memos to the bureaucracy expressing his perspectives through a series of queries that the staff would have to address. The questions were not just idle musings. Rather, according to Rice, they "implicitly—and sometimes explicitly—criticized what State or the NSC was doing." Even if the memos did not challenge the decisions made in internal meetings, "they left the impression that it was Don imparting new wisdom or making an important recommendation."[25]

Powell's approach to the rivalry was more traditional: he leaked. Powell had excellent relations with the press and used them to advance his point of view on administration deliberations. As Rumsfeld complained, "There was a lot of leaking out of the State Department, and the president knew it." The leaking, Rumsfeld felt, had a purpose: "most of it ended up making the State Department look good." The leaking went to both the daily press but also to the first draft of history, in the form of *Washington Post* reporter Bob Woodward's ongoing chronicles of the Bush administration. As ex–Pentagon and White House aide Matt Latimer later noted, Woodward's books "tended to heavily favor Condi Rice and Colin Powell's versions of events." As Washington insiders had long understood, Woodward's books treated those who leaked the information much better than those who did not. In a classic sign of one hand scratching the other, Latimer noted that Woodward later returned the favor, pressing his friend—and source—Powell for secretary of Defense early in the Obama administration. Rice also agreed that State was a prime source of leaks, but she thought that the department was foolishly misguided. As Rice put it, "I could never understand why it was career-enhancing for State to tell the press that Colin was losing every bureaucratic battle." This was more so given that it was not true: "In fact," she wrote, "State was winning its share."[26]

As Rumsfeld noted, choosing not to leak to the press put him at a disadvantage: "We didn't do that in the Pentagon. I insisted we not do it." Rumsfeld made a similar claim in his memoir, stating that he had "made a point of repeatedly telling those I worked with at the Pentagon not to speak to the press against State, the CIA, the White House, or any members of the administration—no matter how strong the temptation." Like Ed Meese in the Reagan administration, Rumsfeld chose to avoid leaking to the press and suffered as a result.[27]

Despite the non-confrontational ethic, Rumsfeld angrily complained to Powell directly about the leaking. According to Rumsfeld's memoir, State leaks "were so brazen that I finally mentioned them to Powell," saying, "Colin, we have a problem." His specific concern was that Deputy Secretary Armitage "was again feeding the press his version of the events." (Note the "again.") An angered Rumsfeld recalled telling Powell, "Armitage has been badmouthing the Pentagon all over town. It's been going on for some time and it's only gotten worse." Rumsfeld added, "I don't know what the hell is in Armitage's craw, but I'm tired of it." Powell could also grow angry at his contretemps with Rumsfeld, telling Rice at one point that "One of us needs to go."[28]

Powell's response to the accusation was noncommittal, as usual. Powell told Rumsfeld that "he would look into it," and then charged that Rumsfeld's deputy Paul Wolfowitz was doing some leaking of his own. Unsurprisingly, little came of the accusation and counter-accusation exchange. As Undersecretary for Policy Doug Feith explained, "It is true that there were policy differences between them (and among others at those meetings), but their personal interactions tend to be cordial and their policy differences generally produced no actual clash." The Powell-Rumsfeld fights took place in many fora, but rarely face-to-face.[29]

Feith remembers an instructive example of their non-direct confrontation. At one point, Rumsfeld was so annoyed by anonymous State Department sniping about Rumsfeld's memos that he decided to take matters into his own hands. He began handing his memos directly to Powell, signaling that anyone else who saw the memos would have received them from Powell, thereby making Powell responsible for any press leaks about their content. According to Feith, this strategy was effective, as "Nasty comments about Rumsfeld memos soon subsided...." As this episode shows, the fighting between the two men was taking place on many levels, as each combatant sought to get the edge on the other through almost every means—apart from actually discussing their problems with one another.[30]

## Real Hatred, Real World Implications

The internal rivalries in the Bush national security team would have real world implications. As Rice noted, "Leaks are debilitating, sowing distrust among the officials who have to work together and coloring the president's options." The lack of trust made it harder to have honest conversations among senior level officials. As Rice, who was supposed to manage the process, complained, "the president knew that Don and Colin did not get along, and decision making was difficult." Over time, as things got more complicated in Iraq, matters worsened. As Rice put it, "My task was to work around the personal distrust between the two men, a task that became harder as the problems became more difficult."

The lack of trust made for an inferior process. Rumsfeld disliked principals meetings—the high-level meetings designed to frame decisions for the president—but Rice observed that his warring with Powell ironically increased the need for principals meetings: "we would have had fewer Principals meetings had the distrust between Don and Colin not made the levels below the secretaries largely incapable of making decisions." According to Rice, Rumsfeld did not trust the Pentagon bureaucracy and second-guessed his own lieutenants, which further contributed to the need for additional meetings at the principals level. Decisions made at the deputy level were not really decisions if the cabinet officials would not accept them. As Rice wrote, "The atmosphere in the Pentagon was one where nothing was really settled until the secretary had opined."[31]

A problematic process led to problematic decisions. The war in Iraq did not go well. State and Defense should have cooperated on rebuilding Iraq, with Defense supplying security and State building a civil society and effective governance structures. Instead, Iraq descended into civil war, and State and Defense engaged in mutual finger-pointing. While the successful 2007 "surge" of U.S. troops helped reassert American control, it came after too many years of bloodshed and internal U.S. disagreements. At this point, though, both Rumsfeld and Powell were gone. Powell left after Bush's first term, thinking that Rumsfeld would be leaving as well. When Powell learned that Rumsfeld was staying, he tried to remain in place, but it was too late. Bush kept Rumsfeld but would replace Powell with Rice. Rumsfeld himself lasted until the next election and was replaced after Republicans lost control of Congress in November of 2006.

## The Vice President's Office

The Bush national security rivalries would also have deeply personal implications. The strange thing about internal rivalries is that they take place among people who nominally are on the same team. Disagreements, even if intense, should theoretically never get too personal. The combatants in earlier administrations might have leaked against one another, tried to advance themselves at the expense of others, or even tried to get rivals fired or moved, but the actions came within limits. George Marshall chose never to speak Clark Clifford's name, and Larry Speakes tried to make David Gergen look bad with a diminishing nickname, but rivals have not sought to destroy one another permanently. Most see each other on a day to day basis and tend to have relatively pleasant interactions face to face. This changed in the Bush administration, as the rivalries intensified and the stakes behind the disputes became higher than ever.

One Bush administration dispute stands out. As with so many earlier internal administration fights, it began with a leak. In 2003, a former

U.S. ambassador named Joe Wilson wrote a *New York Times* op-ed bitterly criticizing the Bush administration's Iraq War policies. Shortly afterwards, a Robert Novak column reported that Wilson's wife was a CIA operative named Valerie Plame. Leaking the name of a covert CIA operative is against the law, and the Justice Department launched an investigation to learn who had leaked Plame's name and position.[32]

The identity of the leaker would not remain secret. Shortly after Justice started the investigation, Novak wrote a column giving readers clues regarding the identity of the leaker, noting that he was a "senior administration official" and "not a partisan gunslinger." Armitage read the column in October of 2003 and immediately recognized himself as the source. He even called Powell, his boss, to tell him that "I'm sure he's talking about me." The State Department then notified the Justice Department—meaning that Justice was aware that Armitage was the leaker at the outset of the investigation—but the investigators pointedly did not inform the White House Counsel that Armitage had leaked the information. Incredibly, Powell and Armitage admitted intentionally withholding this information from the White House Counsel for fear of being embarrassed in the internal disputes between State, Defense, and the White House.[33]

The implications of this intentional omission were staggering. By not revealing that Armitage was the leaker, Powell and Armitage allowed Justice's investigation to continue. Attorney General John Ashcroft recused himself from the investigation, leading Deputy Attorney General James Comey to appoint Patrick Fitzgerald to pursue the matter. Even though Fitzgerald knew from the outset that Armitage was the leaker, he continued to investigate, grilling White House aides including Karl Rove, Andy Card, and the vice president's Chief of Staff Lewis "Scooter" Libby about the leak. During those grillings, Libby's recollection of events differed from some of Fitzgerald's other witnesses, including *New York Times* reporter Judy Miller. Miller later revealed that Fitzgerald both pressured her to give testimony damning of Libby and withheld information that would have exonerated Libby. She later recanted the testimony that helped get Libby convicted for lying under oath and sentenced to thirty months in prison, a $250,000 fine, and the loss of his law license. Bush would commute Libby's sentence so he served no jail time—he was pardoned by President Donald Trump in 2018—but the whole episode might never have taken place had Armitage publicly admitted what he had done. Armitage watched the entire episode from the sidelines as his colleague, albeit one with whom he had disagreed, was convicted of a crime that should never have been investigated in the first place. This was truly a new low in the history of White House internal strife.

It is therefore unsurprising that Cheney had little use for Comey when they sat next to each other at a cabinet meeting. This was shortly after Comey had made the decision to appoint Fitzgerald. According to Comey, he introduced himself to Cheney saying, "Mr. Vice President, I'm Jim Comey from Justice." Cheney did not even look at Comey and said, "I know. I've seen you on TV," taking a swipe at Comey's well-deserved reputation for being a publicity seeker. Cheney then continued to ignore Comey as they waited awkwardly for the meeting to begin.[34]

Cheney's aides could play rough as well. The best-known internal brawler on the Cheney team was David Addington, Cheney's chief counsel and later his chief of staff. A former CIA lawyer, Addington was famous for being willing to engage in bureaucratic tussles to get his way. Addington recognized that imposing a cost on opposition to policies he and the vice president advocated was an effective internal tool. He and Comey would lock horns on the issue of post 9/11 surveillance plans. In one White House meeting, Comey asserted that "no lawyer could rely upon" a 2001 Department of Justice opinion justifying an NSA surveillance program. Addington stepped in, saying, "I'm a lawyer and I did." Comey claims to have stared at the vice president as he responded to Addington, "no good lawyer."[35]

Dislike for Addington and the White House's approach to the surveillance programs led "St. Jim," as Comey was referred to by those who disliked him, to submit a classified memo officially laying out Comey's and Justice's objections to the "Stellar wind" surveillance program.

Doing this created a permanent record, and in Comey's own words, was a "jerk move." Comey justified himself in this course of action, saying "the time to be a jerk was now."[36]

Addington angered others in the administration as well. His hardball approach earned him the internal nickname Keyser Söze, after the ruthless, mysterious mob boss in the 1995 film, *The Usual Suspects*. Addington was adamant about protecting America from future attacks at all costs. Unlike Powell and Rumsfeld, however, he was not shy about confrontation to get his way. Juleanna Glover, a former Addington colleague in the vice president's office, described him as "efficient, discreet, loyal, sublimely brilliant, and, as anyone who works with him knows, someone who, in a knife fight, you want covering your back." Those on the other side, who came up against Addington in bureaucratic disagreements, could even face exile. The *New Yorker*'s Jane Mayer listed five lawyers, including Comey, who found themselves leaving either the White House or the administration after coming up against Addington. Even his friends were not spared. In one incident, he and his ally Berenson got in such a heated altercation that other aides heard fists banging against desks behind a closed door.[37]

Addington was not the only person willing to play hardball in the Bush administration. In fact, in 2007, Addington would find himself "Addingtoned" by another skilled player, White House chief of staff Josh Bolten. Addington had encouraged the vice president to sign on to an *amicus curiae* brief in favor of a strict Second Amendment position on the Supreme Court's case, *D.C. vs Heller*, which looked at the constitutional scope of gun control legislation inside the District of Columbia. This position was contrary to that taken by the administration in the solicitor general's brief on the case. Unhappy with this apparent act of disloyalty to the administration, and with the president's permission, Bolten went to see Cheney and told him that signing the brief had been "a process foul," still a grave sin on the domestic side of the Bush White House. Cheney explained to Bolten that he had acted in his "capacity as *president of the Senate*," rather than as vice president. Bolten then went to see Addington and took Addington to task on the issue. Addington made the same argument, explaining to Bolten that he was paid by the Senate, not the White House. Bolten's stark reply made his displeasure clear: "Understood, but if we have another episode like this, I will make sure that all of your belongings and your mail are forwarded to your tiny office in the Senate and you won't be welcome back inside the gates of the White House."[38] Bolten was a tough bird. Former White House aide Matt Latimer likened meeting with him to getting "a proctology exam from a doctor with cold hands."[39] He clearly had no patience for legalistic games when it came to the White House policy process.

The Bolten-Addington incident was indicative of a notable change that had taken place in the last years of the administration. While Cheney was indeed a dominant player in the administration's first six years, his influence waned after Bolten ascended to the position of chief of staff. On several issues far more significant than the Heller case, such as negotiations with North Korea and whether to bomb the Syrian nuclear reactor, Bush acted in ways that were contrary to Cheney's preferences. Towards the very end of the administration, when Cheney insisted that Bush pardon Libby, President Bush, acting in part on Bolten's advice, refused to do so.[40]

## Unknown Unknowns: The Strangest Rivalry

Bush clearly knew about the fights on his national security team. There was too much noise in the press, Rice was too close to him not to have spoken up, for him not to have known. He would even joke about the tensions in front of Powell and Rumsfeld themselves.[41] And Bolten clearly let Bush know that he planned to address the Addington-Cheney issue. But it is also clear that while Bush knew about the Powell-Rumsfeld-Rice-Cheney infighting, he chose not to address it in a meaningful way, given what the nation was facing after 9/11. It does make some sense that he, as a former governor with limited foreign policy experience, would be reluctant to shed himself of seasoned foreign policy advisors.

Furthermore, Bush would be far from the only president unwilling to act in the face of warring aides. Some presidents, including Clinton and Carter, even intentionally kept in-fighting aides together, hoping to get better results from the creative tension than they could from aides marching in lockstep.

This does not mean that things were perfect in the Bush presidency on the domestic side of the house. The Bush administration domestic shop did score well on the three factors that limit internal disagreement: the president had little patience with it; the administration was broadly conservative; and process was taken seriously. But even here, sometimes surprising challenges appeared.

The strangest rivalry in the Bush administration was one that the president did not know about until it was featured prominently in a venerable American magazine. It took place within the Bush speechwriting team, which got high marks for not only its work but also its teamwork. Bush received a lot of criticism in the press, with the notable exception of the speechwriting shop. As it turned out, though, some elements of teamwork were missing, something discovered in an ugly public way.

Throughout Bush's first term, his top speechwriter, former Senate aide Michael Gerson, earned praise as one of the all-time great speechwriters. Gerson headed a famed "troika" of speechwriters who marched in lockstep creating Bush's best-known remarks circulated both inside and outside of the administration. The speechwriting team of Gerson, Matthew Scully, and John McConnell wrote the president's most important speeches in an unusually collaborative manner, with the three of them crafting and recrafting in front of a single screen until they got things right.

In this case, however, the team was a team in name only. Gerson himself got glowing press throughout the administration. Those press accolades stuck in the craw of Gerson's colleagues, but their unhappiness did not make it into the press or even White House gossip. This impression of unity in the speechwriting shop ended in September of 2007, when

Scully, with little advance public warning, published a 10,000-word piece in *The Atlantic* eviscerating Gerson. In Scully's telling, Gerson was a shameless credit-grabber who diminished his own colleagues while advancing himself. Scully went on in tremendous detail describing episodes in which Gerson had taken credit for something written by the "troika," and how he went out of his way to highlight himself as the sole speechwriter to journalists and to the senior staff. The examples abounded: Gerson would try to prevent his colleagues from emailing with senior staff so that upper management would think only Gerson had worked on the speech. Gerson would fail to introduce colleagues to prominent journalists like E. J. Dionne. While colleagues worked away on speeches, Gerson would be visiting with reporters to explain the speechwriting process. Scully even charged that the phrase "pulling a Gerson" had come to mean taking credit for work not one's own.[42]

The piece was remarkably well-crafted, as if Scully wanted to highlight his impressive talents while going after a colleague he felt had diminished them. Yet if Scully expected that the world would shower him with accolades and acknowledge him as the real genius behind Bush's speeches, he would be disappointed. There was little external impact on Gerson's successful post–White House life. He did not lose his *Washington Post* column, which Scully had cited as evidence that "the Washington establishment has raised him up as one of its own." Gerson defenders such as Peter Wehner wrote in *National Review* that Gerson was a generous boss who shared credit with others, including, Wehner showed, with Scully on multiple occasions. Journalist Tim Noah, covering the affair for *Slate*, read the piece, and concluded, "Memo to self: Be nice to Matthew Scully." Noah guessed that Scully was jealous that Gerson scored a syndicated column while Scully had tried and failed to do so. Peter Baker did some digging and reminded readers that Scully had previously trashed his colleagues in the first Bush administration, writing in the *Washington Post* that Bush had "a staff of self-promoters" well-practiced in "sycophancy and self-aggrandizement." *The Atlantic* piece raised questions about hiring someone with a history of undercutting his own team in public. The entire ugly episode left both men sullied. Still, if Scully's motivation had been to raise questions about the myth of Gerson as the solitary genius behind Bush's best-known speeches, he had certainly chosen a forum and a method for successfully doing so.[43]

As the Scully-Gerson incident demonstrates, even a president who is interested in limiting internal strife may find it hard to do so. The Bush administration shows that a president can have little tolerance for back-biting, be adamant on process, and even encourage ideological comity, and still be whipsawed by internal rivalries in the snake pit that is the modern White House. Sometimes it is external events, such as a foreign policy crisis, that can upset carefully laid plans. At other times, it can be something as simple as an ambitious staffer who gets better press than jealous colleagues can tolerate.

# CHAPTER 11

# BARACK OBAMA
## Conflict in the Era of "No Drama Obama"

There is a momentary historical challenge in writing about the staff tensions in the administration of Barack Obama. The official oral histories do not yet exist, and staff memoirs and other histories are only now starting to trickle out; there will be more in the years ahead. The big story is over, but many of the smaller stories are still being written.

Another aspect to the challenge is the administration's belief that it was above rivalries. Obama pushed the idea of himself as "No Drama Obama," someone with little patience for internecine warfare. Obama's staff picked up the No Drama mantle, emphasizing in both off- and on-the-record conversations how little staff tension they saw in the Obama administration. In addition, they stressed how they consciously looked to avoid the inner turmoil that plagued recent Democratic White Houses and presidential campaigns such as those of Bill Clinton and John Kerry. As Dan Pfeiffer, a senior aide in the Obama White House, wrote, "A number of our staff were veterans of the Kerry campaign, which was known for a poisonous culture of leaks, backstabbing, and jockeying for power and access. This was not something we could risk repeating. We didn't."[1]

Pfeiffer was fundamentally correct in his assessment about the Kerry campaign. It was legendary for its internal fights. In one story that was infamous within Democratic circles, veteran communications aide Howard Wolfson started work at the Kerry campaign on a Monday and was so unhappy with the poisonous atmosphere there that he left for lunch on that Wednesday, never to return.[2]

The Obama team was determined to be different—because Obama was determined to be different. Obama had a burning desire to win, but he also had a strong distaste for disagreement and contentiousness. As Pfeiffer told campaign staffers, they should work under the following guidelines: "Loyal to one another, total commitment to a cause, empowerment and inclusion, and no leaks." Obama's senior team vigilantly policed these standards in its selective hiring and management of the campaign: "People who didn't adhere to these principles didn't get through the door, and the few that did ended up working a backwater field office in a noncompetitive state."[3]

Other rules Pfeiffer detailed specifically aimed at minimizing conflict included "No a\*\*holes," and "No leaks." On the first point, Pfeiffer stressed the need for staffers to be "nice." Specifically, they wanted no prima donnas on the team. When it came to leaks, Pfeiffer reinforced that this rule came straight from the top, noting that "Barack Obama famously hates leaks." Pfeiffer noted only one instance during the campaign in which there had been an unauthorized anonymous quote from a senior campaign official in the press and, even in that circumstance, "we found that person. . . ." As a result of this team focus and discipline, Pfeiffer declared that "Our 2008 campaign was famously leak-free."[4] This claim was not just a belief of the Obama campaign staff. Journalists saw it as well. In June of 2008, *Politico*'s Ben Smith and David Paul Kuhn noted in a passage typical of the media coverage at the time that Obama's "campaign has been a model of leak-free discipline and clear lines of authority."[5]

Kuhn and Smith further observed that the Obama campaign team also aimed to eradicate one of the underlying causes of leaks: a poor process. One thing that leads to leaks is a process that leaves participants feeling as if their voices are unheard—and that rivals' voices are heard. Having seen process challenges lead to infighting and leaking in earlier Democratic administrations and presidential campaigns, the Obama team had a blunt and profane rule about this: "Don't f*** the structure." As Pfeiffer put it, "This was a core principle of the management of the campaign." What they meant by this was that "If you had a concern or an idea, you were obligated to go through the chain of command." The Obama campaign was serious and unforgiving on this point. According to Pfeiffer, "If someone went into [campaign manager David] Plouffe's office with a complaint or concern without going through the proper channels, they were ushered out and not welcomed back."[6] Obama's focus on a clean process was something that would carry over to the White House as well. As Obama speechwriter David Litt recalled in his memoir of his time in the White House, "Obama's process was defined not by infighting or caution but by an ironclad if unwritten rule: Everyone stayed in their lane."[7]

The rules Pfeiffer described worked to an impressive degree. The combination of a principal actively opposed to conflict and a team committed to putting aside egos and jockeying for the sake of winning can go a long way in minimizing some of the backbiting that has characterized other administrations. But another factor, found in places like Pfeiffer's account but also conversations with Obama aides, was the commitment of the Obama team to the "No Drama Obama" narrative. A similar dynamic took place in Bush 43 as well, with the comments from White House aides like Karl Rove, Tim Goeglein, and John DiIulio about the comity among the Bush domestic policy team. Many smart political teams have understood that not only is minimization of conflict a political good, but so is a public narrative about presenting a disciplined and united front.

Obama aides also tend to stress the degree to which they all got along *with Obama*. There is a familial tone to many of the early Obama memoirs, with aides noting the ways that they admired and looked up to the president. To be sure, reverence towards the principal is a common thread in many—although certainly not all—White House staff memoirs, but the Obama team seemed to go even further than was typical. Obama deputy chief of staff Alyssa Mastromonaco recalled in her memoir that Obama called her to wish condolences over the death of her beloved cat. Mastromonaco appreciated the call, and even teared up over it, but she also felt that in the "grand scheme of things I knew that I did not rank." As she put it, describing her boss in the most glowing terms, "Barack Obama, graduate of Columbia University and Harvard Law School, broker of normalized relations between the United States and Cuba, and the nation's first black president, does not have time to call a 39-year-old woman to offer his condolences for the loss of her cat."[8]

Finally, and in contrast to the Clinton administration, Obama's team had less of a fundamental ideological conflict. There are always going to be differences, to be sure, but Obama was a representative of the left side of the Democratic Party. He had challenged Hillary Clinton from the left, and famously had the most liberal voting record in the United States Senate during his brief time there.[9] In the Obama administration, there was less tension between the moderates of the Democratic Leadership Council and the liberals who dominated the administration because Obama, unlike Bill Clinton, had not needed the DLC to get elected. The Obama administration presented a moderate facade to a liberal ideology and had little internal dissent on the overarching point, even if there were disagreements on specific policies. In this way, going into the administration, the Obama team appeared to have absorbed the three key lessons of minimizing conflict: a commitment to build an ideologically unified team; a clear and fair policy and management process; and a principal who frowned on internal strife—and his team knew it.

And yet, as the history of every administration has shown, there is always going to be some degree of conflict and friction. The Obama team stayed together for the most part during the 2008 campaign, but keeping comity in an administration is more challenging. Once an administration begins, the stakes are much higher from both a personal and a policy standpoint. Career-defining jobs are on the line, and policy decisions matter and have real-world implications. Pfeiffer himself notes that once the election was over, he was more prone to violate some of the rules he so carefully adhered to during the campaign. In one telling instance during the transition, Pfeiffer was approving press releases and noted the announcement of a new White House communications director, the very job he wanted and expected. He was unhappy both with the decision and the way he found out about it: "Not only did I not get it, but this was the professional equivalent of being broken up with via a Post-it note. This was messed up."[10]

The new White House communications director was Ellen Moran. Pfeiffer would serve as her deputy. Not only had Moran not been on the campaign, but she had supported Hillary Clinton over Obama in the primaries. "I went into a blind rage," Pfeiffer confessed. "I sent several tirades masquerading as emails to the people well above me on the food chain," a clear violation of the "Don't f*** the structure" maxim he emphasized in his memoir. Moran lasted only a few months—having a frustrated deputy did not help—at which point Pfeiffer was again passed over, this time for Anita Dunn. Dunn also did not last long, and Pfeiffer eventually got the job he wanted before the first year was out. Tellingly, Pfeiffer does not even mention Moran by name in his memoir. This absence suggests that he was not fully over the incident in 2018 when his memoir came out, ten years after the snub took place.[11]

## The Gender Divide

As Pfeiffer's experience shows, there are always going to be dustups, even in a "no drama" administration. Yet, surveyed over the full eight years, the Obama team was successful in avoiding any single, defining conflict between powerful and well-entrenched aides. There was no Baker versus Meese, no Kissinger versus Rogers, no Brzezinski versus Vance, let alone anything even close to LBJ versus RFK. Nevertheless, the Pfeiffer incident showed something new at work, internal tensions based on a gender divide. Press reports suggested that Pfeiffer, who was a more traditional pick for the communications director role given his having held the position on the campaign, was passed over because of higher level concerns that there were too many male staffers in the press and communications shops.[12]

Binders full of men indeed dominated the Obama campaign. Anita Dunn, who did hold a senior role on that 2008 Obama campaign, noted the challenge that women faced in trying to get top jobs in the Obama White House. As Dunn told the *Washington Post* in 2009, "If you didn't come in from the campaign, it was a tough circle to break into. Given the makeup of the campaign, there were just more men than women."[13]

The gender differences manifested in multiple ways. Given the dearth of women from the core campaign team, the Obama transition had to bring in women from the outside, such as Moran, who had not even had a role on the Obama team after the party coalesced around Obama following the primaries. Bringing in new people in this way could alienate those passed over for top jobs, such as Pfeiffer, which in time set them up for likely failure. Apparently, this happened to Moran, who left after a few months for a job as chief of staff at the Department of Commerce, not a typical career move for a top communications aide at the White House.

Another female outsider brought in with little experience in Obama-world was the economist Christina Romer. A well-known economist from the University of California at Berkeley, Romer was Obama's first chair of the Council of Economic Advisers (CEA). Romer was not only new to the Obama team, but she was also new to the sharp-elbowed and tight-knit group of Obama economic advisers, which included Larry Summers, Gene Sperling, Tim Geithner, and Alan Krueger. These advisers had long histories together, dating back to the Clinton administration, and, club-like, played competitive tennis matches together. Noam Scheiber, who chronicled their relationships on and off the tennis court, characterized their intense interactions as a "frivalry." The legendary tennis coach Nick Bollettieri, whose tennis academy some of the "frivals" attended annually, observed about them that "Those guys are very, very competitive.... Holy sh*t. There's no friendship on the friggin' court. They want to beat the sh*t out of everybody."[14]

Unsurprisingly, it was hard for an outsider, and a woman, like Romer to join this closed circle. As Romer complained to the *New Yorker*'s Ryan Lizza, "I'm the quintessential outsider here."[15] Reporters often highlighted tensions between Romer and Summers, who was Obama's director of the National Economic Council (NEC). Friction between the CEA head and the NEC director is common, as the lines of authority make it unclear who is, in fact, the chief economic advisor. The NEC head is supposed to run the economic policy process, while the CEA head supplies economic advice and guidance from a team of academic economists. The NEC head is typically closer to the president, while the CEA head usually has a more impressive academic pedigree. This was not the case under Obama, as Summers was not only assertive in the policy process, but he was also a well-known academic economist in his own right from a family of famous economists.

Romer and Summers clashed early on over Obama's controversial stimulus package. This was one of the administration's first big legislative initiatives, and, as it turned out, one of only a handful of major pieces of legislation to pass on Obama's watch, along with the Affordable Care Act and the Dodd-Frank banking regulations. The clashes between Summers and Romer began over classic sources of White House tension, policy, and process. On the policy side, Romer argued in favor a larger stimulus, well over a trillion dollars, to get the economy moving. Summers, in contrast, felt that such a large package would never pass Congress. As head of the policy process, Summers worked to keep out Romer's larger number from the memo on the subject that made its way to the president.[16] Even if Summers was right about the politics, excluding Romer's recommendation was using control of the policy process to exclude her perspective, a process no-no in the Obama White House.

Summers's hard-ball decision was saddled with gender-related baggage. As president of Harvard in the 2000s, Summers had openly speculated that women might be less represented in the sciences because they had less of an aptitude for the hard sciences. Summers's speculations led to his humiliating ouster as Harvard president in 2006. The incident would make him particularly vulnerable to accusations of gender bias. Romer did just that. She suggested that Summers was excluding her from meetings because she was a woman. This was a dangerous charge to make in the Obama White House, and Summers shot back at her, "Don't you threaten me." "Don't you bully me," Romer responded, and she went to White House chief of staff Rahm Emanuel to demand that she wouldn't be excluded from meetings in the future.[17]

Romer won that battle with Summers. Going forward, Emanuel assured her that she would be able to attend economic policy meetings. But as it turned out, neither she nor Summers would be long for the White House. Summers's departure, which needed to happen before January of 2011 to keep his coveted tenured status at Harvard, appeared long-planned and voluntary. But Romer's departure tale was more out of the ordinary. Late in the summer of 2010, she voiced some concerns about her role on the White House staff. Perhaps seeking affirmation, she suggested to some senior staff, "Well, maybe I should leave." The response she got may not have been what she was looking for: "Let's announce it." Romer had planned to stay through January but left in September due to this hurried effort to announce a departure that she had not planned. Noam Scheiber, the best chronicler of the travails of the Obama economic team, suggests that the top staff at the White House considered her "shrill" and incompetent, which hastened the acceptance of her exit. The fights with Summers did not help much, either, but the result of her search for a supportive word was a shove out the door. Scheiber quotes an anonymous White House aide who acknowledged Romer's rushed departure: "I think she ended up feeling pushed."[18]

Romer was not the only female White House aide who felt she was a victim of gender-based treatment in the Obama administration. Mastromonaco, for example, admitted to being "starstruck" over her first encounter with Summers, which she called "one of many nerdy celebrity sightings at the transition office." Her mooning ended quickly, however, when Summers "whirled around and asked me to get him a Diet Coke." Mastromonaco was mortified, as her "admiration turned to contempt. The gall! The nerve! The bad man! I was so offended."[19]

Mastromonaco's reaction to Summers's request was revealing. While she did "begrudgingly" get him that Diet Coke—Summers would later keep a refrigerator full of the product in his White House office—she also "decided to write him off forever as a douche bag." She resolved to register her pique, in a passive-aggressive way by, as she confessed, "rolling my eyes (internally) every time he spoke." At times, she would even let herself give an occasional eye roll externally. Mastromonaco did eventually warm up to Summers, who helped her understand technical economic concepts, but her first reaction to the Diet Coke offense was telling.[20]

The women of the Obama White House saw themselves as a team among themselves. There was a regular dinner of female Obama senior staffers where they discussed issues specific to being women working at senior levels in the administration. According to Mastromonaco, the purpose of the dinners was "To support one another through the gender imbalance in the West Wing." The senior staff women even had a gender specific name for themselves, "the Vagiants." This gynocentric self-designation was off-putting to some of the pro-Obama but less senior aides not in the Vagiant club. As Obama stenographer Beck Dorey-Stein wrote, "Why does 'Vagiant' make me feel bad...I wouldn't especially love it if the men in the West Wing nicknamed themselves the 10-Inch Senior Staffs." The Vagiants also appeared to have certain privileges not granted to other aides. As Dorey-Stein observed, with more than a touch of envy regarding their leave to wear brighter colors than lower-level White House staffers could, "Only the Vagiants can wear any shade from the J. Crew catalog."[21]

The "Vagiants" joined together in an alliance to advance the ideas of women in the administration. The tactic they adopted was named "amplification." It called for the women to echo the views of other women, and specifically to agree with comments other female aides made in meetings. The *Washington Post*'s Juliet Eilperin took note of the amplification stratagem and wrote that "it forced the men in the room to recognize the contribution—and denied them the chance to claim the idea as their own." Eilperin also quoted Obama senior advisor Valerie Jarrett's approving comment on these efforts: "It's fair to say that there was a lot of testosterone flowing in those early days. Now we have a little more estrogen that provides a counterbalance."[22]

The Obama women would also occasionally pursue gender-specific crusades, often to the confusion of the men with whom they worked. Mastromonaco, for example, spends three pages detailing her ongoing effort to get a tampon dispenser placed in the women's bathroom in the West Wing. At the end of this successful effort, she announced it at the White House senior staff meeting. She admits that none of the male staffers opposed the idea, and with her announcement they offered no opinions on the matter. Yet, Mastromonaco was thrilled, saying, "No one said a word, but it felt really good."[23]

Gender-based concerns could elicit other clear violations of the Pfeiffer rules for Obama staffers. When a *New York Times* article noted that Mastromonaco had long managed Obama's "logistical and travel arrangements" and described her—quite senior—position of deputy chief of staff as "responsible for overseeing scheduling, personnel and much more," she interpreted it as a gender-based slight. The article also called her one of a number of "well-regarded women" in senior slots, although the coverage also noted that none of those women were being considered for the position of chief of staff at that time, during the beginning of Obama's second term.[24]

Mastromonaco was extremely unhappy with the article. By her own admission, she "went apesh*t," and griped that if a male aide such as Jim Messina had received a similar appointment, "they would have said he ran the White House." She blamed the *Times* slight on colleagues diminishing her position in conversations with the press and felt that it was an instance of not supporting team members. As she complained in her memoir, "You don't talk about your colleagues on background, and you definitely don't on-the-record them."[25]

Mastromonaco's reaction to the perceived slight did not fit in to the "No Drama Obama" ethic. When she received the offending article in a group email that went to the entire White House senior staff, she "replied-all with a very cutting, infuriated response." White House counsel Kathy Ruemmler "amplified" via reply-all as well, echoing Mastromonaco's concerns. Mastromonaco was still angry, but she thought that was the end of the matter: "I was fuming but I didn't think it was a big deal."[26]

The next day, Obama summoned her to his office. She was not sure why—the White House deputy chief of staff is typically in regular contact with the president, on a wide-ranging set of issues. Obama greeted her with, "So, I hear you sent quite an email." Mastromonaco was surprised by this and "started going over that distribution list in my head to figure out who had narc'd on me," with a thought towards who "deserves another irrational email." Obama sensed what she was thinking and cut off that train of thought, saying, "It doesn't matter who came to talk to me." He then scolded her a bit over the email, telling her that "I could not send emails like that because they—I am paraphrasing—freak everyone out." The message was clear: "When the president of the United States tells you your words are powerful, it can be pretty shocking." She also admitted that she had miscalculated, recalling that "I honestly didn't think anyone would give a sh*t if I sent a snippy email."[27]

The story is revealing on a few levels. It shows that No Drama Obama was a good theory, but it did not always work in practice. One of the ways it broke down was that burgeoning gender consciousness often magnified perceived slights. But also, to his credit, Obama was willing to confront staffers directly to enforce the No Drama Obama rules. He was always willing to make clear that he wanted to keep internal dissent to a minimum. When he fired General Stanley McChrystal over disrespectful comments about senior administration members published in *Rolling Stone*, he called his national security team together to impose order. At the meeting, he made his desire to avoid backstabbing clear, telling the assembled staff that, "If people can't pull together as a team, then other people are going to go. I mean it."[28]

## The Night Stalker

The Obama women may have been unhappy about the number of women compared to men in the Obama White House, but there is little doubt that Obama's most powerful aide was a woman. Senior Advisor Valerie Jarrett knew Barack and Michelle Obama longer than anyone, even before they were married; outlasted and even encouraged the exit of multiple chiefs of staff; and had access to the first couple that most White House aides could only dream of. By day she was a White House aide, attending meetings with the rest of the staff and calling Obama, "Mr. President." At night, however, she would go to the White House residence with the first couple, hang out with them, and revert to calling the president "Barack." Her regular nocturnal opportunities to convey her policy views directly to the president outside the normal channels in this way earned her the nickname of "The Night Stalker."[29]

Jarrett resented the implication that she took advantage of her closeness to the president and first lady. When challenged on this, she denied violating the process, declaring that "If I have something to say, I don't hold back in meetings so I can have a private conversation with the president." She spoke in terms that would resonate with the Obama White House ethos, saying, "I respect the process." While she acknowledged spending time with the first couple in the residence, she claimed that the visits were for friendship, not policy reasons: they would talk about the kids and shows they liked such as *Downton Abbey*.[30]

Other aides contradicted Jarrett's claim of innocuous evening visits. Given her importance in the White House and closeness to the president, they would not do so on the record. Anonymous aides felt that Jarrett kept her own counsel in official meetings during the day, only to make her case to the president in private. This alienated her colleagues, one of whom complained, "If you have a dissenting view, say it in the room. If you want to advocate for something, do it in the room, not later with the president."[31]

One aide who did not cower before Jarrett was Press Secretary Robert Gibbs. Gibbs had worked for Obama's successful Senate campaign in 2004 and continued to advise Obama when he became a senator. Gibbs was known for an aggressive approach to communications, which occasionally ruffled the feathers of both allies and adversaries. Jarrett was one of those who did not like Gibbs's style, and she would tell other aides—and presumably the president and first lady—that Gibbs was overly abrasive in the press secretary role.[32]

Gibbs differed from other aides not only in style but in background as well. Unlike many in the Obama circle, he was not an Ivy Leaguer, having attended North Carolina State, and may have had a bit of a chip on his shoulder about it. In one meeting, when Gibbs and Wisconsin grad Mastromonaco were the lone non–Ivy Leaguers at a meeting of White House economic advisors, Peter Orszag, Princeton '91, asked them if they ever felt out of place in that company. Mastromonaco's face flushed with embarrassment, but Gibbs was defiant, telling Orszag, "Well, we all ended up at the same table, didn't we? Seems like we got a bargain!"[33]

According to the *New York Times* reporter Jodi Kantor, Gibbs and Jarrett had a significant blow up over a problematic quote by Mrs. Obama. While the Obamas were on a trip to France, a story appeared that Michelle told French first lady Carla Bruni-Sarkozy that she found living in the White House to be "hell." The press team scrambled to respond and issued a denial from the first lady, snuffing out the story before it could make much of a splash in the American press. The next day, Jarrett said at the White House senior staff meeting that the first lady was dissatisfied with the response to the "hell" quote. Gibbs, who had been pleased with their successful effort to contain the quote, exploded at Jarrett. Despite Emanuel's effort to hold him off—"Don't go there Robert, don't do it"—Gibbs went there: "F*ck this, that's not right. I've been killing myself on this, where's this coming from?" When he asked Jarrett to get specific about the first lady's complaints, she demurred, angering Gibbs further. "What the f*ck do you mean? Did you ask her?" When Jarrett said something about the speed of the response, Gibbs asked, "Why is she talking to you about it? If she has a problem she should talk to me." Jarrett was unhappy and told Gibbs, "You shouldn't talk like that," which really angered Gibbs. "You don't know what the f*ck you're talking about," he shouted. Jarrett remained preternaturally calm but made sure to show her closeness to the first couple, saying "The first lady would not believe you're speaking this way." This last comment really set off Gibbs, who shouted, "Then f*ck her too," and left the room.[34]

The aftermath of the Gibbs blowup was telling. Emanuel was unusually quiet in response, telling the remaining staff that "Everyone knows Robert has done a really good job on this." The staff agreed not to tell either of the Obamas about the fight, and an unaware Obama even called Gibbs into the Oval Office to let him know that he had done a good job on the "hell" story. As for Gibbs, he later believed that Jarrett made up the fact that Mrs. Obama was unhappy. Gibbs felt that Jarrett had been suggesting that she had inside knowledge of the first lady's thinking when she had not even discussed the matter with her. From then on, Gibbs said, he "stopped taking her at all seriously as an adviser to the president." As Gibbs saw it, Jarrett's "viewpoint in advising the president is that she has to be up and the rest of the White House has to be down."[35] Gibbs would end up leaving after two years, while Jarrett would remain until the end of the administration.

Several of the Chicagoans clashed with Jarrett as well, according to reports. She differed with Obama's first two chiefs of staff, as well as Senior Advisor David Axelrod. Early on, when Axelrod received Secret Service protection because of an active threat, Jarrett insisted on such protection as well.[36] Emanuel, who had a keen understanding of power dynamics, was wary of her from the outset. He tried to get her appointed to Obama's Senate seat so that he would not have to deal with her in the White House. The first lady, who wanted Jarrett nearby, vetoed that plan.[37]

Taking on Emanuel as chief of staff was not for the faint-hearted. A famously tough and profane operator, Emanuel had a legendary temper and expected to run things his way as chief of staff. He had a sign on his desk reading "Undersecretary For Go F*** Yourself"—a gift from his brothers—and was prone to berate younger aides with insults like "Take your f***ing tampon out of your mouth and tell me what you have to say."[38] These kinds of stories abound, and could begin to sound like urban legends, but they were true. As Ben Rhodes wrote about Emanuel, "The caricature of Rahm is that he swore all the time, and he did."[39]

Obama was aware of his tendencies and hired him, nonetheless. Obama once even joked that a childhood accident that sliced off part of Emanuel's middle figure "rendered him practically mute."[40]  On another occasion, Deputy Chief of Staff Jim Messina, who had been hired without Emanuel's approval, had a temper tantrum regarding congressional negotiations over the Affordable Care Act. Obama told him to stop it: "Hey. Stop. Rahm's supposed to be the screamer. You're supposed to be the calm one. Don't switch roles." As the story shows, Obama knew

President Barack Obama meets with former Chief of Staff and Chicago Mayor-elect Rahm Emanuel. The famously profane Emanuel had a sign on his desk reading "Undersecretary for Go F*** Yourself," but would find himself less influential than the softer-spoken friend of the first couple, Valerie Jarrett. *Official White House photo by Pete Souza*

about Emanuel's temper and found it useful, but he also had little patience with similar displays by other staff members.[41]

Given Emanuel's combative nature, aides and outsiders alike bucked him at their peril. Even so, Emanuel was right to be wary of Jarrett. In addition to her tendency to circumvent the process, there was also the problem of her enabling Obama. As one senior aide noted—anonymously—"It's tough to have her around when you're trying to tell the president, 'Well, no, I think this is wrong.' Because she's always there saying, 'Oh, *yes*, it's fine.'" The chief of staff must be able to tell the president no, and Jarrett wanted to keep saying yes.[42]

Emanuel could not compete with Jarrett. Even though he also knew Obama from Chicago, Jarrett's relationship was longer and deeper. Emanuel could have all the profane tantrums he wanted, but Jarrett was closer to the president. It also did not help that Jarrett learned about Emanuel's effort to keep her out of the White House, adding to the distrust between the two. Emanuel left shortly after Gibbs did. As the *Weekly Standard*'s Matthew Continetti joked, Emanuel's struggles with Jarrett "led to Emanuel's sudden discovery that he had always wanted to be mayor of Chicago."[43]

Emanuel spun his departure as completely voluntary. In Brian Abrams's oral history of the Obama administration, Emanuel argued that Obama always knew that Emanuel wanted to return to Chicago to run for mayor. As Emanuel recalled, "So one day Mayor [Richard M.] Daley announced he wasn't running. We talked about it. There's not a lot of intrigue. I moved back to Chicago on October 3, I think it was." Yet Emanuel was also tired of the fighting, not only with Jarrett but with other aides as well. According to some reports, Obama was tired of it as well, not raising much of an objection when Emanuel announced he was leaving.[44]

To replace Emanuel, Obama selected another Chicagoan, William Daley, from the famous Chicago political dynasty. Daley was a surprise choice, both to the staff and to himself. The White House staff saw him as a conservative outsider. Ben Rhodes's description of Daley, starting with his hairlessness, is telling. According to Rhodes, Daley was "a bald, Chicago-accented centrist who'd recently been hired as Chief of Staff to make deals with Republicans."[45]

For his part, Daley had issues with the White House staff as well. According to the journalist Chuck Todd, Daley "had never met a group of people more disdainful of Congress than the White House staff he worked with."[46] Daley also felt like an outsider among them, noting that "even though I knew Valerie and a few others, I wasn't that close with any of the people. Plouffe I didn't know at all. I mean, I met him but didn't pretend to know him." What made things worse was that the team he inherited was not his own, and he had little ability to make changes to the staff. As Daley complained, "the entire team was people who had been together from the very beginning, no doubt about it. That made it difficult, and all the slots were all filled. There was no full-scale sort of change beyond *We'll change the guy at the top—chief of staff role—and see if that makes a big difference.*"[47]

Although Daley faced difficulties with the staff, his biggest challenge was with Jarrett. The problems included minor inconveniences, like having to share a speechwriter with her, as well as more significant ones on policy. The biggest disagreement between them came on the 2011 contraception mandate. Catholic Daley wanted a limited imposition of the requirement that healthcare providers pay for contraceptive coverage. He was particularly concerned with how moderates and Catholics would view an expansive requirement, but that is exactly what Jarrett wanted. When the more expansive version appeared, causing the very political upheaval and controversy that Daley had feared, he called Health and Human Services Secretary Kathleen Sibelius to complain. When Daley asked her why she had acted without White House authorization, she let him know that she had not. At that point, Daley understood what had happened: "It was then made clear to me that, no, there were senior White House officials who had been involved and supported this."[48] As an anonymous White House advisor told the *New York Times* about the president's management of the situation, "Valerie is effectively the chief of staff, and he knows, but he doesn't know." Overall, Daley had even worse relations with Jarrett than Emanuel had. Because of incidents like these, Daley could not even tolerate being in the same room as Jarrett.[49]

After Emanuel and Daley left, Obama took a different approach to his chiefs of staff. Their replacements would have much less confrontational tacks towards the powerful Jarrett, including temporary placeholder Pete Rouse and former budget director Jack Lew. Denis McDonough, Obama's final chief of staff, saw what had happened to his first term predecessors and was much more accommodating of Jarrett. He described Jarrett as an asset rather than a liability to being chief of staff, explaining that, "VJ makes my job easier, not harder. The fact that she's close to the president and to the first lady. That coupled with the fact that she is a consummate professional."[50] McDonough clearly saw the risks of antagonizing her, and instead tried to placate her, a strategy that seemed to work for him.

Other staff members also capitalized on Jarrett's appreciation of flattery. The *New York Times*'s Mark Leibovich reported that after his paper's Jo Becker wrote a critical piece about Jarrett, some White House staffers compiled a sycophantic memo called "The Magic of Valerie," which heaped enough praise on Jarrett to placate a North Korean dictator. Examples included "The magic of Valerie is her intellect and her heart"; "Valerie is the perfect combination of smart, savvy and innovative"; and "Valerie has an enormous capacity for both empathy and sympathy." Leibovich added that his favorite of the 33 (!) bullet points was the incomplete "Valerie is someone here who other people inside the building know they can trust. (need examples.)"[51]

McDonough was a good flatterer, an apparent requirement for the job, but he also had the advantage of being an Obama person. Both Emanuel and Daley were outsiders to Obama world, their Chicago origins aside. In fact, according to 2008 Obama campaign aide and official White House videographer, Arun Chaudhary, "It wasn't until Denis that the Obama inner circle had been represented by a chief of staff." McDonough's close understanding of the Obama world allowed him to manage the Valerie Jarrett dynamic, and to remain in the chief of staff role without some of the pitfalls that had tripped up Emanuel and Daley. Unlike the three chiefs of staff who served in the first term—four if you count interim chief Rouse—McDonough served as Obama's chief of staff, if not his most powerful aide, for the entire second term.[52]

## The Generational Divide

McDonough was not only inner circle, but he also came from the foreign policy side of the operation. He had brought the youthful speechwriter Ben Rhodes onto the Obama team, and he and Rhodes were leading members of the younger generation of Obama foreign policy aides. Chuck Todd, in his history of the Obama White House, characterized Rhodes and McDonough as "the two most political members of the national security team."[53]

The Rhodes-McDonough alliance spoke to an added divide in the administration, a generational one. Older aides, many of whom had worked for Bill Clinton's administration, took a different approach from the younger, often more liberal, Obama aides. Tension between the Obama world and the Clinton team dated back to the struggle between Obama and Hillary for the Democratic nomination. Rhodes recalled being told by a friend that he should not work for Obama, since Clinton foreign policy guru "Richard Holbrooke's keeping a list of everyone who goes to work for Obama."[54]

As it turned out, Holbrooke himself would end up working for Obama. Obama let Secretary of State Hillary Clinton staff the State Department with her loyalists, including Holbrooke, who served as special advisor for Pakistan and Afghanistan. There were some limits, though. She tried to hire poison pen journalist and Clinton fixer Sidney Blumenthal on her team, but David Axelrod vetoed it. Beyond that, though, Clinton had a lot of latitude to select her own team. But that does not mean that Obama and his team embraced Holbrooke and his approach. Once, after a typical Holbrooke policy briefing that was a didactic history lesson, Obama was nonplussed. "Do people really *talk* like that?" he asked.[55]

The locus of Obama's foreign policy came from the White House, not the State Department. One of the most influential players was Rhodes. In a legendary *New York Times Magazine* piece on Rhodes, David Samuels compared Rhodes to Holden Caulfield in J. D. Salinger's *The Catcher in the Rye*, and characterized Rhodes as "the Boy Wonder of the Obama White House." Rhodes's youth aside, he was closely in sync with Obama's foreign policy thinking. As Samuels wrote about Rhodes's links to Obama, "Nearly everyone I spoke to about Rhodes used the phrase 'mind meld' verbatim."[56]

The Obama-Rhodes "mind meld" rejected the older generation of Democratic foreign policy thinking. As Rhodes wrote in his memoir, this younger generation was heavily influenced by Samantha Power, who would serve as an NSC staffer and later Obama's U.N. ambassador. Power had written the Pulitzer Prize–winning book, *A Problem from Hell*, which was a bible of sorts to young foreign policy experts on the left. Power's approach, Rhodes wrote, favored an "interventionist America that promoted human rights and prevented atrocities," while at the same time "standing apart from many liberal interventionists who were co-opted by the Bush crowd."[57]

The differences between the older, more Clintonite, foreign policy hands and the younger, Power-influenced group manifested in several ways. One was on Israel. The younger crowd was far more critical of Israel and much more sympathetic towards the Palestinian argument. Rhodes even admits that his empathetic view of the Palestinians as compared to the Israelis led to Emanuel granting Rhodes the nickname "Hamas," as in "Hamas over here is going to make it impossible for my kid to have his f***ing bar mitzvah in Israel." Some people might have objected to having the name of a terrorist organization as a nickname. Rhodes included the designation in his memoir.[58]

Another important distinction related to the reaction to the Arab Spring. In this case, the older, more experienced hands argued for caution, but the younger Rhodes and Power set wanted to see faster change. Rhodes noted several times that there was a generational aspect to this divide, writing that "The main driver of opinion seemed to be generational, with the younger staff pressing for change." He also observed that his outspoken advocacy for his approach had advantages and disadvantages. In one meeting, where he criticized corrupt autocrats, he observed that "The people at the table sat there grimly; the young people on the back bench loved it. I was inspired by the moment; I was also making enemies."[59]

It's not surprising that Rhodes's disruptive approach made him some enemies. He rejected the Democratic foreign policy establishment in stark terms, referring to it as "The Blob." As Rhodes's friend, Obama speechwriter Jon Favreau, said of him, "He truly gives zero [expletive] about what most people in Washington think." Favreau framed this as a form of high mindedness: "he's always seen his time there as temporary and won't care if he's never again invited to a cocktail party, or asked to appear on 'Morning Joe,' or inducted into the Council on Foreign Relations hall of fame or whatever the hell they do there." (Of course, after the administration, Rhodes became a frequent guest on *Morning Joe*).[60]

In the end, Rhodes's rivalry was not with an individual but with a mindset. He also had the support of his boss the president in taking on the established foreign policy experts. Even when Rhodes overreached, as in his many damning comments about "the blob" and the journalists he manipulated on behalf of the White House, Obama's criticism of him was soft. According to Rhodes, following the Samuels piece, Obama just asked him one question: "Why were you so eager to talk about how the sausage gets made?"[61]

No Drama Obama was fine with Rhodes's drama because it was in pursuit of Obama's foreign policy vision. While Obama did not want to see tension and made it clear to his staff that he had little tolerance for it, in the Obama White House it surfaced in areas where Obama was willing to let it happen. The gender divide is a core aspect of Democratic politics, and Obama couldn't have stopped it even if he was inclined to act. Jarrett was one of his oldest friends and received more leeway than other staffers, especially over those who were not core Obama people. And the foreign policy disagreements stemmed from a fundamental ideological divide within Democratic foreign policy circles. No Drama Obama was theoretically against internal conflict, except when conflict was to his advantage. Then he was not always above the fray.

# THE LESSONS OF FIGHTING AT THE HIGHEST LEVEL

Infighting has been constant in every presidential administration since George Washington. As former White House speechwriter Bill McGurn said in 2018, "All White Houses have internal wars. Most White Houses keep them internal."[1]

Still, internal rivalries have accelerated in the modern presidency, especially with the advent of the high-profile White House staff. With the acceptance of the Brownlow report's recommendations in the late 1930s, a new force was unleashed on the White House grounds. In many ways, Brownlow's determination that the "the president needs help" has helped the presidency but created new challenges for every president since then. It clearly worsened infighting and gave more opportunities for rivals to undercut one another. At the same time, the creation of high-profile White House aides and an all-encompassing media put more scrutiny on the West and East Wings of the White House. This, in turn, raised the stakes for participants.

At the individual level, it is an undisputed fact that a successful star-making role in the White House can lead to riches and many career opportunities. In contrast, a failed White House tenure can lead to tremendous frustration and a lifetime of jealousy, regret, self-doubt, and fewer, if any, future opportunities. The magnitude of the stakes at the individual level helps make rivalries in the White House potentially crippling for a president. When taken with the daily crush of stories about staff dysfunction in the White House, it is not surprising that the casual observer may see interpersonal relations in the White House today as worse than they have ever been.

## Nothing New under the Sun?

While the Trump White House is indeed replete with wild energy and rivalries, it is hard to say from the perspective of the past seventy-five years that any of the current rivalries are worse or more intense than Kissinger-Rogers under Nixon or Vance-Brzezinski under Carter. Furthermore, it is unclear yet whether the rivalries in the Trump White House will match the personal cost felt in some earlier administrations. One hopes that lamentable episodes like the criminal conviction of Lewis "Scooter" Libby stemming from rival Richard Armitage's deliberate silence will be exceptions rather than the rule.

Many of the underhanded tactics used against administration rivals by Trump aides have been deployed before. As with earlier White Houses, most of the nasty tactics had to do with shaping media coverage. In the Trump administration, *Axios*'s Jonathan Swan reported that rivals leak to the press using the vocabulary or diction of others. In the Reagan and Bush administrations, leakers would use big, polysyllabic words like "inchoate" or crutch phrases such as "and the like" to throw suspicion for a leak onto Dick Darman and Don Regan, respectively.

Another reality is the desire for White House staffers to get ahead of any story about themselves. For instance, Trump's first White House press secretary, Sean Spicer, made a point of telling the media he was resigning—not fired. As Spicer wrote in his memoir, "With all of the media reports on White House palace intrigue, one in which backstabbing daggers are fashioned from leaks, somebody would surely try to sell the story that I have been pushed out."[2] In the Carter administration, Mark Siegel resigned over frustrations he faced in making the case for Carter's Middle East policy to the Jewish community, only to have the administration tell the media that he was fired. David Frum would have a similar experience in the George W. Bush administration as his resignation was interpreted by some as a firing.

Even during outbursts and physical threats during routine disagreement, the Trump White House is comfortably in the mainstream of recent history—though a little more colorful. Few were surprised when the story came out that Secretary of Defense James Mattis told Press Secretary Sean Spicer to stop asking him to go on Sunday shows, warning him that "I've killed people for a living. If you call me again, I'm going to f***ing send you to Afghanistan. Are we clear?"[3] In another instance, White House chief of staff and ex-general John Kelly grabbed former Trump campaign manager Corey Lewandowski by the collar and tried to eject him from the White House. In the Ford administration, embattled chief of staff and former general Al Haig physically grabbed an aide to obstreperous Ford advisor Robert Hartmann and told him, "If you have any influence over that fat Kraut, you tell him to knock it off or he's going to be the first stretcher case coming out of the West Wing."[4]

There have also been many cases in which White House players cut each other off and refused to speak. In the Trump world, communications aide Hope Hicks and strategist Steve Bannon halted personal exchanges after they disagreed on the statement President Trump made about Donald Trump Jr.'s meeting with the Russians. In the Truman administration, Secretary of State George Marshall was so angry with Clark Clifford for successfully making the case for recognizing Israel, that he not only stopped speaking to Clifford but never again uttered Clifford's name for the rest of his life. Similarly, Judge William Clark stopped speaking to his fellow Californian Michael Deaver after Deaver opposed Clark's attempt to join the troika atop the Reagan White House and make it into a foursome. Ignoring is never helpful in any White

House, but it is a human tendency, seen among children on playgrounds and old married couples, as well as bitter work rivals.

White House battles, which transcend policy to become personal, are often expressed in verbal abuse. Like earlier administrations, the Trump administration is filled with nicknames and factions, with the Bannonite wing of the White House derisively referring to Jared Kushner and Ivanka Trump as "Jarvanka" and "the Democrats." Trump chief of staff John Kelly called the youthful looking Hope Hicks "the high schooler," and anonymous Trump aides referred to Deputy Chief of Staff Kirstjen Nielsen as "Nurse Ratched" of *One Flew Over the Cuckoo's Nest* fame because of her attempts to impose a buttoned-down policy process. And Trump himself was famous for his use of nicknames against his rivals, something his aides clearly noticed and emulated. Steve Bannon thought that Trump's use of nicknames reflected Carl Jung's *Memories, Dreams, Reflections*, and his nicknames were "Jungian archetypes," or part of Trump's conscious and unconscious mind. Spicer, less pretentiously, said that Trump "was a master of branding and psyching out his opponents by defining them with nicknames that stuck."[5]

Yet nicknaming has long been a tactic among presidential rivals. In the Reagan administration, Larry Speakes admitted in his memoir that he tried to diminish his rival David Gergen by tagging Gergen as "the tall guy," which was later shortened to just "Tall." Obama national security advisor General James Jones called younger national security aides with whom he clashed "the water bugs." While nicknaming is a storied part of White House rivalries, one type of White House nickname was unique to the Trump administration. This was the emoji nickname, which could not have appeared earlier for technological reasons but will certainly appear in the future. In the Trump White House, short-lived but voluble communications aide Anthony Scaramucci was depicted in text messages as 🤪, "Globalist" economic advisor Gary Cohn was 🌍 , and Chief of Staff Reince Priebus, who was often called Prancer, had a reindeer emoji: 🦌.[6]

In the Trump administration, once things get personal, friendships, even existing ones, can go out the window. Trump son-in-law Jared

Kushner was surprised to find that his campaign friendship with Steve Bannon was no longer operational once they had opposing policy views in the White House. Unhappy to be on the receiving end of a series of Bannon leaks, Kushner was supposed to have asked, "What's up with Steve? I don't understand. We were so close."[7] Scaramucci's eventful eleven days in the Trump White House taught him a similar lesson, which he expressed afterwards in the unique style of "The Mooch." When one gets to the White House, he said, "The first pill you take is the 'anti-friendship' pill. You can be my friend for 30 years, but I'm gonna stab your eyeball out with an ice pick if it gets me more power."[8] Even here, though, this kind of distasteful behavior has been witnessed before, as Cy Vance and Zbig Brzezinski had dinner together on the night of Carter's election and talked excitedly about the prospects of working together, only to be at each other's throats throughout the Carter administration. On Day One in the Carter White House, Brzezinski was already demanding that the direct line between the secretary of state and the national security advisor be cut because he worked for the president, not for Vance.

The process is crucial to keeping order in any White House, so it is unsurprising that process manipulation has played a key role in White House infighting under Trump. Bob Woodward famously reported that Gary Cohn would take papers off Trump's desk to prevent policies favored by rival aides from being endorsed by the president. This behavior was not unique in the annals of White House infighting. In the Ford administration, Bob Hartmann was even worse, hovering by the president's desk so that he could intercept documents he disagreed with and pass them to leak-hungry columnists Rowland Evans and Robert Novak. Hartmann would also place papers not previously seen by other staff in front of the president for his signature, thereby completely subverting the internal-staffing process. Hartmann's interventions were so frequent and disruptive that Don Rumsfeld and Dick Cheney launched a strategic gambit to get Hartmann moved away from his perch adjoining the Oval Office.

As is always the case in any organization, absence of an orderly chain of command and well-understood roles and responsibilities made proximity to ultimate authority (in this case the president) the de facto policy process. In the early days of Trump's presidency, Trump's top aides would all travel with him to prevent key policy decisions from being made in their absence. This, too, has happened before. The troika of top aides surrounding Ronald Reagan made sure none of the three would see Reagan alone lest they get private time with the president to make the case against the others. This tendency became so pronounced that other aides saw their continual presence around the president as an opportunity to get things done without interference from the higher ups. Reagan himself recognized what they were up to, joking during the troika's joint visit to Reagan's hospital bed after his shooting that he was not aware they had been planning a "staff meeting."

Working in the White House, Trump aides showed typical awareness of the historical record in conducting their internecine warfare. Sharp-elbowed aide Omarosa Manigault Newman surreptitiously tape-recorded conversations with fellow aides using a recording device hidden in a pen. She even recorded her own firing at the hands of Chief of Staff John Kelly in the secure White House Situation Room. Sean Spicer took such copious notes during his tenure in the White House that a fellow aide told *Axios*'s Mike Allen that "People are going to wish they'd been nicer to Sean.... He was in a lot of meetings."[9]

Here as well, White House tape recordings and copious notes are obviously nothing new. At a far more powerful level, Johnson and Nixon recorded their conversations; the Nixon tapes were key to the Watergate scandal and coverup, while Johnson's tapes remain an excellent guide to politics in Washington. Furthermore, note-taking by future memoirists is old news as well. Richard Nixon used to introduce speechwriter—and author of a later memoir—William Safire by saying, "This is Safire, absolutely trustworthy, worked with us in '60. But watch what you say, he's a writer."[10] Safire, far from irked, liked the quote so much that it adorned the back cover of his memoir, *Before the Fall*. Similarly, Dean Rusk later explained that his depiction as silent and Buddha-like in

Arthur Schlesinger's memoir stemmed from his desire to guard his words in front of the loose-lipped Schlesinger.

Even without electronic means, the "memo to file" has long been a way to memorialize conversations and incidents to protect oneself and undercut others. Undersecretary of State Robert Lovett did this back in the Truman administration with a memo to file that spoke of actions by the "President's political advisers," prompting White House aide Clark Clifford to recall later that "I knew exactly whom Lovett meant when he referred to 'the President's political advisers.'" James Comey did something like this to Vice President Cheney's staff, creating a permanent record of his objections to the "Stellar Wind" surveillance program and even acknowledging that his own action was "a jerk move."

Not only has White House infighting been a relative constant since the advent of the White House staff, the tactics themselves are time-tested. There is just more media attention than ever today, since with the proliferation of smartphones and other electronic means of communication there are more platforms for unscrupulous aides to share their insider perspectives with the media and others.

## The Three-Part Test

The focus on internal administration rivalries raises questions in a democracy. As voters, should we care if Official A hates and undercuts Official B? Is it possible that rivalries in an administration can bring about better results, which Doris Kearns Goodwin suggests? History does not have a pat answer, but disciplined presidents with equally disciplined processes have the potential to get more out of their staffs and mitigate conflict.

What has happened under Trump is a case study in whether infighting as a strategy works. The Trump White House checked the box on all three indicators of internal dissent laid out in the introduction. On the ideological front, the Trump administration had not only the binary conservative versus liberal, but three groups: so-called globalists like economic advisor

Gary Cohn and presidential son-in-law Jared Kushner; traditional Republicans like former chief of staff Reince Priebus; and Trump loyalists like Steve Bannon and Kellyanne Conway. The three groups allied and opposed each another, issue by issue, with the president himself appearing to take different sides at various times. The three groupings, coupled with a continuing uncertainty over the president's ideological leanings, meant that White House infighting had an ideological as well as a personal aspect. Fighting with colleagues can have added value if it increases the odds of getting an ideological win. Furthermore, ideological alliances can paper over personal differences, while ideological disagreements can worsen those differences.

On the process front, the Trump White House has had a more raucous and less orderly approach than some of its predecessors. The creation of two power centers at the beginning, headed by Bannon as senior advisor and Priebus as chief of staff, guaranteed a disorderly process. Following on the initial set up was the president's own willingness to make decisions without following the process, the high turnover of White House personnel, and the lack of experience among many top aides. Subsequent chiefs of staff John Kelly and Mick Mulvaney each tried to impose more order, but the Trump administration has never been a buttoned-down, process-driven entity. As a result, process has mattered less, thereby giving incentive to circumvent the process to achieve policy goals or power.

As for the third factor, presidential tolerance, Trump made it clear in both word and deed that he did not mind unrest on his team. When asked about stories of infighting in the White House, Trump responded that strife did not bother him; he encouraged it. "I like conflict," he told reporters, elaborating that "I like having two people with different points of view. And I certainly have that. And then I make a decision. I like watching it. I like seeing it and I think it is the best way to go."[11]

Critics with short memories may have thought his comments had a component of bluster or rationalization to them, but his actions suggest otherwise. In one amusing story from the campaign, Hope Hicks and press aide A. J. Delgado got in a screaming match about a media mix-up on the campaign plane, Trump Force One, while standing near Trump. Trump was reading a newspaper at the time, but put down the paper long enough to shout, "Cat Fight." He then picked up the paper again and continued reading. This is not the action of a leader who wishes to stamp out arguments among his staff.[12]

Trump's willingness to tolerate fighting continued after the campaign and into his presidency. As Chris Christie, who claimed to have turned down offers for multiple administration roles, described Trump's attitude towards staff warfare: "Donald seemed content to let them all fight it out."[13]

## Method or Just Madness?

Trump's preference for conflict is real, but he also has a competing interest in order. His move to bring in Department of Homeland Security secretary John Kelly as chief of staff in July of 2017 reflected an instinctive, if temporary, interest in a more orderly process, at least until Kelly himself fell out of favor and eventually left at the end of 2018. Even the chaotic eleven-day reign of Scaramucci as communications director found Scaramucci trying—and failing—to end leaking and infighting in the communications shop. In addition, the various efforts to root out and identify leakers, including the search for the anonymous administration author of an anti-Trump *New York Times* op-ed in September of 2018, meant that there were limits to types of dissent that the president and his administration were willing to tolerate. Just as Obama's "No drama Obama" approach did not eliminate infighting in the Obama White House, Trump's "I like conflict" comments, and actions, did not mean that all fighting was, or would be, tolerated. It is a matter of degree and preference set by the president, and Obama and Trump have practiced both approaches as managers and image-conscious leaders.

Trump may be the rare president willing to say, "I like conflict," but other presidents have wanted or tolerated conflict when it suited their purposes. Truman, for example, recognized that Clark Clifford's argument with George Marshall over Israel was "rough as a cob," but he also set up the circumstances in which it happened and supported Clifford. Conflict has a powerful role in American administrations, as in all aspects of life, and is a key takeaway from White House infighting.

Head coaches and managers in sports have long recognized its potential as well. The idea behind putting together a successful team is not to maximize comity but to maximize effectiveness. The success of famously fractious baseball teams like the 1972–1974 Oakland As or the 1977–1978 New York Yankees shows that internal dislikes and disagreements do not preclude great results, and may spur them. In the 2014 Super Bowl, the Seattle Seahawks crushed the Denver Broncos 43–8, even though Seahawks wide receiver Percy Harvin gave teammate Golden Tate a black eye in the week leading up to the game.[14]

In both sports and politics, media attention plays a significant role. Media focus on internal disagreements has increased over time with the twenty-four-hour news cycle and proliferations of media platforms. White House infighting is another form of entertainment to many in the media and increases viewers, readership, and advertisements; on the internet it can also be clickbait. While there is no doubt that the Trump administration has plenty of internal disagreements, the media's intense scrutiny of every disagreement does highlight many disputes that might not have surfaced until the publishing of post-presidency memoires. With the Obama administration, for example, post-administration memoirs revealed plenty of internal fights that few outside the White House knew about while Obama was in the Oval Office.

The American people, over their long history, have a tendency to elect presidents who are the opposite of their predecessors, often in reaction to the previous four or eight years. After the gut-based decision making of the Bush White House in war, the electorate favored Obama's more dovish approach. And after eight years of Obama's insistence on comity within his administration and the country at large, the American people, through the electoral college vote, favored a candidate who appeared to relish conflict, personally and politically.

A president has quite a bit of power in controlling the level of internal disputes that take place within an administration. Some presidents will like creative tension paraded before them, while others will avoid it. Knowing the history behind White House infighting, often portrayed as primetime soap opera by the media, can help leaders in politics, business, or sports understand better the role of conflict and its larger benefits to an organization, but also its capacity to sink the best of leaders.

# Acknowledgments

The idea for this book came from a conversation with Bob Greene of Cazenovia College. He was interviewing me for a book of his own on George W. Bush when he asked me about my next project. This book stemmed from that conversation. Once I had the idea, I started asking my kitchen cabinet what they thought of the concept. Clinton and Obama White House veteran Ken Baer thought it was a "very cool idea"; John McConnell, who worked for both Bushes and has been reading my manuscripts for over two decades, immediately leapt on board; brother and fellow historian Gil Troy said, "I think it's a great idea." And the ever-skeptical Alan Rechtschaffen even said, "I would read that book," thereby sealing the deal.

I also have to thank my informal committee on titles and covers. Dan Huff came up with the title in a flash over a lunch conversation at the home of Sam Melamed. Constant advisor Matt Gerson has been promoted to senior vice president for titles, even though he did not come up with this one. Mark Hemingway, Bethany Mandel, Juleanna Glover, Austen Furse, Jeremy Katz, Josh Raffel, Stephen Ford, Victoria Davis, Scott Yonover, Sam Garfield, Lanhee Chen, Abby Wisse Schachter, Matt Solomson, and Noam Neusner were always ready to weigh in on key decisions by text.

Jonah Goldberg, Brian Montgomery, Stanley Kurtz, Senator Ben Sasse, Ambassador Norm Eisen, Steve Hess, Professor David Eisenhower, Peter Baker, Secretary Mike Leavitt, Seth Leibsohn, and Vin Cannato provided helpful early insights. Brian Hook, who has seen his share of infighting in multiple administrations, encouraged me by laughing at many of the stories that would appear in the book. Matt Robinson, as usual, read every word and helped shape and improve the entire manuscript.

Talented interns Sasha Grujin, Madeleine Nagle, Jay Mens, and especially Liam Gorman provided invaluable research. Kara Jones was particularly helpful during the research and proposal phases.

Howard Mortman and his wizardly mastery of the C-SPAN archives highlighted certain stories that otherwise would not have been unearthed for this project. Larry Rothenberg's steel trap memory also provided me with one great story that I would not have found without him.

As they have with my previous books, my Hudson Institute colleagues listened to my thoughts on how to approach this book and responded with voluminous and helpful thoughts of their own. Thanks to John Weicher, Chris DeMuth, Abe Shulsky, Doug Feith, Joel Scanlon, Thomas Duesterberg, John Fonte, Jonas Parello-Plesner, Chris Sands, Scooter Libby, Ken Weinstein, Hank Cardello, Sean Kelly, and Justin Smith for their participation in the process.

A special thank you to the talented team at Regnery. Trusty agent Alex Hoyt brought the concept their way. Publisher Alex Novak signed off on the product—and contributed an excellent preface. (Alex's late father, Bob Novak, was helpful as well—his long-standing syndicated column had some of the best stories I found on infighting in the White House.) Other appreciated assistance came from editor Stephen Thompson, Tom Spence, Kylie Frey, Nicole Yeatman, Jennifer Duplessie, Mark Bloomfield, Kathryn Riggs, and of course the redoubtable Marji Ross.

My family had to endure a largely absent relative for long periods as I tried to juggle work and a looming book deadline. My parents and in-laws, Bernard and Elaine Troy and Drs. Ray and Vita Pliskow, are always so supportive. It is much appreciated. Mother-in-law Vita once again proofread the draft and caught many mistakes. Brothers Dan and Gil Troy, and sisters-in-law Dr. Cheryl Troy and Linda Adams, are great sounding boards. My nieces and nephews—Aaron, Lia, Yoni, Leora, Ariel, Aviv, and Dina—endure (barely) my book-related postings on the United Troy Family WhatsApp group. Thanks to my wife, Kami, and kids—Ezra, Ruthie, Rina, and Noey—for their patience with me, if not with the book itself. I look forward to their help on the selling part, where the fun really begins.

# THE INFIGHTING SCORECARD

I n the modern presidency, as in most organizations, the three leading causes of staff infighting are ideological differences, undefined processes, and leadership's tolerance of staff infighting and discord. Controlling these three factors does not guarantee teamwork and effectiveness, however. History attests to the fact that an ideologically unified administration does have fewer contentious internal debates, but too much unity brings with it challenges of group think and ossification. As political scientist, former White House aide, and distinguished Senator Daniel Patrick Moynihan observed, "In unanimity one often finds a lack of rigorous thinking." On the other hand, a White House divided along clear ideological lines quickly devolves into factionalism. For this reason, a successful executive must deftly balance the ideological differences, clearly delineate process and lines of accountability, and set the tone for natural personal differences without tolerating outright discord. Balancing these three factors properly positions the combined team to achieve organizational goals.

| President | Ideological Discord (low to high) | Process (tight to loose) | Tolerance for Infighting (low to high) | Result |
|---|---|---|---|---|
| Truman | Mostly low, except on select issues | Tight, but early in the development of a White House staff | Low, except when needed | Relatively non-contentious White House environment, but the president was willing to foster conflict when necessary |
| Eisenhower | Low, except when the president wanted some | Tight, with a military mindset | Low, but willing to experiment on select issues | Ike preferred not to see conflict, but was willing to set some up to get better results |
| Kennedy | Low | Loose—no chief of staff | Seemingly low, and yet tolerated it | Despite protestations against mistreating the vice president, Kennedy allowed his brother to torment LBJ, with far-reaching implications |
| Johnson | Very low, especially with respect to the Vietnam War | Extremely tight | Very low, to the point of inhibiting dissenting views | Relatively little infighting among staff, but also insufficient airing of dissenting views |
| Nixon | High on both foreign and domestic | Tight—imperial presidency | High—set up relationships prone to conflict | Desire for total control led to paranoia, and conflict persisted throughout the administration. The extremes likely contributed to the Watergate scandal |
| Ford | Moderate | Extremely loose—did not assert control | Reputation for excessive niceness allowed it to fester | One of the most rivalry-filled and chaotic administrations in history |
| Carter | High, especially on foreign policy | Loose—refusal to have chief of staff | High, willing to put up with ongoing tension | Conflict abounded, and the president was not able to control it |

| President | Ideological Discord (low to high) | Process (tight to loose) | Tolerance for Infighting (low to high) | Result |
|---|---|---|---|---|
| **Reagan** | High among staff, but little confusion about where the president stood | Tight, with clear lines of authority | Relatively high—"You fellas work it out" | Bitter and persistent conflict at the staff level in the first term, followed by conflict between the first lady and the chief of staff in the second term |
| **Bush 41** | High on domestic policy, low on foreign policy | Tight, power concentrated up top | Low, yet often unwilling to address head on | Had an effective foreign policy team, but domestic team dysfunction contributed to a 1992 reelection loss |
| **Clinton** | Inherently high, but shifted according to external events | Loose and somewhat freewheeling | High, even fostered at times | Tension-filled first term calmed down in a second term as the external impeachment threat served as a unifying factor |
| **Bush 43** | High on domestic policy, low on foreign policy | Aimed for a tight process | Low, but often unwilling to address | Smooth-running domestic operation; chaotic national security team with bitter rivalries among top leaders |
| **Obama** | Low, but gender issues emerged | Very tight—"Don't f*** the structure" mantra—but certain aides given more leeway | Low—"No drama Obama" | Low in conflict in press accounts, but details of conflict emerged in later accounts |
| **Trump** | High, especially on trade and immigration | Largely loose, but with periodic changes in approach | High—"I like conflict" | Conflict-filled, especially on areas of ideological disagreement |

# WHITE HOUSE NICKNAMES

## KENNEDY ADMINISTRATION

### Lyndon Johnson

"Rufus Cornpone"

"Judge Crater" (referring to a judge who, like the vice president, had "disappeared")

"Huckleberry Capone"—used by Ethel Kennedy

### Vice President and Mrs. Johnson

"Uncle Cornpone and his Little Pork Chop"—used by the "Hickory Hill Gang" of Robert Kennedy allies

### Robert F. Kennedy

"Sonny Boy"—used by Lyndon Johnson

## NIXON ADMINISTRATION

### Richard Nixon

"That Madman," "Our Drunken Friend," and "The Meatball Mind"— used by Henry Kissinger

"Old Man," "Rufus," "The Leader of the Free World," and, in his diaries, "P."—used by Chief of Staff H. R. Haldeman

### H. R. Haldeman and John Ehrlichman

"The Germans"

**Labor Secretary Peter Brennan**
"Secretary Bunker"

**Ethnic Outreach Staffer Mike Balzano**
"The Garbage Man"

**OMB Director Caspar Weinberger**
"Cap the Knife"

**Diane Sawyer**
"The Tall Girl"—used by Nixon

## FORD ADMINISTRATION

**Bob Hartmann**
"Fat Kraut"
"SOB" (Note: Hartmann jokingly insisted that it stood for Sweet
  Ol' Bob)

## CARTER ADMINISTRATION

**Hugh Carter**
"Cousin Cheap"

**National Security Advisor Zbigniew Brzezinski**
"Woody Woodpecker"

## REAGAN ADMINISTRATION

**David Gergen**
"The Tall Guy"
"Tall"
"Professor Leaky"

**Don Regan Aides David Chew, Al Kingon, Tom Dawson, and Dennis Thomas**
"The Mice"

**Ed Meese's briefcase**
"A Briefcase without a Bottom"
"The Black Hole"
"The Meesecase"

## GEORGE H. W. BUSH ADMINISTRATION

**Hanns Kuttner**
"The Fontmeister"

## CLINTON ADMINISTRATION

**Harold Ickes**
"The Garbage Man"
"Director of the Sanitation Department"

**Dick Morris**
"The Unabomber"

**Leon Panetta, Harold Ickes, and George Stephanopoulos**
"The Thugocracy"

**George Stephanopoulos**
ABC News "Comment*raitor*"

**Sidney Blumenthal**
"Sid Vicious"
"GK" (for Grassy Knoll)

**Mack McClarty**
"Mack the Nice"

## GEORGE W. BUSH ADMINISTRATION

**Vice Presidential Chief of Staff David Addington**
"Keyser Söze"

**James Comey**
"Saint Jim"

## OBAMA ADMINISTRATION

**Ben Rhodes**
"Hamas"

**Secretary of Defense Robert Gates**
"Yoda"

## TRUMP ADMINISTRATION

**Hope Hicks**
"Hopey"
"The High Schooler" (used by John Kelly)

**Chief of Staff John Kelly**
"The Church Lady"

**Deputy Attorney General Rod Rosenstein**
"Mr. Peepers"

**Attorney General Jeff Sessions**
"Mr. Magoo"
"Benjamin Button"

**Kirstjen Nielsen**
"Nurse Ratched"

## Zachary Fuentes
"ZOTUS"
"Prime Minister"

## Gary Cohn
"Globalist Gary"

## Anthony Scaramucci
"The Mooch"

## Jared Kushner and Ivanka Trump
"Jarvanka"
"The Democrats"

# Notes

## Introduction

1. "Steve Bannon Takes the Stage at Delivering Alpha," interview with CNBC's Michelle Caruso, July 18, 2018, https://www.cnbc.com/video/2018/07/18/steve-bannon-delivering-alpha.html?play=1.
2. Jonathan Swan, "1 Fun Thing: The Legend Lives On," Axios, August 6, 2017, https://www.axios.com/axios-sneak-peek-2469600856.html; Mara Siegler, "The Mooch Rips 'Loser' Steve Bannon at Hanukkah Party," *New York Post*, December 19, 2017, https://pagesix.com/2017/12/19/the-mooch-rips-loser-steve-bannon-at-hanukkah-party/.

## Chapter 1: Truman and Ike

1. Duane Tananbaum, *Herbert H. Lehman: A Political Biography* (Albany: State University of New York Press, 2016), 162.
2. Stephen Hess, *Organizing the Presidency* (Washington: Brookings, 1988), 45.
3. Peter Rodman, *Presidential Command: Power, Leadership, and the Making of Foreign Policy from Richard Nixon to George W. Bush* (New York: Knopf, 2009), 22.
4. Alonzo Hamby, "Insecurity and Responsibility," in *Leadership in the Modern Presidency*, ed. Fred Greenstein (Cambridge: Harvard, 1988), 62.
5. Clark M. Clifford, "Oral History Interviews," Harry S. Truman Presidential Library and Museum, https://www.trumanlibrary.org/oralhist/cliford.htm.
6. Ibid.
7. Martin Tolchin, "The Presidency: Whether Counsel or Counselor, It's a Key Role," *New York Times*, February 24, 1986, http://www.nytimes.com/1986/02/24/us/the-presidency-whether-counsel-or-counselor-it-s-a-key-role.html.
8. Ibid.
9. Marilyn Berger, "Clark Clifford, a Major Adviser to Four Presidents, Is Dead at 91," *New York Times*, October 11, 1998, http://www.nytimes.com/1998/10/11/us/clark-clifford-a-major-adviser-to-four-presidents-is-dead-at-91.html.

10. Clifford, "Oral History Interviews."
11. Ibid.
12. Harry S. Truman, *Memoirs: Years of Trial and Hope, 1946–1952* (Garden City: Doubleday, 1956), 162.
13. Clifford, "Oral History Interviews."
14. Michael T. Benson, *Harry S. Truman and the Founding of Israel* (Westport: Praeger, 1997), 156.
15. Clark M. Clifford and Richard C. Holbrooke, *Counsel to the President: A Memoir* (New York: Random House, 1991), 12.
16. Benson, *Truman and the Founding of Israel*, 157.
17. Clifford and Holbrooke, *Counsel to the President*, 15.
18. The Soviet Union was the first country to recognize Israel *de jure* on May 17, 1948; Truman was the first to recognize Israel de facto, on May 14, 1948.
19. Truman, *Memoirs*, 164.
20. Clifford and Holbrooke, *Counsel to the President*, 23–24.
21. Ibid., 13, 9.
22. Hamby, "Insecurity and Responsibility," 66.
23. Benson, *Truman and the Founding of Israel*, 156.
24. David McCullough, *Truman* (New York: Simon & Schuster, 2003), 659.
25. Tevi Troy, *What Jefferson Read, Ike Watched, and Obama Tweeted: 200 Years of Popular Culture in the White House* (Washington: Regnery History, 2013), 183.
26. Hess, *Organizing the Presidency*, 2, 45.
27. Clifford and Holbrooke, *Counsel to the President*, 5.
28. Rodman, *Presidential Command*, 19.
29. Hess, *Organizing the Presidency*, 45.
30. Rodman, *Presidential Command*, 24.
31. Dwight Eisenhower, *Mandate for Change: The White House Years, 1953–1956* (Garden City: Doubleday, 1962), 140.
32. Merle Miller, *Plain Speaking: An Oral Biography of Harry S. Truman* (New York: Berkeley, 1973), 373.
33. Hess, *Organizing the Presidency*, 59–60.
34. Fred Greenstein, ed., *Leadership in the Modern Presidency* (Cambridge: Harvard, 1988), 86.
35. Hess, *Organizing the Presidency*, 72.
36. Dwight D. Eisenhower, "Statement by the President Announcing the Appointment of Harold Stassen as Special Assistant to the President for Disarmament Studies," March 19, 1955, Public Papers of the President, 1955, Number 57.

37. David Tal, "The Secretary of State versus the Secretary of Peace: The Dulles-Stassen Controversy and US Disarmament Policy, 1955–58," *Journal of Contemporary History* (October 2006): 721–40.
38. Lawrence S. Kaplan, *Harold Stassen: Eisenhower, the Cold War, and the Pursuit of Nuclear Disarmament* (Lexington: University Press of Kentucky, 2018), 94.
39. Tal, "The Secretary of State versus the Secretary of Peace."
40. Ibid.
41. Stephen Kinzer, *The Brothers: John Foster Dulles, Allen Dulles, and Their Secret World War* (New York: Henry Holt, 2013), 39.
42. John Kelly, "More on Dulles, the Man and the Airport," *Washington Post*, December 8, 2012, https://www.washingtonpost.com/local/more-on-dulles-the-man-and-the-airport/2012/12/08/9e838b14-401a-11e2-bca3-aadc9b7e29c5_story.html?utm_term=.8c0b62a554c1.
43. Mark Russell, "DULL, DULLER, DULLES," *New York Times*, July 13, 1986, http://www.nytimes.com/1986/07/13/books/dull-duller-dulles.html.
44. Dwight D. Eisenhower, "Letter Accepting Resignation of Harold E. Stassen, Special Assistant to the President," February 15, 1958, http://www.presidency.ucsb.edu/ws/index.php?pid=11274/.

## Chapter 2: John F. Kennedy

1. Bradley Patterson, *The White House Staff: Inside the West Wing and Beyond* (Washington: Brookings Institution Press, 2000), 3.
2. Garry Wills, "America's Nastiest Blood Feud," the *New York Review of Books*, May 24, 2012, http://www.nybooks.com/articles/2012/05/24/americas-nastiest-blood-feud/.
3. Michael O'Brien, *John F. Kennedy: A Biography* (New York: Thomas Dunne Books, 2005), 733.
4. Jeff Shesol, *Mutual Contempt: Lyndon Johnson, Robert Kennedy, and the Feud That Defined a Decade* (New York: W. W. Norton & Co., 1997), 10.
5. Ibid., 52–54. Before becoming a liberal president himself, where he championed civil rights and the Great Society, Senator Johnson was a conservative Southern Democrat.
6. Arthur M. Schlesinger Jr., *A Thousand Days: John F. Kennedy in the White House* (New York: Houghton Mifflin, 1965), 48–56.
7. Jeffrey K. Smith, *Bad Blood: Lyndon B. Johnson, Robert F. Kennedy, and the Tumultuous 1960s* (Bloomington: AuthorHouse, 2010), 119.
8. Jonathan Darman, *Landslide: LBJ and Ronald Reagan at the Dawn of a New America* (New York: Random House, 2014), 16.

9. Robert A. Caro, *The Passage of Power* (New York: Alfred A. Knopf, 2012), 205.
10. Carl Brauer, "The Endurance of Inspirational Leadership," in *Leadership in the Modern Presidency*, ed. Fred Greenstein (Cambridge: Harvard, 1988), 62.
11. Shesol, *Mutual Contempt*, 78.
12. Caro, *The Passage of Power*, 262.
13. Ibid., 262–63.
14. Evan Thomas, *Robert Kennedy: His Life* (New York: Simon & Schuster, 2000), 290; Caro, *The Passage of Power*, 198; Lawrence O'Donnell, *Playing with Fire: The 1968 Election and the Transformation of American Politics* (New York: Penguin Press, 2017), 86.
15. Caro, *The Passage of Power*, 90; Califano, *The Triumph and Tragedy of Lyndon Johnson*, 279.
16. Theodore C. Sorensen, *Kennedy* (New York: Harper & Row, 1965), 261.
17. Ibid., 5.
18. Stephen Hess, *Organizing the Presidency* (Washington: Brookings, 1988), 76.
19. "Executive Branch Civilian Employment Since 1940," Historical Federal Workforce Table, Office of Personnel Management, https://www.opm.gov/policy-data-oversight/data-analysis-documentation/federal-employment-reports/historical-tables/executive-branch-civilian-employment-since-1940/. Of course, this two million workers figure does not include contractors, military personnel, or postal workers, which would swell the size of the workforce to an estimated seven to nine million people.
20. Hess, *Organizing the Presidency*, 83.
21. Jeremy Suri, *The Impossible Presidency: The Rise and Fall of America's Highest Office* (New York: Basic, 2017), 189. In the twenty-first century, this kind of entrenched bureaucracy that was resistant to change would be characterized as the Deep State.
22. Peter Rodman, *Presidential Command: Power, Leadership, and the Making of Foreign Policy from Richard Nixon to George W. Bush* (New York: Knopf, 2009), 31.
23. Schlesinger, *A Thousand Days*, 72.
24. Tevi Troy, *Intellectuals and the American Presidency: Philosophers, Jesters, or Technicians?* (Lanham: Rowman and Littlefield, 2002), 21.
25. Ibid., 27. In later years, this "neutral figure" role would become a specialty of David Gergen.
26. Steven Levingston, *Kennedy and King: The President, the Pastor, and the Battle Over Civil Rights* (New York: Hachette Books, 2017), 89.

27. Schlesinger, *A Thousand Days*, 72–73.
28. Ibid., 138.
29. Richard Aldous, *Schlesinger: The Imperial Historian* (New York: W. W. Norton & Company, 2017), 285.
30. Schlesinger, *A Thousand Days*; Sorensen, *Kennedy*.
31. David E. Bell, recorded interview by Robert C. Turner, July 11, 1964, John F. Kennedy Library Oral History Program, https://www.jfklibrary.org/Asset-Viewer/Archives/JFKOH-DEB-01.aspx.
32. Theodore Sorensen, "Arthur M. Schlesinger, Jr., 1917–2007," *The American Prospect*, March 16, 2007, http://prospect.org/article/arthur-m-schlesinger-jr-1917-2007.
33. Rosenman held the position under Roosevelt as well.
34. Richard E. Neustadt, *Presidential Power and the Modern Presidents: The Politics of Leadership from Roosevelt to Reagan* (New York: Free Press, 1990), 222.
35. Troy, *Intellectuals and the American Presidency*, 19.
36. Hess, *Organizing the Presidency*, 81.
37. Michael Medved, *The Shadow Presidents* (New York: Times Books, 1979), 272.
38. Troy, *Intellectuals and the American Presidency*, 27–29.
39. Aldous, *Schlesinger*, 297.
40. Ibid., 207–8.
41. Ibid., 208.
42. Troy, *Intellectuals and the American Presidency*, 33.
43. Schlesinger, *A Thousand Days*, 16.
44. Aldous, *Schlesinger*, 223; Troy, *Intellectuals and the American Presidency*, 29.
45. Sorensen, *Kennedy*, 288.
46. Joseph W. Alsop, recorded interview by Elspeth Rostow, June 26, 1964, John F. Kennedy Library Oral History Program, https://www.jfklibrary.org/Asset-Viewer/Archives/JFKOH-JWA-02.aspx.
47. Robert W. Komer, recorded interview by Dennis J. O'Brien, December 22, 1969, John F. Kennedy Library Oral History Program, https://archive2.jfklibrary.org/JFKOH/Komer,%20Robert%20W/JFKOH-ROWK-05/JFKOH-ROWK-05-TR.pdf.
48. Troy, 33.
49. Alsop, recorded interview.
50. Sorensen, *Kennedy*, 289.
51. Chester Bowles, *Promises to Keep: My Years in Public Life, 1941–1969* (New York: Harper and Row, 1971), 364.
52. Sorensen, *Kennedy*, 289–90.
53. Alsop, recorded interview.

54. Sorensen, *Kennedy*, 290.
55. Aldous, *Schlesinger*, 314.
56. Sorensen, "Arthur M. Schlesinger, Jr.," *The American Prospect*.
57. Aldous, *Schlesinger*, 315–16.
58. Mark White, *Kennedy: A Cultural History of an American Icon* (New York: Bloomsbury, 2013), 95.
59. Aldous, *Schlesinger*, 331. "We Try Harder" was the well-known slogan of Avis Rent A Car, which was consistently ranked second behind Hertz among car rental companies.
60. Ibid., 325.
61. Rodman, *Presidential Command*, 32.
62. Drew Pearson, *Washington Merry-Go-Round: The Drew Pearson Diaries, 1960–1969* (Lincoln: Potomac Books, 2015), 348.

## Chapter 3: LBJ

1. James J. Best, "Who Talked to the President When? A Study of Lyndon B. Johnson," *Political Science Quarterly* 103, no. 3 (Autumn 1988), 543.
2. Denise Gamino, "Longtime LBJ Aide Mildred Stegall Finally Tells Her Story," *Austin-American Statesman*, February 13, 2011, http://www.statesman.com/news/local/longtime-lbj-aide-mildred-stegall-finally-tells-her-story/c2sFEFnrKMgguG8zLYvKVK/.
3. Charles Wesley Roberts, *LBJ's Inner Circle* (New York: Delacorte Press, 1965), 43.
4. George E. Reedy, *Lyndon B. Johnson: A Memoir* (Kansas City: Andrews and McMeel, Inc., 1982), 43–44.
5. Robert Dallek, *Flawed Giant: Lyndon Johnson and His Times, 1961–1973* (New York: Oxford University Press, 1998), 66.
6. Best, "Who Talked to the President When?" 543, 545.
7. Dallek, *Flawed Giant*, 68.
8. Larry L. King, "Bringing Up Lyndon: As the Twig Is Bent, So the Tree Is Inclined," *Texas Monthly* (January 1976), https://www.texasmonthly.com/politics/bringing-up-lyndon/.
9. Best, "Who Talked to the President When?" 539–40.
10. Dallek, *Flawed Giant*, 68.
11. King, "Bringing Up Lyndon."
12. Jeff Shesol, *Mutual Contempt: Lyndon Johnson, Robert Kennedy, and the Feud That Defined a Decade* (New York: W. W. Norton & Co., 1997), 296, 325.
13. Doris Kearns Goodwin, *Lyndon Johnson and the American Dream* (New York: St. Martin's Press, 1991), 176; King, "Bringing Up Lyndon."
14. Joe Califano, *The Triumph and Tragedy of Lyndon Johnson* (New York: Simon and Schuster, 1991), 171.

15. Peter Rodman, *Presidential Command: Power, Leadership, and the Making of Foreign Policy from Richard Nixon to George W. Bush* (New York: Knopf, 2009), 34.

16. Matt Schudel, "W. Marvin Watson Jr., a Top White House Aide to Lyndon B. Johnson, Dies at 93," *Washington Post*, November 28, 2017, https://www.washingtonpost.com/local/obituaries/w-marvin-watson-jr-a-top-white-house-aide-to-lyndon-b-johnson-dies-at-93/2017/11/28/a351b7d8-d43f-11e7-95bf-df7c1 9270879_story.html?utm_term=.f64ef8690963.

17. Nicholas Katzenbach, *Some of It Was Fun: Working with RFK and LBJ* (New York: W. W. Norton, 2008), 203.

18. Ibid., 202–3. Unfortunately, Katzenbach did not explain the details of his leak, claiming that he had "forgotten the subject matter" beyond the fact that it was about "some proposed changes, I think, in legislation.

19. Jeremy Suri, *The Impossible Presidency: The Rise and Fall of America's Highest Office* (New York: Basic, 2017), 212.

20. Douglas Martin, "Nicholas Katzenbach, Trusted Adviser to J.F.K. and L.B.J., Dies at 90," *New York Times*, May 9, 2012, http://www.nytimes.com/2012/05/10/us/nicholas-katzenbach-1960s-political-shaper-dies-at-90.html. Johnson, concerned about Katzenbach's loyalty—Bobby had recommended him as a successor—did initially offer the position to Clark Clifford, who said no. Clifford would later serve as Johnson's secretary of defense in 1968.

21. Shesol, *Mutual Contempt*, 295, 298.

22. Rowland Evans and Robert Novak, *Lyndon B. Johnson: The Exercise Of Power: A Political Biography* (New York: New American Library, 1966), 355.

23. Diana McLellan, "Talk of Two Towns," *Washington Post*, September 24, 1995, https://www.washingtonpost.com/archive/entertainment/books/1995/09/24/talk-of-two-towns/a99d99dd-82c6-4ca5-83ad-07a3e6fd5b50/?utm_term=.41d8eedc2653.

24. Dallek, *Flawed Giant* 57–56.

25. Ibid., 55.

26. Evans and Novak, *Lyndon B. Johnson*, 345.

27. Ibid., 342.

28. Tevi Troy, *Intellectuals and the American Presidency: Philosophers, Jesters, or Technicians?* (Lanham: Rowman and Littlefield, 2002), 47.

29. Stephen Hess, *Organizing the Presidency* (Washington: Brookings, 1988), 88.

30. Evans and Novak, *Lyndon B. Johnson*, 343.

31. Hess, *Organizing the Presidency*, 88, 100.

32. Eric Goldman, *The Tragedy of Lyndon Johnson* (New York: Knopf, 1969), 18.
33. Troy, *Intellectuals and the American Presidency*, 50.
34. Schudel, "W. Marvin Watson Jr., a Top White House Aide to Lyndon B. Johnson, Dies at 93."
35. Shesol, *Mutual Contempt*, 119.
36. Dallek, *Flawed Giant*, 58.
37. Robert A. Caro, *The Passage of Power* (New York: Alfred A. Knopf, 2012), 579.
38. Dallek, *Flawed Giant*, 57.
39. Shesol, *Mutual Contempt*, 123.
40. Kearns Goodwin, *Lyndon Johnson and the American Dream*, 199–201.
41. Dallek, *Flawed Giant*, 135.
42. Kearns Goodwin, *Lyndon Johnson and the American Dream*, 201.
43. Ibid.
44. Reedy, *Lyndon B. Johnson*, 140–41; Stuart Eizenstat, *President Carter: The White House Years* (New York: St. Martin's Press, 2018), 90.
45. Tom Lehrer, "Whatever Became of Hubert?" (1965), YouTube, April 9, 2016, https://www.youtube.com/watch?v=C11ZNuVSBMU.
46. Joseph A. Califano Jr., *The Triumph and Tragedy of Lyndon Johnson* (New York: Simon and Schuster, 1991), 64, 69.
47. Shesol, *Mutual Contempt*, 260.
48. Ibid., 261.
49. Hess, *Organizing the Presidency*, 89.
50. Kearns Goodwin, *Lyndon Johnson and the American Dream*, 318.
51. Mark White, "Going to War in Vietnam: George Ball's Dissent in the 1960s," *American Diplomacy*, April 2007, http://www.unc.edu/depts/diplomat/item/2007/0406/whit/white_ball.html.
52. Ibid.
53. Lyndon B. Johnson, *The Vantage Point: Perspectives on the Presidency, 1963–1969* (New York: Holt, Rinehart And Winston, 1974), 147.
54. W. Marvin Watson and Sherwin Markman, *Chief of Staff: Lyndon Johnson and His Presidency* (New York: Thomas Dunne Books, 2004), 154.
55. David Halberstam, *The Best and the Brightest* (New York: Random House, 1972), 246.
56. Robert W. Komer, recorded interview by Dennis J. O'Brien, December 22, 1969, John F. Kennedy Library Oral History Program, https://archive2.jfklibrary.org/JFKOH/Komer,%20Robert%20W/JFKOH-ROWK-05/JFKOH-ROWK-05-TR.pdf.
57. Ibid.
58. White, "Going to War in Vietnam."

59. Larry Berman, "Paths Chosen and Opportunities Lost," *Leadership in the Modern Presidency*, ed. Fred Greenstein (Cambridge: Harvard, 1988), 163.
60. Kearns Goodwin, *Lyndon Johnson and the American Dream*, 318.
61. Ibid., 320.
62. Lawrence O'Donnell, *Playing with Fire: The 1968 and the Transformation of American Politics* (New York: Penguin Press, 2017), 109.
63. Shesol, *Mutual Contempt*, 378, 392.
64. Kearns Goodwin, *Lyndon Johnson and the American Dream*, 321.
65. Shesol, *Mutual Contempt*, 390, 391.
66. Kearns Goodwin, *Lyndon Johnson and the American Dream*, 320–21.
67. Shesol, *Mutual Contempt,* 390–91.
68. Townsend Hoopes, "Disagreement between Them," *The Atlantic*, October 1969, https://www.theatlantic.com/magazine/archive/1969/10/the-fight-for-the-presidents-mind-and-the-men-who-won-it/303584/.
69. Marilyn Berger, "Clark Clifford, a Major Adviser to Four Presidents, Is Dead at 91," *New York Times*, October 11, 1998, http://www.nytimes.com/1998/10/11/us/clark-clifford-a-major-adviser-to-four-presidents-is-dead-at-91.html.
70. Ibid.
71. Hoopes, "Disagreement between Them."
72. Ibid.
73. Reedy, *Lyndon B. Johnson*, 152.
74. Clark M. Clifford and Richard C. Holbrooke, *Counsel to the President: A Memoir* (New York: Random House, 1991), 488.
75. Transcript, McGeorge Bundy Oral History Interview I, 1/30/69, by Paige E. Mulhollan, Internet Copy, LBJ Library.
76. Califano, *The Triumph and Tragedy of Lyndon Johnson*, 18.
77. O'Donnell, *Playing with Fire*, 167.

## Chapter 4: Nixon

1. Stephen Hess, *The Professor and the President: Daniel Patrick Moynihan in the Nixon White House* (Washington: Brookings Institution Press, 2015), xv.
2. Patrick J. Buchanan, *Nixon's White House Wars: The Battles That Made and Broke a President and Divided America Forever* (New York: Random House, 2017), 12.
3. Alvin S. Felzenberg, *A Man and His Presidents: The Political Odyssey of William F. Buckley Jr.* (United States of America: Yale University Press, 2017), 106.

4.  Walter Isaacson, *Kissinger: A Biography* (New York: Simon & Schuster, 2013), 511; Robert Dallek, "The Kissinger Presidency," *Vanity Fair*, May 2007, https://www.vanityfair.com/news/2007/05/kissinger200705.

5.  Milton Viorst, "William Rogers Thinks Like Richard Nixon," *New York Times*, February 27, 1972, http://www.nytimes.com/1972/02/27/archives/william-rogers-thinks-like-richard-nixon-rogers-thinks-like-nixon.html.

6.  Bernard Gwertzman, "Rogers Quits, Kissinger Named," *New York Times*, August 23, 1973, http://www.nytimes.com/1973/08/23/archives/rogers-quits-kissingernamed-rogers-resigns-kissinger-named.html.

7.  Niall Ferguson, interview for "Uncommon Knowledge," January 25, 2018, https://www.hoover.org/research/niall-fergusons-square-and-tower-0.

8.  Viorst, "William Rogers Thinks Like Richard Nixon."

9.  Peter Rodman, *Presidential Command: Power, Leadership, and the Making of Foreign Policy from Richard Nixon to George W. Bush* (New York: Knopf, 2009), 37–38.

10. Chris Whipple, *The Gatekeepers: How the White House Chiefs of Staff Define Every Presidency* (New York: Crown, 2017), 28.

11. Rodman, *Presidential Command*, 39.

12. Ibid., 41.

13. James P. Pfiffner, "The President's Chief of Staff: Lessons Learned," *Presidential Studies Quarterly* 23, no. 1 (Winter, 1993), 82–85.

14. Shirley Anne Warshaw, *Guide to the White House Staff* (Thousand Oaks: CQ Press, 2013), 210.

15. James Pfiffner, *The Modern Presidency* (Boston: Wadsworth, 2010), 68.

16. Roger Porter, *Presidential Decision Making: The Economic Policy Board* (Cambridge University Press, 1980), 237, fn 13.

17. John Ehrlichman, *Witness to Power: The Nixon Years* (New York: Simon & Schuster, 1982), 110–12.

18. Ibid.

19. Robert Dallek, *Nixon and Kissinger: Partners in Power* (New York: Harper's, 2007), 102.

20. Isaacson, *Kissinger*, 198.

21. Robert Dallek, "The Kissinger Presidency," *Vanity Fair*, May 2007, https://www.vanityfair.com/news/2007/05/kissinger200705; Dallek, *Nixon and Kissinger*, 352.

22. John W. Dean, *Blind Ambition: The White House Years* (New York: Simon & Schuster, 1976), 29.

23. Ibid., 29–30.

24. Buchanan, *Nixon's White House Wars*, 41. Sears would continue to maintain powerful enemies. He was forced off the Reagan campaign in

1980 after tossing a power struggle with Mike Deaver, but not before Sears had purged many of the "Californians" from the Reagan team.

25. Margaret MacMillan, *Nixon and Mao: The Week That Changed the World* (New York: Random House, 2006), 200.

26. David Rothkopf, *Running the World: The Inside Story of the National Security Council and the Architects of American Power* (New York: Public Affairs, 2005), 135.

27. MacMillan, *Nixon and Mao*, 75, 60.

28. Dallek, *Nixon and Kissinger*, 222.

29. Isaacson, *Kissinger*, 198, 251.

30. Rodman, *Presidential Command*, 76.

31. Ibid., 55, 76.

32. Richard Nixon And Henry A. Kissinger, transcript, June 13, 1971, Miller Center Presidential Recordings, http://prde.upress.virginia.edu/conversations/4002137.

33. Viorst, "William Rogers Thinks Like Richard Nixon."

34. Ibid.

35. Niall Ferguson, "The Secret to Henry Kissinger's Success," *Politico*, January 20, 2018, https://www.politico.com/magazine/story/2018/01/20/henry-kissinger-networking-216482.

36. Isaacson, *Kissinger*, 356.

37. Dallek, *Nixon and Kissinger*, 212.

38. Buchanan, *Nixon's White House Wars*, 56.

39. Dallek, *Nixon and Kissinger*, 251, 211; Dallek, "The Kissinger Presidency."

40. Isaacson, *Kissinger*, 211–12.

41. Buchanan, *Nixon's White House Wars*, 175.

42. Ibid., 239.

43. Ferguson, interview for "Uncommon Knowledge."

44. Isaacson, *Kissinger*, 197.

45. Robert Dallek, "Q&A with Robert Dallek," C-SPAN, April 18, 2007, https://www.c-span.org/video/?197600-1/qa-robert-dallek.

46. Isaacson, *Kissinger*, 503.

47. Rodman, *Presidential Command*, 59.

48. Harold Jackson, "William Rogers," *The Guardian*, January 4, 2001, https://www.theguardian.com/news/2001/jan/05/guardianobituaries.haroldjackson.

49. Isaacson, *Kissinger*, 503.

50. Ehrlichman, *Witness to Power*, 94–97.

51. Seymour M. Hersh, "Kissinger and Nixon in the White House," *The Atlantic*, May 1982, https://www.theatlantic.com/magazine/archive/1982/05/kissinger-and-nixon-in-the-white-house/308778/.

52. Rodman, *Presidential Command*, 59.
53. Henry Kissinger, *White House Years* (New York: Simon and Schuster, 1979), 33.
54. Buchanan, *Nixon's White House Wars*, 32, 175; Patrick J. Buchanan, "Q&A with Pat Buchanan," C-SPAN, May 25, 2017, https://www.c-span.org/video/transcript/?id=55942. Of course, Buchanan himself also had to be educated in the ways of the White House. In one telling incident, William Safire used the "passion for anonymity" line in advising Buchanan not to take credit for Nixon's Colorado Springs address. Buchanan, however, would learn that Safire had an ulterior motive: "Shortly afterward, National Review would reveal that it had discovered the author of Nixon's terrific speech at the Air Force Academy—Bill Safire. I have been had. I said to myself my naive self, so this is how the game is played." Buchanan, *Nixon's White House Wars*, 49.
55. Tevi Troy, *Intellectuals and the American Presidency: Philosophers, Jesters, or Technicians?* (Lanham: Rowman & Littlefield, 2002), 90, 106; Hess, *The Professor and the President*, 37–38.
56. Troy, *Intellectuals and the American Presidency*, 92.
57. Hess, *The Professor and the President*, 110–11.
58. Albert R. Hunt, "When Nixon Listened to Liberal Moynihan," *Bloomberg*, December 28, 2014, https://www.bloomberg.com/view/articles/2014-12-28/when-nixon-listened-to-liberal-moynihan.
59. Troy, *Intellectuals and the American Presidency*, 106–8.
60. Ibid., 108.

## Chapter 5: Gerald Ford

1. Peter Rodman, *Presidential Command: Power, Leadership, and the Making of Foreign Policy from Richard Nixon to George W. Bush* (New York: Knopf, 2009), 83.
2. Stephen Hess, *Organizing the Presidency* (Washington: Brookings, 1988), 134.
3. Ibid.
4. Rodman, *Presidential Command*, 85.
5. Robert Schlesinger, "RIP Bob Hartmann, 'SOB,'" HuffPost, April 22, 2008 (updated May 25, 2011), https://www.huffingtonpost.com/robert-schlesinger/rip-bob-hartmann-sob_b_98033.html.
6. David S Broder, *Behind the Front Page* (New York: Simon & Schuster, 1987), 56.
7. Seymour M. Hersh, "The Pardon: Nixon, Ford, Haig, and the Transfer of Power," *The Atlantic*, August 1983, https://www.theatlantic.com/magazine/archive/1983/08/the-pardon/305571/.

8.  Shirley Anne Warshaw, *Guide to the White House Staff* (Thousand Oaks, California: CQ Press, 2013), 170–71; Robert Hartmann, interview with Martha Kumar, White House Interview Program, Transition Interviews, November 22, 1999, https://www.archives.gov/files/presidential-libraries/research/transition-interviews/pdf/hartmann.pdf.

9.  Hartmann, interview with Martha Kumar.

10. Patrick J. Buchanan, *Nixon's White House Wars: The Battles That Made and Broke a President and Divided America Forever* (New York, Random House, 2017), 384.

11. Being written off certainly did not happen to Gergen, as he would go on to serve in both the Reagan and Clinton administrations. David Gergen, "Oral History," Gerald R. Ford Oral History Project, October 8, 2010, https://geraldrfordfoundation.org/centennial/oralhistory/david-gergen/.

12. "Fat Kraut" was of course a reference to Hartmann, who was both portly and had a German sounding last name. Seymour M. Hersh, "The Pardon: Nixon, Ford, Haig, and the Transfer of Power," *The Atlantic*, August 1983, https://www.theatlantic.com/magazine/archive/1983/08/the-pardon/305571/.

13. Gergen, "Oral History."

14. Ron Nessen, *Making the News, Taking the News: From NBC to the Ford White House* (Middleton: Wesleyan University Press, 2011), 98.

15. Donald Rumsfeld, *When the Center Held: Gerald Ford and the Rescue of the American Presidency* (New York: Free Press, 2018), 50.

16. Rowland Evans and Robert Novak, "Mr. Ford's Advisers: Gen. Haig Must Go," *Washington Post*, September 8, 1974, http://www.washingtonpost.com/wp-dyn/content/article/2009/08/07/AR2009080702990.html.

17. Robert Novak, *The Prince of Darkness: 50 Years Reporting in Washington* (New York: Three Rivers Press, 2007), 255.

18. Rumsfeld, *When the Center Held*, 50.

19. Hartmann, interview with Martha Kumar.

20. Richard Reeves, "The Manipulated President," *New York Magazine*, September 29, 1975, 7.

21. Shirley Anne Warshaw, *Powersharing: White House-Cabinet Relations in the Modern Presidency* (Albany: SUNY Press, 1996), 76.

22. Warshaw, *Guide to the White House Staff*, 171.

23. Chris Whipple, *The Gatekeepers: How the White House Chiefs of Staff Define Every Presidency* (New York: Crown, 2017), 50–51.

24. Ron Nessen, *Making the News, Taking the News: From NBC to the Ford White House* (Middleton: Wesleyan University Press, 2011), 112.

25. Buchanan, *Nixon's White House Wars*, 384.

26. Andrew Downer Crain, *The Ford Presidency: A History* (London: McFarland & Company, 2014), 17.

27. Roger Porter, "Roger Porter Oral History," Gerald R. Ford Oral History Project, October 8, 2010, https://geraldrfordfoundation.org/centennial/oralhistory/roger-porter/.

28. Tevi Troy, *Intellectuals and the American Presidency: Philosophers, Jesters, or Technicians?* (Lanham: Rowman & Littlefield, 2002), 123.

29. Ibid.

30. Nessen, *Making the News, Taking the News*, 113.

31. Warshaw, *Guide to the White House Staff*, 170.

32. Whipple, *The Gatekeepers*, 53.

33. Ibid.

34. Thomas M. DeFrank, *Write It When I'm Gone: Remarkable Off-the-Record Conversations with Gerald R. Ford* (New York: Putnam, 2007), 43.

35. Jonathan Martin, "A Political Junkie's Guide to Dick Cheney's Memoir," *Politico*, August 28, 2011, https://www.politico.com/news/stories/0811/62194_Page3.html.

36. Ibid.

37. Gergen, "Oral History."

38. Tom Korologos, Gerald R. Ford Oral History Project, May 21, 2009, https://geraldrfordfoundation.org/centennial/oralhistory/tom-korologos/.

39. Ron Nessen, Gerald R. Ford Oral History Project, January 28, 2009, https://geraldrfordfoundation.org/centennial/oralhistory/ron-nessen/.

40. Whipple, *The Gatekeepers*, 67.

41. Schlesinger, "RIP Bob Hartmann, 'SOB'"; Rumsfeld, *When the Center Held*, 66.

42. Porter, "Roger Porter Oral History."

43. Dennis Hevesi, "Robert Hartmann, 91, Dies; Wrote Ford's Noted Talk," *New York Times*, April 19, 2008, http://www.nytimes.com/2008/04/19/us/politics/19hartmann.html.

44. Yanek Mieczkowski, *Gerald Ford and the Challenges of the 1970s* (Lexington: University Press of Kentucky, 2005), 34.

45. Troy, *Intellectuals and the American Presidency*, 123.

46. Whipple, *The Gatekeepers*, 66–67.

47. Gergen, "Oral History."

48. Mieczkowski, *Gerald Ford and the Challenges of the 1970s*, 160–61.

49. Karen M. Hult and Charles E. Walcott, "Separating Rhetoric from Policy: Speechwriting under Gerald Ford and Jimmy Carter," in *White House Studies Compendium*, ed. Robert W. Watson (New York: Nova Science Publishers, 2007), 358–59.

50. Mieczkowski, *Gerald Ford and the Challenges of the 1970s*, 140, 165; Rumsfeld, *When the Center Held*, 50.

51. Mieczkowski, *Gerald Ford and the Challenges of the 1970s*, 140, 165.

52. Martin Crutsinger, "Ford's WIN Buttons Remembered," *Washington Post*, December 28, 2006, http://www.washingtonpost.com/wp-dyn/content/article/2006/12/28/AR2006122801002.html.

53. Robert Hartmann, *Palace Politics: An Inside Account of the Ford Years* (New York: McGraw-Hill, 1980), 397.

54. Porter, "Roger Porter Oral History."

55. Richard Cheney, C-SPAN interview with Carl Rutan, "House Republican Policy Committee: Representative Dick Cheney Talked about Leading the House Republican Policy Committee and Its Function," C-SPAN, June 25, 1984, https://www.c-span.org/video/?124382-1/republican-policy&start=1157.

56. Michael Medved, *The Shadow Presidents* (New York: Times Books, 1979), 338.

57. Whipple, *The Gatekeepers*, 54–55.

58. Karen M. Hult and Charles E. Walcott, "Separating Rhetoric from Policy: Speechwriting under Gerald Ford and Jimmy Carter," 361.

59. Porter, "Roger Porter Oral History."

60. Richard B. Cheney, "Oral History, Secretary of Defense," Miller Center, March 16, 2000–March 17, 2000, https://millercenter.org/the-presidency/presidential-oral-histories/richard-b-cheney-oral-history-secretary-defense.

61. Whipple, *The Gatekeepers*, 71.

62. Donald Rumsfeld, *Known and Unknown: A Memoir* (New York: Penguin, 2011), 179.

63. Hartmann, interview with Martha Kumar.

64. Hartmann, *Palace Politics*, 431–34.

65. Rodman, *Presidential Command*, 93.

66. Gilbert King, "Past Imperfect: A Halloween Massacre at the White House," *Smithsonian*, October 25, 2012, http://blogs.smithsonianmag.com/history/2012/10/a-halloween-massacre-at-the-white-house/#ixzz2h2lK1255.

67. Ibid.

68. Richard B. Cheney and Elizabeth Cheney, *In My Time: A Personal and Political Memoir* (New York: Threshold, 2011), 92.

69. Rodman, *Presidential Command*, 85.

## Chapter 6: Jimmy Carter

1. Edward Walsh, "Carter Names 12 Key Staff Aides," *Washington Post*, January 15, 1977, https://www.washingtonpost.com/archive/

politics/1977/01/15/carter-names-12-key-staff-aides/38a5c4a6-98f7-4f94-9487-11659d59bed1/?utm_term=.d626e3b7b4be.

2.  Martin Schram, "Jack Watson—Full Circle at the White House," *Washington Post*, June 15, 1980, https://www.washingtonpost.com/archive/politics/1980/06/15/jack-watson-full-circle-at-the-white-house/7346747a-a220-44d1-b145-9747995c07cf/?utm_term=.d0da9a9fcfa8.

3.  Ibid.

4.  Chris Whipple, *The Gatekeepers: How the White House Chiefs of Staff Define Every Presidency* (New York: Crown, 2017), 82–83.

5.  Ibid., 82.

6.  Stephen Hess, *Organizing the Presidency* (Washington: Brookings, 1988), 146.

7.  Stuart Eizenstat, "Oral History," Presidential Oral Histories, Jimmy Carter Presidency, Miller Center, January 29, 1982, and January 30, 1982, https://millercenter.org/the-presidency/presidential-oral-histories/stuart-eizenstat-oral-history-assistant-president.

8.  Stuart Eizenstat, *President Carter: The White House Years* (New York: St. Martin's Press, 2018), 76.

9.  Eizenstat, "Oral History."

10. Ibid.; Eizenstat, *President Carter*, 78.

11. Ibid.

12. Jimmy Carter, *Keeping Faith: Memoirs of a President* (New York: Bantam, 1982), 60.

13. Eizenstat, "Oral History."

14. Ryan Lizza, "Battle Plans: How Obama Won," *The New Yorker*, November 17, 2008, https://www.newyorker.com/magazine/2008/11/17/battle-plans.

15. Jack Watson Jr., "Oral History," Presidential Oral Histories, Jimmy Carter Presidency, Miller Center, https://millercenter.org/the-presidency/presidential-oral-histories/jack-h-watson-jr-oral-history-transition-director.

16. Eizenstat, *President Carter*, 75.

17. Whipple, *The Gatekeepers*, 82.

18. Schram, "Jack Watson—Full Circle at the White House."

19. Watson Jr., "Oral History."

20. Eizenstat, *President Carter*, 632, 76.

21. Hedrick Smith, *Power Game: How Washington Works* (New York: Ballantine Books, 1988), 337–39.

22. James Fallows, "The Passionless Presidency," *The Atlantic*, May 1979, https://www.theatlantic.com/magazine/archive/1979/05/the-passionless-presidency/308516/.

23. Hess, *Organizing the Presidency*, 143.
24. Fallows, "The Passionless Presidency." For his part, Eizenstat asserts that Fallows's claim that Carter scheduled the White House tennis courts is "a lie." He also adds, for good measure, that Fallows did not seem to be working as hard as perhaps he should have been in the White House: "Fallows was an especially avid player and frequently used the court. (I am glad he had the time for such indulgences, courtesy of the president. I certainly did not!)" Eizenstat, *President Carter*, 711.
25. Hess, *Organizing the Presidency*, 143.
26. Smith, *Power Game*, 109.
27. Charles Gati, "Zbigniew Brzezinski: The Professor-Strategist 1928–2017," *Politico*, December 28, 2017, https://www.politico.com/magazine/story/2017/12/28/zbigniew-brzezinski-carter-obituary-216174.
28. Bernard Gwertzman, "Vance and Brzezinski: Feuding Chapter by Chapter," *New York Times*, May 26, 1983, http://www.nytimes.com/1983/05/26/us/vance-and-brzezinski-feuding-chapter-by-chapter.html?pagewanted=all.
29. Eizenstat, *President Carter*, 66; Whipple, *The Gatekeepers*, 82.
30. Eizenstat, *President Carter*, 73; Watson, "Oral History."
31. Eizenstat, *President Carter*, 66.
32. Cyrus Vance, *Hard Choices: Four Critical Years in Managing America's Foreign Policy* (New York: Simon & Schuster, 1983), 30.
33. Betty Glad, *An Outsider in the White House: Jimmy Carter, His Advisors, and the Making of American Foreign Policy* (Ithaca: Cornell University Press, 2009), 27; Eizenstat, *President Carter*, 66.
34. Vance, *Hard Choices*, 34.
35. Erwin C. Hargrove, *Jimmy Carter as President: Leadership and the Politics of the Public Good* (Baton Rouge: Louisiana State University Press, 1998), 118; Vance, *Hard Choices*, 36–37.
36. Vance, *Hard Choices*, 36–37; Zbigniew Brzezinski, "Oral History," Presidential Oral Histories, Jimmy Carter Presidency, Miller Center, https://millercenter.org/the-presidency/presidential-oral-histories/zbigniew-brzezinski-oral-history-assistant-president.
37. Vance, *Hard Choices*, 37; Glad, *An Outsider in the White House*, 30.
38. National Security Archive, "The Carter-Brezhnev Project, "W. Averell Harriman papers," https://nsarchive2.gwu.edu/carterbrezhnev/salt_ii_ebb.html; Sally Quinn, "Zbigniew Brzezinski: Insights, Infights, Kissinger and Competition," *Washington Post*, December 21, 1979, https://www.washingtonpost.com/archive/lifestyle/1979/12/21/zbigniew-brzezinski-insights-infights-kissinger-and-competition/3dd68d37-23e7-4c6d-88c3-247aaaaac89b/?utm_term=.c11b9c8d1685; Walter Isaacson and Evan Thomas, *The Wise Men: Six Friends and the World They Made* (New York: Simon & Schuster, 1986), 727.

39. Sally Quinn, "Zbigniew Brzezinski: Insights, Infights, Kissinger and Competition," *Washington Post*, December 21, 1979.
40. Eizenstat, *President Carter*, 591.
41. Glad, *An Outsider in the White House*, 29–33; Eizenstat, *President Carter*, 98, 589.
42. Glad, *An Outsider in the White House*, 29–33; Rodman, *Presidential Command*, 121, 123.
43. Rowland Evans and Robert Novak, "Brzezinski Now Controls Foreign Policy," *Rochester Democrat and Chronicle*, June 7, 1978, 17.
44. Brzezinski, "Oral History."
45. Ibid.
46. Ibid.
47. Ibid.
48. General William Odom, quoted with other NSC staff in Zbigniew Brzezinski, "Oral History."
49. Eizenstat, *President Carter*, 736.
50. Jimmy Carter, "Oral History," Presidential Oral Histories, Jimmy Carter Presidency, Miller Center, https://millercenter.org/the-presidency/presidential-oral-histories/jimmy-carter-oral-history-president-united-states.
51. Richard Burt, "Zbig Makes It Big," *New York Times*, July 30, 1978, www.nytimes.com/1978/07/30/archives/zbig-makes-it-big-zbig-makes-it-big.html.
52. Quinn, "Zbigniew Brzezinski: Insights, Infights, Kissinger and Competition."
53. Peter Beinart, *The Icarus Syndrome: A History of American Hubris* (New York: Harper, 2010), 214.
54. Lawrence Wright, *Thirteen Days in September: Carter, Begin, and Sadat at Camp David* (New York: Alfred A. Knopf, 2014), 160; Eizenstat, *President Carter*, 510.
55. Charles Kirbo, "Oral History," Presidential Oral Histories, Jimmy Carter Presidency, Miller Center, https://millercenter.org/the-presidency/presidential-oral-histories/charles-kirbo-oral-history-advisor-close-friend; Carter, "Oral History"; Eizenstat, "Oral History."
56. Quinn, "Zbigniew Brzezinski: Insights, Infights, Kissinger and Competition."
57. Jimmy Carter, *White House Diary* (New York: Farar, Straus, and Giroux, 2010), 289.
58. Ibid., 364, 425.
59. Bernard Gwertzman, "Vance and Brzezinski: Feuding Chapter by Chapter," *New York Times*, May 26, 1983, http://www.nytimes.

com/1983/05/26/us/vance-and-brzezinski-feuding-chapter-by-chapter.
html?pagewanted=all.

60. Eizenstat, *President Carter*, 409, 537.
61. Ibid., 494, 496, 537–39.
62. Ibid., 491–92.
63. Ibid., 492.
64. Rowland Evans and Robert Novak, "Vance and Those Pygmies in the White House," *The Tennessean*, May 1, 1980, 9.
65. James Schlesinger, "Oral History," Presidential Oral Histories, Jimmy Carter Presidency, Miller Center, https://millercenter.org/the-presidency/presidential-oral-histories/james-schlesinger-oral-history-secretary-energy.

## Chapter 7: Rivalries under Reagan

1. Peter Robinson, "The Ricochet Podcast," Episode 360, "Sajak and Yoo," July 24, 2017, https://ricochet.com/podcast/ricochet-podcast/sajak-and-yoo/.
2. Rowland Evans and Robert Novak, *The Reagan Revolution* (New York: Elsevier-Dutton Publishing, 1981), 67.
3. Martin Anderson, *Revolution: The Reagan Legacy* (Stanford: Hoover Institution Press, 1988), 215–16; Bob Spitz, *Reagan: An American Journey* (New York: Penguin, 2018), 427, 433, 435.
4. Edwin Meese, *With Reagan: The Inside Story* (Washington: Regnery, 1992), 5; Steven F. Hayward, *The Age of Reagan: The Fall of the Old Liberal Order: 1964–1980* (New York: Crown Publishing, 2001), 642; Spitz, *Reagan*, 447.
5. Lou Cannon, "Life After Sears," *Washington Post*, March 8, 1980, https://www.washingtonpost.com/archive/politics/1980/03/08/life-after-sears/b0e7ffe0-a322-4189-a64a-b7fb753757bd/?utm_term=.24c96b473e09.
6. Lou Cannon, *President Reagan: The Role of a Lifetime* (New York: Simon & Schuster, 1991), 70.
7. Chris Whipple, *The Gatekeepers: How the White House Chiefs of Staff Define Every Presidency* (New York: Crown, 2017), 106; Spitz, *Reagan*, 469.
8. Peggy Noonan, *What I Saw at the Revolution: A Political Life in the Reagan Era* (New York: Ballantine, 1990), 173.
9. David Stockman, *The Triumph of Politics: Why the Reagan Revolution Failed* (New York: Public Affairs, 1986), 82. While Baker had indeed managed the Bush campaign, the responsibility for the "voodoo economics" line was speechwriter Pete Teeley. When the phrase led to continued criticism of Bush from conservatives, he chided his

speechwriter, saying, "You know Teeley, that's the only goddamned memorable thing you've ever written for me." Jon Meacham, *Destiny and Power: The American Odyssey of George Herbert Walker Bush* (New York: Random House, 2015), 235.

10. Stockman, *The Triumph of Politics*, 82.

11. Whipple, *The Gatekeepers*, 108.

12. Louise Sweeney, "Reagan's Velvet Hammer," *Christian Science Monitor*, January 2, 1981, https://www.csmonitor.com/1981/0102/010254.html.

13. Whipple, *The Gatekeepers*, 104.

14. H. W. Brands, *Reagan: The Life* (New York: Anchor, 2015), 245.

15. Sweeney, "Reagan's Velvet Hammer"; Cannon, *President Reagan*, 112.

16. James P. Pfiffner, "The President's Chief of Staff: Lessons Learned," *Presidential Studies Quarterly* 23, no. 1; "Democracy in Transition," (Winter, 1993), 77–102; Brands, *Reagan*, 245.

17. Spitz, *Reagan*, 427; Hedrick Smith, *The Power Game: How Washington Works* (New York: Ballantine Books, 1988), 313.

18. George P. Shultz, *Shultz, Turmoil and Triumph: My Years as Secretary of State* (New York: Charles Scribner's Sons, 1993), 12.

19. Brands, *Reagan*, 379–80; Cannon, *President Reagan*, 113.

20. Brands, *Reagan: The Life*, 379–80; Clayton E. McManaway, "Oral History," in "Alexander Haig's Fall from Grace," Association for Diplomatic Studies and Training, https://adst.org/2016/06/alexander-haigs-fall-grace/; Anne Edwards, *The Reagans: Portrait of a Marriage* (New York: St. Martin's, 2003), 202; Don Oberdorfer and Martin Schram, "Haig Believes a Reagan Aide Is Campaigning Against Him," *Washington Post*, November 4, 1981, https://www.washingtonpost.com/archive/politics/1981/11/04/haig-believes-a-reagan-aide-is-compaigning-against-him/a3bc44b0-02b8-48f9-bef5-06c80dacfcc3/?utm_term=.eb5face2e802. Haig's rapid fall from grace became a widely recognized joke. In 1982 episode of *Police Squad*, Leslie Nielsen's Lt. Frank Drebin opens a bay in the morgue to discover a photo of Al Haig in there. See https://www.youtube.com/watch?v=GQ1-CKhiFGQ; Shultz, *Turmoil and Triumph*, 12.

21. Smith, *The Power Game*, 318.

22. Bill Moyers, "Illusions of News," in *The Public Mind: Image & Reality*, prod. Richard Cohen, PBS, WETA, Washington, and WNET, New York, November 22, 1989, https://billmoyers.com/content/illusions-news/.

23. Mark Hertsgaard, *On Bended Knee: The Press and the Reagan Presidency* (New York: Farrar, Straus, Giroux, 1988), 46.

24. Richard Reeves, *President Reagan: The Triumph of Imagination* (New York: Simon and Schuster, 2005), 13.

25. Edwin Meese, *With Reagan: The Inside Story* (Washington: Regnery, 1992), 109.
26. Reeves, *President Reagan*, 86.
27. William Niskanen, *Reaganomics: An Insider's Account of the Policies and the People* (New York: Oxford University Press, 1988), 299–300; Stockman, *The Triumph of Politics*, 91; Robert Novak, *The Prince of Darkness: 50 Years of Reporting in Washington* (New York: Crown, 2007), 388.
28. Brands, *Reagan*, 46.
29. Stockman, *The Triumph of Politics*, 49.
30. Meese, *With Reagan*, 205.
31. Cannon, *President Reagan*, 191; Bob Spitz, *Reagan*, 427.
32. Noonan, *What I Saw at the Revolution*, 34.
33. Larry Speakes and Robert Pack, *Speaking Out: The Reagan Presidency from Inside the White House* (New York: Avon Books, 1989), 244; Spitz, *Reagan*, 506.
34. Stockman, *The Triumph of Politics*, 120.
35. Edmund Morris, *Dutch: A Memoir of Ronald Reagan* (New York: Random House, 1999), 431–32.
36. Noonan, *What I Saw at the Revolution*, 110.
37. Smith, *The Power Game*, 320–21; Cannon, *President Reagan*, 433.
38. Meese, *With Reagan*, 80.
39. David Gergen, *Eyewitness to Power: The Essence of Leadership Nixon to Clinton* (New York: Simon & Schuster, 2003), 180.
40. Cannon, *President Reagan*, 555, 493.
41. Gil Troy, *Morning in America: How Ronald Reagan Invented the 1980s* (Princeton: Princeton University Press, 2005), 237.
42. Cannon, *President Reagan*, 555.
43. Pfiffner, "The President's Chief of Staff: Lessons Learned," 51.
44. Mark Weinberg, *Movie Nights with the Reagans: A Memoir* (New York: Simon & Schuster, 2018), 190.
45. Peter Wallison, *Ronald Reagan: The Power of Conviction and the Success of His Presidency*, (Cambridge: Perseus Books Group, 2004), 169.
46. Cannon, *President Reagan*, 500.
47. Smith, *The Power Game*, 323.
48. Pfiffner, "The President's Chief of Staff: Lessons Learned," 90.
49. Noonan, *What I Saw at the Revolution*, 120.
50. Ibid.
51. Reeves, *President Reagan*, 113.
52. Dinesh D'Souza, *Ronald Reagan: How an Ordinary Man Became an Extraordinary Leader* (New York: Free Press, 1997), 223.

53. Cannon, *President Reagan*, 566.
54. Anderson, *Revolution*, 204–5.
55. Bernard Weinraub, "The White House Crisis: Regan's Exit was Inevitable, Baker's Entrance a Surprise," *New York Times*, March 1, 1987, https://www.nytimes.com/1987/03/01/us/the-white-house-crisis-regan-s-exit-was-inevitable-baker-s-entrance-a-surprise.html; Whipple, *The Gatekeepers*, 146.
56. Weinraub, "The White House Crisis."
57. D'Souza, *Ronald Reagan*, 223.
58. Alex Horton, "The Only Communications Director Booted Faster Than Scaramucci Had Been Outed for Nazi Ties," *Washington Post*, July 31, 2017, https://www.washingtonpost.com/news/retropolis/wp/2017/07/31/the-only-communications-director-booted-faster-than-scaramucci-had-been-outed-for-nazi-ties/?utm_term=.b18d55670b90&wpisrc=nl_daily202&wpmm=1.
59. D'Souza, *Ronald Reagan*, 223.
60. Stockman, *The Triumph of Politics*, 119.
61. Smith, *The Power Game*, 303.
62. Chris Sommerfeldt, "President Ronald Reagan Would Switch Off His Hearing Aids to Tune Out His Wife During Dinner," *New York Daily News*, April 3, 2018, http://beta.nydailynews.com/news/national/president-reagan-turn-hearing-aids-tune-wife-article-1.3912617.
63. "President Reagan's management style is dictated, in part, by..." UPI, August 27, 1986, https://www.upi.com/Archives/1986/08/27/President-Reagans-management-style-is-dictated-in-part-by/9872525499200/.
64. Wallison, *Ronald Reagan*, 17.

## Chapter 8: George H. W. Bush

1. Tevi Troy, *Intellectuals and the American Presidency: Philosophers, Jesters, or Technicians?* (Lanham: Rowman and Littlefield, 2002), 161; Jon Meacham, *Destiny and Power: The American Odyssey of George Herbert Walker Bush* (New York: Random House, 2015), 235.
2. Larry Speakes, *Speaking Out* (New York: Charles Scribner's Sons, 1988), 85–86.
3. James Pinkerton, "Oral History," Deputy Assistant to the President for Policy Planning, Miller Center, February 6, 2001, https://millercenter.org/the-presidency/presidential-oral-histories/james-p-pinkerton-oral-history-deputy-assistant.
4. George Bush, *All the Best, George Bush: My Life in Letters and Other Writings* (New York: Scribner, 2013), 17.

5. Chris Whipple, *The Gatekeepers: How the White House Chiefs of Staff Define Every Presidency* (New York: Crown, 2017), 7, 164–65, 171.

6. Rowland Evans and Robert Novak, "Sniping at Sununu," *Washington Post*, December 12, 1988, https://www.washingtonpost. com/archive/opinions/1988/12/12/sniping-at-sununu/b830a336-e5d9-49c0-bfcc-9aa072933da5/?utm_term=.5e4c9cad0b6e; Robert Novak, *The Prince of Darkness: 50 Years of Reporting in Washington* (New York: Crown, 2007), 459–61.

7. John Harwood, "Dad's Adviser Darman Is Far from Inner Circle," *Wall Street Journal*, August 2, 2000, https://www.wsj.com/articles/SB965192527144739797.

8. Marjorie Williams, "The Long and the Short of Richard G. Darman," *Washington Post Magazine*, July 29, 1990, https://www.washingtonpost. com/archive/lifestyle/magazine/1990/07/29/the-long-and-the-short-of-richard-g-darman/1850c303-c86c-4ca9-a047-32da064a6436/?utm_term=.1e47b7c673a4.

9. Smith, *The Power Game*, 314.

10. Anderson, *Revolution*, 240.

11. Ibid.

12. Lou Cannon, *President Reagan: The Role of a Lifetime* (New York: Simon & Schuster, 1991), 113.

13. Williams, "The Long and the Short of Richard G. Darman"; Novak, *The Prince of Darkness*, 405.

14. Anderson, *Revolution*, 240.

15. William Niskanen, *Reaganomics 300*; Marjorie Williams, "The Long and the Short of Richard G. Darman."

16. John H. Sununu, *The Quiet Man: The Indispensable Presidency of George H. W. Bush* (New York: Broadside Books, 2015), 49.

17. John Sununu, "Oral History," Chief of Staff, Miller Center, November 9, 2000, https://millercenter.org/the-presidency/presidential-oral-histories/john-h-sununu-oral-history-062000-white-house-chief.

18. Ibid.

19. Bob Woodward, "Origin of the Tax Pledge," *Washington Post*, October 4, 1992, https://www.washingtonpost.com/archive/politics/1992/10/04/origin-of-the-tax-pledge/b669c4fc-79b2-4d2d-8289-c0398e3e2895/?utm_term=.a01373494306.

20. Sununu, *The Quiet Man*, 164.

21. Williams, "The Long and the Short of Richard G. Darman."

22. Steven Mufson "In Heat of Battle, Darman Put Taxes Back on the Table," *Washington Post*, January 26, 2008, http://www.washingtonpost.com/wp-dyn/content/article/2008/01/25/AR2008012503158.html.

23. "Bush Jogs on 65th Birthday," UPI, June 12, 1989, https://www.upi. com/Archives/1989/06/12/ Bush-jogs-on-65th-birthday/4372613627200/.
24. Pinkerton Oral History.
25. Dan Quayle, "Oral History," Miller Center, March 12, 2002, https://millercenter.org/the-presidency/presidential-oral-histories/ j-danforth-quayle-oral-history-vice-president-united.
26. Pinkerton, "Oral History."
27. Quayle, "Oral History."
28. Pinkerton, "Oral History."
29. John Podhoretz, *Hell of a Ride: Backstage at the White House Follies, 1989 to 1993* (New York: Simon & Schuster, 1993), 57.
30. David Mervin, *George Bush and the Guardianship Presidency* (New York: Saint Martin's, 1996), 70.
31. Marlin Fitzwater, *Call the Briefing! Bush and Reagan, Sam and Helen: A Decade with Presidents and the Press* (New York: Times Press, 1995), 179.
32. Quayle, "Oral History."
33. Podhoretz, *Hell of a Ride*, 62.
34. Ibid., 61.
35. Charles Kolb, *White House Daze: The Unmaking of Domestic Policy in the Bush Administration* (New York: Free Press, 1994), 47–49.
36. Kolb, *White House Daze*, 47–49.
37. Ibid., 36.
38. James P. Pfiffner, "Democracy in Transition," *Presidential Studies Quarterly* 23, no. 1 (1993), 90.
39. Kolb, *White House Daze*, xvi.
40. Podhoretz, *Hell of a Ride*, 42, 62.
41. Pfiffner, "Democracy in Transition."
42. Sununu, "Oral History."
43. Sununu, *The Quiet Man*, 49; Kolb, *White House Daze*, 35–40.
44. Joel Achenbach, "Feint Dams for Those High-Level Leaks," *Washington Post*, January 18, 1993, https://www.washingtonpost.com/archive/ lifestyle/1993/01/18/feint-dams-for-those-high-level-leaks/ d523350f-8d44-4331-8a8f-ef045ccbcd23/?utm_term=.52d9e2a12cb8.
45. George H. W. Bush White House communications aide Peter Sobich, conversation with the author, March 2018.
46. Pfiffner, "Democracy in Transition."
47. Kolb, *White House Daze*, 25.
48. Ibid., 40–41.
49. Ibid., 44. Recollection of multiple Bush White House aides.

50. William Barr, "Oral History," Miller Center, April 5, 2001, https://millercenter.org/the-presidency/presidential-oral-histories/j-danforth-quayle-oral-history-vice-president-united.

51. Pinkerton, "Oral History."

52. Podhoretz, *Hell of a Ride*, 62.

53. Rowland Evans and Robert Novak, "Darman's Disdain," *Washington Post*, November 23, 1990, https://www.washingtonpost.com/archive/opinions/1990/11/23/darmans-disdain/0974720f-fbc0-453e-a699-f6ea26caf2d7/?utm_term=.8d8a950cd8ad.

54. Pinkerton, "Oral History."

55. Evans and Novak, "Darman's Disdain."

56. Ibid.

57. Pinkerton, "Oral History."

58. Ibid.

59. Ibid.

60. Pinkerton, "Oral History"; Troy, *Intellectuals and the American Presidency*, 165.

61. Sununu, "Oral History."

62. Quayle, "Oral History"; Mervin, *George Bush and the Guardianship Presidency*, 360.

63. Podhoretz, *Hell of a Ride*, 63.

64. Peter Rodman, *Presidential Command: Power, Leadership, and the Making of Foreign Policy from Richard Nixon to George W. Bush* (New York: Knopf, 2009), 180–81.

## Chapter 9: Clinton Administration

1. Gil Troy, *The Age of Clinton: America in the 1990s* (New York: Thomas Dunne Books, 2015), 45.

2. Steve Daley, "'Mainstream' Democratic Group Tries to Push Jackson out of the Spotlight," *Chicago Tribune*, April 21, 1991, http://articles.chicagotribune.com/1991-04-21/news/9102050410_1_democratic-party-jackson-won-t-political-mainstream.

3. Thomas L. Friedman, "The Transition; Democratic Leader and Clinton Friend Gain Major Posts," *New York Times*, December 13, 1992, http://www.nytimes.com/1992/12/13/us/the-transition-democratic-leader-and-clinton-friend-gain-major-posts.html.

4. Leonard Greene, "I Warned Bill I'd Walk If He Had Affairs: Clinton Adviser," *New York Post*, November 26, 2014, https://nypost.com/2014/11/26/i-warned-bill-id-walk-if-he-had-affairs-clinton-adviser/.

5. Joe Conason, "George's Tell-All Reads Like Fine Whine," *Observer*, March 29, 1999, http://observer.com/1999/03/

georges-tellall-reads-like-fine-whine/; Dee Dee Myers, interview for *Frontline*, June 2000, https://www.pbs.org/wgbh/pages/frontline/shows/clinton/interviews/myers.html; Amy Chozick, *Chasing Hillary* (New York: Harper Collins, 2018), 327.

6.   Stephen Hess, "First Impressions: A Look Back at Five Presidential Transitions," Brookings Institution, March 1, 2001, https://www.brookings.edu/articles/first-impressions-a-look-back-at-five-presidential-transitions/; Russell Riley, *Inside the Clinton White House: An Oral History* (New York, Oxford, 2016), 79–80.

7.   Myers, interview for *Frontline*.

8.   Bob Woodward, *The Agenda: Inside the Clinton White House* (New York: Simon & Schuster, 1994), 332.

9.   Michael Duffy, "Thomas McLarty: They Call Him Mack the Nice," *Time*, December 28, 1992, http://content.time.com/time/magazine/article/0,9171,977339,00.html.

10.  David Gergen, "Frontline Interview with Chris Bury," June 2000, https://www.pbs.org/wgbh/pages/frontline/shows/clinton/interviews/gergen.html.

11.  Bill Clinton, *My Life* (New York: Alfred A. Knopf, 2004), 359.

12.  David A. Graham, "How Trump Can Fix His Troubled White House: An Administration in Chaos. An Undisciplined President. A Bloodthirsty Press. A Surfeit of Leaks. Spring 1993 Looked A Lot Like Spring 2017," *The Atlantic*, March 21, 2017, https://www.theatlantic.com/politics/archive/2017/03/clinton-transition-trump-chaos/514760/.

13.  Myers, interview for *Frontline*.

14.  George Stephanopoulos, *All Too Human: A Political Education* (Boston: Little, Brown and Company, 1999), 284.

15.  Graham, "How Trump Can Fix His Troubled White House."

16.  Myers, *Frontline Interview*.

17.  Ibid.

18.  Lloyd Grove, "The White House Kiddie Corps," *Washington Post*, June 1, 1993, https://www.washingtonpost.com/archive/lifestyle/1993/06/01/the-white-house-kiddie-corps/addc5e4e-c694-41db-a037-a75edd840e94/?utm_term=.2048d82cd813.

19.  Elizabeth Drew, *On the Edge: The Clinton Presidency* (New York: Touchstone, 1994), 187.

20.  Grove, "The White House Kiddie Corps." "Sprockets" was an early 1990s *Saturday Night Live* sketch in which Mike Myers (no relation to Dee Dee) played a pretentious German talk show host who dressed in all black clothing.

21.  George Stephanopoulos, interview for *Frontline*, June 2000, https://www.pbs.org/wgbh/pages/frontline/shows/clinton/etc/script.html.

22. Grove, "The White House Kiddie Corps."
23. David Gergen, interview for *Frontline*, June 2000, https://www.pbs.org/wgbh/pages/frontline/shows/clinton/interviews/gergen.html.
24. Woodward, *The Agenda*, 284.
25. Ibid., 328.
26. Ibid.
27. Elaine Sciolino, "State Department Awaits Gergen with Trepidation," *New York Times*, June 29, 1994, https://www.nytimes.com/1994/06/29/us/state-department-awaits-gergen-with-trepidation.html.
28. Myers, interview for *Frontline*.
29. "The Morris Meltdown," *Newsweek*, September 8, 1996, http://www.newsweek.com/morris-meltdown-177794; Dick Morris, "Setting the Record Straight: An Open Letter to Hillary Clinton," *National Review Online*, June 12, 2003, https://www.nationalreview.com/2003/06/setting-record-straight-4limitedgovt/.
30. Dick Morris, interview for *Frontline*, June 2000, http://www.pbs.org/wgbh/pages/frontline/shows/clinton/interviews/morris.html.
31. Ibid.
32. Chris Whipple, *The Gatekeepers: How the White House Chiefs of Staff Define Every Presidency* (New York: Crown, 2017), 205–6.
33. Morris, interview for *Frontline*.
34. Michael Lewis, "Bill Clinton's Garbage Man," *New York Times*, September 21, 1997, https://www.nytimes.com/1997/09/21/magazine/bill-clinton-s-garbage-man.html.
35. Leon Panetta, "Oral History, Director of the Office of Management and Budget; Chief of Staff," UVA Miller Center, January 31, 2003, https://millercenter.org/the-presidency/presidential-oral-histories/leon-panetta-oral-history-director-office-management-and.
36. Whipple, *The Gatekeepers*, 205–6.
37. Morris, interview for *Frontline*.
38. Stephanopoulos, interview for *Frontline*.
39. "Leon Panetta Oral History."
40. Whipple, *The Gatekeepers*, 205–6.
41. Stephanopoulos, *All Too Human*, 329–30.
42. Morris, interview for *Frontline*.
43. Margaret Carlson, "A Tell-All That Doesn't," CNN, March 15, 1999, http://www.cnn.com/ALLPOLITICS/time/1999/03/15/stephanopoulos.html.
44. Stephanopoulos, interview for *Frontline*.
45. Stephanopoulos, *All Too Human*, 329.
46. Stephanopoulos, interview for *Frontline*.
47. Stephanopoulos, *All Too Human*, 331.

48. Ibid., 339.
49. Morris, *Frontline Interview*.
50. Stephanopoulos, *All Too Human*, 414.
51. Ibid., 338, 385; Graham, "How Trump Can Fix His Troubled White House."
52. "Wild Card," *Newsweek*, November 17, 1996, http://www.newsweek.com/wild-card-176404; "On Target," *Newsweek*, November 17, 1996, https://www.newsweek.com/target-176402.
53. "Wild Card," *Newsweek*.
54. Ibid.
55. Stephanopoulos, interview for *Frontline*; "The Morris Meltdown," *Newsweek*, September 8, 1996, https://www.newsweek.com/morris-meltdown-177794.
56. Stephanopoulos, *Frontline Interview*; Stephanopoulos, *All Too Human*, 423; Richard L. Berke, "Call Girl Story Costs President a Key Strategist," *New York Times*, August 30, 1996, https://www.nytimes.com/1996/08/30/us/call-girl-story-costs-president-a-key-strategist.html.
57. Stephanopoulos, *Frontline Interview*; Morris, *Frontline Interview*; Stephanopoulos, *All Too Human*, 385.
58. Robert Novak, *The Prince of Darkness: 50 Years of Reporting in Washington* (New York: Crown, 2007), 536.
59. Peter Baker, *The Breach: Inside the Impeachment and Trial of William Jefferson Clinton* (New York: Simon and Schuster: 2000), 39.
60. "Clinton Apologizes to Cabinet," CNN, September 11, 1998, http://www.cnn.com/ALLPOLITICS/stories/1998/09/11/cabinet.reax/.
61. James Carville, interview for *Frontline*, PBS Frontline, 2000, https://www.pbs.org/wgbh/pages/frontline/shows/clinton/interviews/carville.html; Troy, *The Age of Clinton*, 218.
62. Carl M. Cannon, "'Far-Right Conspiracy' a Gift from Blumenthal," *Baltimore Sun*, February 15, 1998, http://articles.baltimoresun.com/1998-02-15/news/1998046033_1_aide-sidney-blumenthal-white-house-al-gore.
63. Michael Powell, "Blumenthal, Giving as Good as He Gets," *Washington Post*, September 25, 1998, http://www.washingtonpost.com/wp-srv/politics/special/clinton/stories/blumenth092598.htm; Cannon, "'Far-Right Conspiracy' a Gift from Blumenthal."

## Chapter 10: George W. Bush

1. John Burke, *Becoming President: The Bush Transition, 2000–2003* (Boulder: Lynne Rienner, 2004), 119.
2. Richard Brookhiser, "Close Up: The Mind of George W. Bush," *The Atlantic*, April 2003, https://www.theatlantic.com/magazine/archive/2003/04/close-up-the-mind-of-george-w-bush/303399/.

3. Timothy S. Goeglein, *The Man in the Middle: An Inside Account of Faith and Politics in the George W. Bush Era* (Nashville: B&H Publishing Group, 2011), 33.
4. Elisabeth Bumiller, "An Influential Bush Adviser, Karen Hughes, Will Resign," *New York Times*, April 24, 2002, https://www.nytimes.com/2002/04/24/us/an-influential-bush-adviser-karen-hughes-will-resign.html; Burke, *Becoming President*, 119.
5. John DiIulio, "John DiIulio's letter," *Esquire*, May 22, 2007, http://www.esquire.com/news-politics/a2880/dilulio/. Mayberry was the small fictional North Carolina community spoofed in *The Andy Griffith Show*.
6. Brookhiser, "Close Up"; Ken Auletta, "Bush's Press Problem," *New Yorker*, January 19, 2004, https://www.newyorker.com/magazine/2004/01/19/bushs-press-problem.
7. Brookhiser, "Close Up"; "Decision Making Style," *Frontline PBS*, October 12, 2004, http://www.pbs.org/wgbh/pages/frontline/shows/choice2004/bush/style.html.
8. Peter Rodman, *Presidential Command: Power, Leadership, and the Making of Foreign Policy from Richard Nixon to George W. Bush* (New York: Knopf, 2009), 237; author recollections of Card "pep talks"; Brookhiser, "Close Up," *The Atlantic*; Peter Baker, *Days of Fire: Bush and Cheney in the White House* (New York: Anchor Books, 2014), 5, 17; Lois Romano, "George Walker Bush, Driving on the Right," *Washington Post*, September 24, 1998, B1, http://www.washingtonpost.com/wp-srv/politics/campaigns/wh2000/stories/whbush092498.htm.
9. Chris Whipple, *The Gatekeepers: How the White House Chiefs of Staff Define Every Presidency* (New York: Crown, 2017), 164.
10. I was once accused of committing a "process foul" while serving in the Bush 43 White House. It turns out that I had not done what I was accused of, but the accusation, coming from the chief of staff's office and coupled with a closed door and a raised voice, was chilling.
11. Tevi Troy, "Low Profiles Make a Winning Team," *Politico*, February 10, 2011, https://www.politico.com/news/stories/0211/49179_Page2.html.
12. Michael Isikoff, "The Man Who Said Too Much," *Newsweek*, September 3, 2006, http://www.newsweek.com/man-who-said-too-much-109351.
13. Bob Woodward, *Plan of Attack* (New York: Simon and Schuster, 2004), 433.
14. Condoleezza Rice, *No Higher Honor: A Memoir of My Years in Washington* (New York: Crown Publishing Group, 2011), 20, 17.
15. Donald Rumsfeld, *Known and Unknown: A Memoir* (New York: Penguin Group, 2011), 325, 327; Rick Klein, "Rumsfeld to Diane

Sawyer: 'It's Possible' Troop Decisions Were a Mistake in Iraq," ABC News, February 7, 2011, https://abcnews.go.com/Politics/donald-rumsfeld-diane-sawyer-exclusive-interview-troop-decisions/story?id=12853695.

16. Peter Rodman, *Presidential Command: Power, Leadership, and the Making of Foreign Policy from Richard Nixon to George W. Bush* (New York: Knopf, 2009), 248.

17. Marcus Mabry, *Twice As Good: Condoleezza Rice and Her Path to Power* (New York: Modern Times, 2007), 152; Rodman, *Presidential Command*, 249.

18. Rodman, *Presidential Command*, 249.

19. Melvyn P. Leffler, "Trust but Clarify: George W. Bush's National Security Team Was Beset with Rivalries," Miller Center, http://firstyear2017.org/essay/trust-but-clarify.

20. Jane Mayer, "The Hidden Power: The Legal Mind Behind the White House's War on Terror." *The New Yorker*, July 3, 2006, https://www.newyorker.com/magazine/2006/07/03/the-hidden-power.

21. Rice, *No Higher Honor*, 16.

22. Whipple, *The Gatekeepers*, 243.

23. Rice, *No Higher Honor*, 16.

24. Klein, "Rumsfeld to Diane Sawyer: 'It's Possible' Troop Decisions Were a Mistake in Iraq."

25. Rice, *No Higher Honor*, 16.

26. Ibid., 21.

27. Klein, "Rumsfeld to Diane Sawyer: 'It's Possible' Troop Decisions Were a Mistake in Iraq"; Matt Latimer, "George Bush Memoir: Ex-Aide Matt Latimer On George W. Bush's 'Decision Points,'" *The Daily Beast*, November 9, 2010, http://www.thedailybeast.com/george-bush-memoir-ex-aide-matt-latimer-on-george-w-bushs-decision-points; Donald Rumsfeld, *Known and Unknown: A Memoir* (New York: Penguin Group, 2011), 504.

28. Rumsfeld, *Known and Unknown*, 504.

29. Ibid., 504; Douglas J. Feith, *War and Decision: Inside the Pentagon at the Dawn of the War on Terrorism* (New York: Harper, 2008), 62.

30. Feith, *War and Decision*, 61fn.

31. Rice, *No Higher Honor*, 20–22.

32. This is a very brief overview of a long and complex tale, too long to fully recount here. For the interested reader, there are entire libraries devoted to the incident. All that's necessary here is to understand that Plame's name was leaked and the Justice Department sought to uncover the leaker.

33. Isikoff, "The Man Who Said Too Much."

34. James Comey, *A Higher Loyalty: Truth, Lies, And Leadership* (New York: Flatiron Books, 2018), 72.
35. Ibid., 87.
36. Ibid., 98.
37. Ari Shapiro, "Cheney's New Chief of Staff Is Much Like His Boss," *All Things Considered*, November 8, 2005, https://www.npr.org/templates/story/story.php?storyId=4994740; Michael Kranish, "Kavanaugh's Role in Bush-era Detainee Debate Now an Issue in His Supreme Court Nomination," *Washington Post*, July 18, 2018, https://www.sfgate.com/news/article/Kavanaugh-s-role-in-Bush-era-detainee-debate-now-13086506.php; Jane Mayer, "The Hidden Power."
38. Baker, *Days of Fire*, 579.
39. Matt Latimer, *Speech-Less: Tales of a White House Survivor* (New York: Crown, 2010), 156.
40. Baker, *Days of Fire*, 642.
41. In Cabinet meetings I sat in, Bush would get Powell and Rumsfeld to say things in agreement, and then jibe, "Who says they can't get along?"
42. Matthew Scully, "Present at the Creation," *The Atlantic*, September 2007, www.theatlantic.com/magazine/archive/2007/09/present-at-the-creation/306134/.
43. Timothy Noah, "Is Mike Gerson a Glory Hog, or Is His Former Colleague, Matthew Scully Just Unhinged?" *Slate*, August 10, 2007, www.slate.com/articles/news_and_politics/chatterbox/2007/08/is_mike_gersona_glory_hog.html.

## Chapter 11: Barack Obama

1. Dan Pfeiffer, *Yes We (Still) Can: Politics in the Age of Obama, Twitter, and Trump* (New York: Hachette Book Group, 2018), 42.
2. Tevi Troy, "Low Profiles Make a Winning Team," *Politico*, February 10, 2011, https://www.politico.com/story/2011/02/low-profiles-make-a-winning-team-049179.
3. Pfeiffer, *Yes We (Still) Can*, 42.
4. Ibid., 45.
5. David Paul Kuhn and Ben Smith, "Obama Moves Quickly To Reshape DNC," *Politico*, June 13, 2008, https://www.politico.com/story/2008/06/obama-moves-quickly-to-reshape-dnc-011045.
6. Pfeiffer, *Yes We (Still) Can*, 45.
7. David Litt, *Thanks, Obama: My Hopey, Changey White House Years* (New York: HarperCollins, 2017), 61.
8. Alyssa Mastromonaco, *Who Thought This Was a Good Idea? And Other Questions You Should Have Answers to When You Work in the White House* (New York: Hachette Book Group, 2017), 322.

9.  "Fact Check: Is Obama the Most Liberal Senator?" Factcheck.org, September 18, 2008, http://politicalticker.blogs.cnn.com/2008/09/18/fact-check-is-obama-the-most-liberal-us-senator/.
10. Pfeiffer, *Yes We (Still) Can*, 61.
11. Ibid.
12. "White House Communications Chief to Step Down," Associated Press, November 10, 2009, accessed August 8, 2018, https://newsok.com/article/feed/104514/white-house-communications-chief-to-step-down.
13. Juliet Eilperin, "White House Women Want to be in the Room Where It Happens," *Washington Post*, September 13, 2016, https://www.washingtonpost.com/news/powerpost/wp/2016/09/13/white-house-women-are-now-in-the-room-where-it-happens/?utm_term=.345e16968de5.
14. Noam Scheiber, "Moneyball," *The New Republic*, October 12, 2009, https://newrepublic.com/article/70139/moneyball.
15. Ryan Lizza, "Inside the Crisis: Larry Summers and the White House Economic Team," *The New Yorker*, October 12, 2009, https://www.newyorker.com/magazine/2009/10/12/inside-the-crisis.
16. Noam Scheiber, "Exclusive: The Memo that Larry Summers Did Not Want Obama to See," *The New Republic*, February 22, 2012, https://newrepublic.com/article/100961/memo-larry-summers-obama.
17. Jonathan Alter, *The Promise: President Obama, Year One* (New York: Simon and Schuster, 2010), 198.
18. Noam Scheiber, *The Escape Artists: How Obama's Team Fumbled the Recovery* (New York: Simon & Schuster, 2011), 137, 243–44.
19. Mastromonaco, *Who Thought This Was a Good Idea?*, 217–18.
20. Ibid.
21. Ibid., 14; Beck Dorey Stein, *From the Corner of the Oval: A Memoir* (Spiegel & Grau, 2018), 37, 91.
22. Eilperin, "White House Women Want to be in the Room Where It Happens."
23. Mastromonaco, *Who Thought This Was a Good Idea?*, 14–16.
24. Jackie Calmes, "Obama's Chief of Staff Pick Is Said to Be Down to 2," *New York Times*, January 10, 2013, https://www.nytimes.com/2013/01/11/us/politics/lew-to-complete-change-of-obamas-economic-team.html.
25. Mastromonaco, *Who Thought This Was a Good Idea?*, 121–23.
26. Ibid.
27. Ibid.
28. Ben Rhodes, *The World as It Is: A Memoir of the Obama White House* (New York: Random House, 2018), 85.

29. Jo Becker, "The Other Power in the West Wing," *New York Times*, September 1, 2012, https://www.nytimes.com/2012/09/02/us/politics/valerie-jarrett-is-the-other-power-in-the-west-wing.html.

30. Jonathan Alter, *The Center Holds: Obama and His Enemies* (New York: Simon & Schuster, 2013), 139.

31. Ibid., 139.

32. Jodi Kantor, *The Obamas* (New York: Little, Brown and Company, 2012), 237.

33. Mastromonaco, *Who Thought This Was a Good Idea?*, 217–18; for the record, Jarrett went to Stanford and Michigan Law School.

34. Kantor, *The Obamas*, 252–53.

35. Ibid., 254.

36. Rachel Weiner, "White House Wrote Memo on 'Magic' of Valerie Jarrett," *Washington Post*, July 3, 2013, https://www.washingtonpost.com/news/post-politics/wp/2013/07/03/white-house-wrote-memo-on-magic-of-valerie-jarrett/?utm_term=.2c51120dade9.

37. Ibid., 139.

38. Chris Whipple, *The Gatekeepers: How the White House Chiefs of Staff Define Every Presidency* (New York: Crown, 2017), 261.

39. Rhodes, *The World As It Is*, 56.

40. Ryan Lizza, "The Gatekeeper," *The New Yorker*, March 2, 2009, https://www.newyorker.com/magazine/2009/03/02/the-gatekeeper.

41. Brian Abrams, *Obama: An Oral History 2009–2017* (New York: Little A, 2018), 180, 188; Whipple, *The Gatekeepers*, 139.

42. Whipple, *The Gatekeepers*, 263.

43. Matthew Continetti, "The Worst White House Aide," *The Weekly Standard*, January 23, 2012, https://www.weeklystandard.com/matthew-continetti/the-worst-white-house-aide.

44. Brian Abrams, *Obama: An Oral History*, 180, 188; Whipple, *The Gatekeepers*, 269.

45. Rhodes, *The World As It Is*, 113.

46. Chuck Todd, *The Stranger: Barack Obama in the White House* (New York: Little, Brown and Company, 2014), 287.

47. Abrams, *Obama*, 204.

48. Litt, *Thanks, Obama*, 94; Becker, "The Other Power in the West Wing," *New York Times*, September 1, 2012, https://www.nytimes.com/2012/09/02/us/politics/valerie-jarrett-is-the-other-power-in-the-west-wing.html.

49. Whipple, *The Gatekeepers*, 272.

50. Ibid., 282.

51. Mark Leibovich, *This Town: Two Parties and a Funeral—Plus Plenty of Valet Parking!—in America's Gilded Capital* (New York: Penguin Group, 2013), 345–46.
52. Abrams, *Obama*, 203.
53. Todd, *The Stranger*, 353.
54. Rhodes, *The World As It Is*, 17.
55. Carlos Lozada, "Why the Ben Rhodes Profile in the New York Times Magazine Is Just Gross," *Washington Post*, May 6, 2016, https://www.washingtonpost.com/news/book-party/wp/2016/05/06/why-the-ben-rhodes-profile-in-the-new-york-times-magazine-is-just-gross/?utm_term=.9e4208210ed2.
56. David Samuels, "The Aspiring Novelist Who Became Obama's Foreign-Policy Guru," *New York Times Magazine*, May 5, 2016, https://www.nytimes.com/2016/05/08/magazine/the-aspiring-novelist-who-became-obamas-foreign-policy-guru.html.
57. Rhodes, *The World As It Is*, 17.
58. Ibid., 57.
59. Ibid., 101, 103.
60. Samuels, "The Aspiring Novelist Who Became Obama's Foreign-Policy Guru."
61. Rhodes, *The World As It Is*, 370.

## Chapter 12: Conclusion

1. Bill McGurn, "Potomac Watch Podcast," November 15, 2018, https://www.wsj.com/podcasts/opinion-potomac-watch.
2. Sean Spicer, *The Briefing: Politics, the Press, and the President* (Washington: Regnery, 2018), 11.
3. Bob Woodward, *Fear* (New York: Simon and Schuster, 2018), 133.
4. Seymour M. Hersh, "The Pardon: Nixon, Ford, Haig, and the Transfer of Power," *The Atlantic*, August 1983, https://www.theatlantic.com/magazine/archive/1983/08/the-pardon/305571/.
5. David Bossie and Corey Lewandowski, *Let Trump Be Trump: The Inside Story of His Rise to the Presidency* (New York: Center Street, 2017), 102; Spicer, *The Briefing*, 76.
6. Jonathan Swan, "1 Fun Thing: The Mooch 😎 Emoji," Axios, July 23, 2017, https://www.axios.com/axios-sneak-peek-2463714935.html?utm_source=newsletter&utm_medium=email&utm_campaign=newsletter_axiossneakpeek&stream=top-stories.
7. Michael Wolff, "Donald Trump Didn't Want to Be President," *New York Magazine*, January 2018, http://nymag.com/daily/intelligencer/2018/01/michael-wolff-fire-and-fury-book-donald-trump.html.

8.  Mara Siegler, "The Mooch Rips 'Loser' Steve Bannon at Hanukkah Party," *New York Post*, December 19, 2017, https://pagesix.com/2017/12/19/the-mooch-rips-loser-steve-bannon-at-hanukkah-party/.
9.  Mike Allen, "1 Big Thing: Mueller's Tapes, Spicer's Notes," Axios, September 21, 2017, https://www.axios.com/newsletters/axios-am-cdc21b3d-1d60-4865-b11a-a87313252422.html.
10. Tevi Troy, *Intellectuals and the American Presidency: Philosophers, Jesters, or Technicians?* (Lanham: Rowman and Littlefield, 2002), 82.
11. Michelle Mark, "Trump Shoots Down Rumors of White House Chaos, Says Everyone Wants 'A Piece of That Oval Office,'" *Business Insider*, March 6, 2018, https://www.businessinsider.com/trump-says-everyone-wants-to-work-in-white-house-2018-3.
12. Bossie and Lewandowski, *Let Trump Be Trump*, 223.
13. Chris Christie, *Let Me Finish: Trump, the Kushners, Bannon, New Jersey, and the Power of In-Your-Face Politics* (New York: Hachette, 2019), 367.
14. That Seahawks team was a particularly rambunctious bunch. The next year, the Seahawks lost the Super Bowl to the New England Patriots when quarterback Russell Wilson threw an interception on the one-yard line. When the game ended shortly afterwards, the two teams fought each other in the end zone. Some sportswriters even suggested that the team would have been more successful without the internal squabbles, but that is speculation, and the Super Bowl win is an actual fact.

# Index